THINK OUTSIDE
THE BOX OFFICE

The Ultimate Guide to Film Distribution in the Digital Era

First Printing
Copyright c. Jon Reiss 2010. All Rights Reserved
jon@jonreiss.com
www.twitter.com/Jon_Reiss
http://www.facebook.com/thinkoutsidetheboxoffice

Book Layout and Design Will Hays
Cover Design Justin Van Hoy
Book Title by: Susan Graves
Cover Photographer Jay B Sauceda
Assistant Editor Stephanie Bousley
Copy Editor Jennifer Hoche
Website Programmer Kazuha Torisawa

Published by Hybrid Cinema Publishing a division of Hybrid Cinema
ISBN: 9780982576205
The publisher offers special discounts on bulk orders of this book.
For information please contact:
Hybrid Cinema
+1 310-471-7210
hybridcinema@gmail.com

For links, extra documents, distribution and marketing tools go to the Official Book
Website:
www.ultimatefilmguides.com

Grateful acknowledgement is made for permission to reprint the following copyrighted
works: Lance Weiler's Culture Hacker column on Piracy and Torrent Sites and Lance
Weiler's Hope is Missing MIG both originally published in Filmmaker.

Cover photo is from a B-Side screening of Before the Music Dies, Republic Square Park
Austin, Texas June 5, 2006.

For Jill, Sam and Lucie who inspire me every day.

TABLE OF

CONTENTS

Love, Embrace, Share. Curate and Speak Up and Out. The People United Shall Never Be Defeated.

FOREWORD

Our dreams are born out of our pasts, curiously making fantasy rarely relevant to the world we are actually living in — and no where is this more evident than in the dream factory of the film business.

Don't even get me started on Hollywood, but much of so-called "American independent filmmaking" is still fueled by the hopes of industry discovery and colossal riches.

The indie filmmaking process has been romanticized — partially by the misuse of the label "independent" — conjuring up the notion of an individual auteur pulling a fully formed and instantly embraced über-work out of his or her brain and onto screens everywhere. I am not sure that myth ever had any applicability to our world, to the one in which I have experienced laboring in the producing trenches on more than 60 "indie" films in the past two decades, other than helping to inspire a plethora of content that was left begging for a home and an audience. Let's weep for them no longer, though. Change is now the name of the game.

If the past decade and a half of the American independent film movement was defined by the demystification of the development, production, and festival/sales processes, then the coming hours are about demystifying the distribution, marketing, and discovery processes. Filmmakers have generally drunk the Kool-Aid and swallowed the belief that there needed to be a concrete barrier between creation and discovery — the polarization more popularly referred to as art versus commerce. I have heard hordes of directors acquiesce that they must "leave the marketing up to the experts" and they had "too many stories to tell" to get involved in the distribution of the work they helped to produce. There is no future for innovative, diverse, and challenging work if those isolating and defeatist attitudes continue to permeate the community.

Granted, we all have things we do better and enjoy more than some of the most practical aspects of our daily toil. I totally get why some artists find it necessary to seclude themselves from certain influences, practices, and solutions. Yet filmmaking has always been both a collaborative art and an audience-based business. No filmmaker can expect to do it on his or her own. At its most fundamental, cinema is a dialogue between the audience and the screen. These two simple truths are the core principals that will allow for a vibrant movie culture to flourish. Collaboration and dialogue are also the foundation for everything Jon has outlined in precise detail in this book. They should be every filmmaker's mantra for the days ahead.

When filmmakers embrace the dictates of collaboration and dialogue as the governing elements for marketing, distribution, and discovery, grand new possibilities open up to both creators and audiences alike. These next few years of Truly Free Independent Filmmaking will be about erasing the lines between art and commerce, between content and marketing, between the narrative and the sell, and between creation and discovery.

Whether it is that one's body of work is all one story, or that instead of reinventing the wheel each time, we seek to engage our audiences, family, and friends in an ongoing conversation, it is this fundamental mind shift from the way most of the "indie" community approaches their work, its marketing, and its consumption, that will drive the changes to come. Call it what you will, but the movement to engage audiences more fully in an earlier and actual dialogue will ultimately mean that stories are more layered, contextual, and robust than they were in the past — and the possibilities for expansion have just begun to be unearthed. Sure, the cynical say social network outreach is nothing but marketing, but it really is a robust, user-driven dialogue and collaboration, one that can fuel good work finding its appropriate home. It's a new frontier, and the book you are holding is a blazing trail into the discovery of a series of best practices.

While some may like to look at the barrage of change that we've had to endure (i.e., the collapse of mainstream distribution of art and specialized films, the collapse of print journalism and the national dismissal of film criticism, the bottoming out of the DVD market, the continual format wars within corporate media, the bait and switch of "free" content for expensive and "necessary" hardware, and the corporate film industry's rejection of original material in favor of "pre-branded" content — *The Dixie Cup Movie*, anyone?) as understandable cause for alarm, it can also be recognized as a tremendous opportunity. This book is not about marketing *work*, but collaborative practices that will expose us and others to new pleasures.

For as long as we have a free and open Internet, individuals who want to "connect" and not just be sold to, people who embrace the expansive definition of what it means to be human and not just a demographic, citizens who are committed to compassion, empathy, and equal opportunity, and artists who are committed to emotional truth and an evolving definition of cinema, we have ample reason to hope that our filmmaking culture and apparatus can continue to embrace innovative and passionate work.

We are never going to do it on our own. The best practices that Jon lays out for us here may be intimidating initially when reading them on our own, but when we reach out and connect to each other, we can't help but recognize our shared predicament, and with that the necessity of embracing these new practices becomes clear.

It is not a question of "just doing it." We have to get over our collective fear of the future and utilize the benefits of a true community. We need to educate each other, tend to one another's children, and inoculate our villages against the viruses of despair and isolation. What at times seems like a prescriptive for world peace is also a formula for independent film prosperity, once we drill down and get to the specifics as Jon has herein. Eat up every morsel Reiss provides. Internalize it and make it your second skin. Remember the chants and we can make the world a better place:

Seed, Corral, Migrate and Pollinate.

Love, Embrace, Share.

Curate and Speak Up and Out.

The People United Shall Never Be Defeated.

~*Ted Hope*

This book is about connecting filmmakers with audiences and creating long-term relationships with them

INTRODUCTION

The independent film world is abuzz about the collapse of the traditional independent film distribution model.

In recent years, more than 5,000 feature films have been submitted to the Sundance Film Festival annually, and only a few hundred get the golden ticket. Of those accepted, perhaps a handful at best will make a sale that might cover at least half of their production expenses. Another handful might be offered a 20-year deal for all rights to their film — with either a token advance of about $15,000 or no advance at all. No longer can filmmakers expect someone to come and take their film off their hands and guarantee them theatrical release and full recoupment. Any filmmaker who doesn't understand the current state of affairs is going to have a rude awakening.

I had my own rude awakening in 2007 when I brought my film *Bomb It* (a documentary about the global explosion of graffiti art and culture, and the resultant worldwide battle over public space) to the Tribeca Film Festival. We did our festival launch the old-school way:

- We saved our world premiere for a top U.S. film festival that had a history of acquisitions.

- We got a top-class sales agent to marshal the distribution world and get people excited about our film.

- No advance screeners went out to potential buyers.

- We paid a ton of money for a conventional publicist to get the film written up, so potential distributors would know that there was interest in our film.

- We spent more money on a variety of marketing efforts to get our audience into the theaters (the festival's theaters).

- We held off creating DVDs for sale so as not to compet with any potential distributor.

And the results: Each of our five screenings (in 500- to 600-seat venues) was sold out. People lined up around the block; 100 to 200 people were turned away at each screening! The audiences were engaged in the film: People laughed in places that I didn't expect; there were eruptions of applause after the screenings and mobs of adoring fans.

And nothing in terms of sales. No overall deal with an advance that made any financial sense. We were offered extremely low money deals for theatrical and DVD, tied together so that we were sure that we would never see a dime. No television or cable. No foreign. 2007 was the tipping point in the collapse of the studio-based independent distribution model. We did get interest from a few DVD companies — however, none with any significant advance. What the F? The market had changed — drastically.

A week after Tribeca, our film was available for sale on Canal Street — as a bootleg.

We could have sold copies of our film to our enraptured audiences (2,500 people in the theaters, plus the 800 turned away). Converting just 10 percent of those 3,300 would have meant $6,600 in sales.

In short, we received a good, no advance deal from New Video, who also handle our download-to-own digital rights. The DVD was scheduled to be released at the end of May 2008. I was still committed to having a theatrical release. After an unfortunate sidestep with a company who said that they would release the film theatrically, I decided to do a theatrical release on my own, knowing that I had a very small window in which to do so, as determined by my DVD release. I started in January 2008 and ended the official theatrical at the end of June 2008 (note the crossover with the DVD release).

Part of the reason I wrote this book is because I wish I had had it before I released my film. Filmmakers are hungry for information on how to distribute and market their films. Many are shooting themselves in the foot in the process (like I did many times). While there are some disparate sources of information on these new methods, no single resource exists that combines all of the knowledge and tools now available to filmmakers.

Think Outside the Box Office is the first step in filling that void. It is a nuts-and-bolts guide for filmmakers who want to take control of their own destiny and create a strategy that works for their specific film. Each section and the chapters herein address an essential aspect of distribution and marketing and give specific techniques for independent filmmakers to release their films in today's marketplace. It is designed as a first step to develop a series of best practices for filmmakers and other visual media content creators wishing to distribute and market their work.

What I think is more important than a distribution and marketing manual, is that the book serves as a first step to reconceptualizing the way we think about creating and distributing visual media content throughout the world. Some of the most exciting techniques in here, such as transmedia, point to a new way telling stories that a few forward-thinking filmmakers are already experimenting with. These new ways of storytelling will not only help filmmakers get their work out to new audiences, but will expand their creative horizons as well. This book is about connecting filmmakers with audiences and creating long-term relationships with them. It is about thinking outside the box in terms of form and content. It is about embracing the changes in our industry that are facing us all — and using them to spur new creativity.

MY HOPES FOR THE BOOK

My first hope is that the ideas and opinions expressed in this book will cause you to think differently about how you can connect your film to its audience.

My second hope is that you will then use this book to create a strategy to make your film (and career) a success, whatever you define that success to be.

My third hope is that the book contains the practical advice necessary to put that strategy into practice.

My fourth hope is that this book will help you see how new forms of storytelling, distribution, and marketing can expand your creative horizons.

Not every idea, technique or reconceptualization in this book will work for every film or filmmaker. You need to trust your gut and decide what works best for you.

GENESIS/ METHODOLOGY/ EVOLUTION

The concepts and techniques presented in this book took shape over the last five years as result of three simultaneous paths in my life:

- I produced, directed, and sought distribution for my most recent film, *Bomb It*, a feature documentary about the global explosion of street art and graffiti. Part of my continued pursuit of *Bomb It*'s distribution is to use it as a lab for the techniques outlined in this book.

- I created a class at CalArts (California Institute of the Arts), where I teach in the Film Directing Program, titled "Reel World Survival Skills: Everything I Wish I Had Been Taught in Film School." This course concerns practical aspects of being a filmmaker, such as pitching, fundraising, and distribution. Teaching the subject caused me to structure and organize my thoughts about film distribution.

- Based on pursuing a hybrid distribution, split rights path for *Bomb It*, my financier and producer, Jeffrey Levy-Hinte, encouraged me to write about my experience and share it with others. In the summer of 2008 I contacted Scott Macaulay, the editor of *Filmmaker* magazine, and proposed writing an article about my DIY theatrical experience, and he agreed. Based on the success of that article, I wrote two more, one on DVD distribution and one on DVD marketing. I realized that the articles were much longer than Scott had requested and still didn't cover what needed to be covered — so I started to conceptualize this book.

METHODOLOGY

The knowledge used to create the content for the book has been has come from the following sources:

- My personal distribution experience with *Bomb It*, as well as my experience distributing my other features and documentaries for nearly 30 years

- My discussions, both on an ad hoc basis and in the classroom, with filmmakers, distributors, festival programmers, publicists, marketers, etc.

- Interviews that I have conducted over the past several months to explore this subject in more depth.

MY OPINION IS ONE OF MANY

I am opinionated. The people whom I spoke with and interviewed are opinionated. The book's purpose is twofold: to provoke thought and to provide practical tips and techniques.

You must process what I present to you in this book and decide which aspects of it work for your film and career. Not every idea, technique or reconceptualization in this book will work for every film or filmmaker. You need to trust your gut and decide what works best for you.

HOW THE BOOK WILL EVOLVE

Because many people expressed to me the need to get this information into the hands of filmmakers as soon as possible, I began writing in earnest after the Tribeca Film Festival in April 2009 and completed the book in time for a November 2009 launch. If I had waited to complete all of the interviews that I wanted to conduct for this book and worked the book's rough edges into a smoothly polished stone, it would not have been finished for another year.

There is a belief that the landscape of film distribution is changing every week. While in certain respects it is, in other respects there are still constants that will take years to evolve. Most of the information in this book is not time-dependent; however, some of it is and will need to be revised similarly to how computer software is revised. In addition I will continue to rework the book and interview more people. If you bought this book from my website, you will be able to buy subsequent editions of the book at a discount, similar to new software releases.

The book will also change through your participation. I wish to crowdsource the evolution of the book. I will not be asking a variety of people from across the globe to rewrite chunks of the book (although that is a good idea). I would like to include your experiences and knowledge in future editions of the book and the website discussed below.

I invite your feedback, suggestions, comments, and opinions. If you have a lot of experience, I invite you to complete one of my filmmaker surveys so that the breadth of knowledge can be expanded and shared with other filmmakers. Anyone completing this survey will receive a free copy of the next edition of the book. If you have a lot of distribution or marketing experience, I invite you to be interviewed for the web and future editions of the book. I hope to have the chance to interview everyone that is on my expanding list over the course of the next year. If you don't agree with the opinions expressed in the book, write to me and share your opinion with me.

THE WEBSITE

The web component of this book will first provide links to resources indicated in the book, as well as new ones discovered after the book's printing. These resources might be online services, articles, or other sites related to the subject.

The website will be constructed so that you can not only provide feedback and commentary on these resources, but it will be set up so that you can upload any resources that you know about – wiki in nature. Only through your participation can this knowledge grow for all filmmakers. I look forward to your comments, criticisms, rants, and knowledge.

My goal with the website, as it has been with the book, is to create a central locus of all tools, techniques, and opinions about visual media content distribution and marketing.

FOR MORE INFOMATION ON THE BOOK GOTO:

www.ultimatefilmguides.com

I want this book to help film-makers with their careers and career path, not just help them with one film.

WHO THE BOOK WAS WRITTEN FOR

Initially this book was to be written for people who had made a film and needed hard information on how to distribute it.

As I wrote the book, however, I expanded the audience to include people who had not yet made a film or had not made the film they would use this book for. I did this for the following reasons:

- I feel that it is important for filmmakers to consider the distribution and marketing of their films as early in the process as possible, even from inception. The techniques discussed in this book will work best the sooner they are implemented in the filmmaking process.

- I want this book to help filmmakers with their careers and career path, not just help them with one film. I feel that filmmakers should integrate their career paths with the distribution and marketing of their individual films.

I believe that the book also pertains to all forms of visual media content creators, who, for the purposes of this book, I will usually refer to as filmmakers. This includes feature filmmakers and short filmmakers, as well as people creating content specifically for the web. I feel that, just like "traditional" filmmakers, people who make a name for themselves on the web using visual content can use this book to expand their audiences, platforms of release, and resultant revenue. Already many YouTube stars are selling a variety of merchandise, so there is no reason they cannot go on tour and do live events as well. This book will help them, and you, to do that.

Filmmakers must use all techniques and models available to them to create a distribution strategy, and DIY is only one of those elements.

HOW TO USE THIS BOOK

I had been advised by the few intrepid souls who read the early drafts of the book that it is dense, too dense for a casual read. Too much information comes at the reader too fast to absorb in one sitting.

This book is not designed to be read in one sitting. I recommend that you read the first section of the book and then initially skim the rest of the book to get a sense of the breadth and scope of the new landscape of distribution and marketing. As part of that skim, I recommend that you read Chapters 6, 7, 8, 13, 14, 20, and 29 in their entirety, as well as the section introductions and conclusions and the opening paragraphs of every chapter. You can then go back to each chapter as it pertains to you and explore the techniques and suggestions as you need them. A warning: Chapter 9 is particularly dense, especially if you are not ready put your website online.

A shorter way of saying this is: Read the book; if you encounter anything that is too arcane or does not seem to apply to you at this point in time, skip it and come back to it later.

A NOTE ON DIY

When I was at the True/False film festival this past year, an independent distributor came up to me and said, "Oh, you're the DIY guy. I don't believe in DIY."

I feel this needs to be addressed on a few levels.

First, DIY is an attitude, or a point of view, more than anything else. It's a belief that if no one else is going to come along and do it for you, you should do it yourself rather than not doing it at all. For many people, it is more preemptive than that: "Since I believe in my work, I don't need anyone else to come along and be involved. If I believe in my work, I will produce it and get it out into the world."

However, the "yourself" part of DIY does not have to be taken literally. I strongly advocate creating a team to accomplish your release. IndieGoGo's slogan, "Do It With Others," is a bit more apt. In general, films take a team of people to create them and should require a team of people to release them. Even if you don't have much money, you can find people willing to be involved in the release of your film.

Finally, I don't believe in DIY as the only solution. Filmmakers must use all techniques and models available to them to create a distribution strategy, and DIY is only one of those elements. If there are companies willing to give you money to release your film in any medium, and it makes sense financially *and* works within your overall strategy, take it. This is why I prefer the term *hybrid distribution*, coined by distribution strategist Peter Broderick. According to Broderick, hybrid distribution allows filmmakers to combine limited deals with different distribution partners (e.g. educational, theatrical, television, home video) and direct sales from their website.

I would prefer to expand the use of the term hybrid distribution to mean any time a filmmaker or media content creator uses a variety of techniques (conventional and/or unconventional, working with companies and/or DIY, old school and/or new school etc.) in order to distribute and market their content. This definition reflects the necessity to combine all forms and techniques into a new whole.

ACKNOWLEDGMENTS

My Family

This book would not have been possible without the loving support of my wife, Jill, and my children, Sam and Lucie. Not only have they endured the countless years/months/hours of work that it took to release *Bomb It*, but they have also endured the additional months of work that it took to write this book. In order to get the book out for Fall 2009, I even spent a good percentage of our summer vacation writing.

My Philosophical Inspirations

While I have never lost my love of DIY and what it represents on a sociological level (most of my work concerns people who DIY in one way or another), and while I have continued to produce much of my work in a DIY fashion, I have to admit that I was as eager as any other filmmaker to leave the distribution of my films to others.

Lance Weiler and Peter Broderick both reinspired my belief in this process throughout the life of the film. My first partner on *Bomb It*, producer/DP Tracy Wares came to me one day after hearing Peter speak. "We have to retain the right to sell DVDs from our website — that's totally how it's done now and we'll make a ton of money." I rolled my eyes, thinking, "Great, the last thing I want to do is to be sitting in my office shoving DVDs in envelopes and licking stamps." But I got the chance to see one of Peter's presentations and I was hooked.

Right after seeing Peter, I heard about filmmaker Lance Weiler and what he had done to release his film *Head Trauma*. I checked out his incredible website, workbookproject.com, and realized that I needed to learn from this man. So I invited him to be a guest artist in my CalArts class. Lance was passionate about how it was possible to book a theatrical release for yourself, do the publicity for it as well, and sell DVDs both in person and from your website. He outlined a wide range of web-based marketing techniques that had my supposedly tech-savvy graduate students swimming in 0s and 1s.

Without what I learned from Peter and Lance, this book would not only not have been possible, but probably never would have happened.

My Sponsors

Without the continued support and encouragement of Jeffrey Levy-Hinte, the best producer that I have had the pleasure of working with, *Bomb It* could not have been completed or released. Jeff is a renowned producer (*Thirteen, Laurel Canyon, Mysterious Skin, Roman Polanski: Wanted and Desired, High Art*, among others) and is now an acclaimed director (*Soul Power*). While he chuckled as I proceeded with some of the more insane aspects of my DIY strategy, Jeff was the first person to tell me that I should write about my experiences and share them with the filmmaking community.

Jeff said that I should at least contact Scott Macauley, who, besides being a fabled independent producer (*Gummo, Raising Victor Vargas, First Love, Last Rites*, and many more), is also the editor of *Filmmaker* magazine. Scott suggested that I write about my theatrical experience, including the unpleasant story of how I ended up doing it myself. Based upon the success of that article, I wrote two more. Seeming to have a small knack for non-fiction gave me the confidence to write this book.

Ted Hope resides somewhere between psychic sponsor and philosophical inspiration. It was his speech at the 2008 FIND Filmmaker Forum on the need for a Truly Free Film that got me inspired to expand my writing on the subject.

Bomb It Support Team

I couldn't have released *Bomb It* without the following incredible people who worked tirelessly on the release of the film: producers Tracy Wares and Kate Christensen; webmaster Michael Medaglia, who has been my personal tutor in all things web; Lynn Hasty, who worked tirelessly promoting *Bomb It* as my publicist; Harrison Bohrman, who assisted me in the theatrical bookings and deliveries and earned his co-producer credit via that work and a two-year commitment to blog for *Bomb It*; Calder Greenwood, who endlessly revised our key art and graphics into its myriad permutations, usually with no notice whatsoever; and Shepard Fairey and Studio No. 1, who produced a kickass piece of key art.

Several people provided invaluable advice during the process of the release (all of which I have included in the book, of course): publicist Kathleen McInnis; theatrical booker/distributor Gregory Gardner, who taught me how to book my film; consultant Thomas Ethan Harris; and Scott Beibin of the Lost Film Fest, who taught me about street promotion.

Thanks to Luke Marchetti and Janet Brown for helping guide me through the digital rights land mines. John Chang and Brian Olson at Neoflix for patiently showing me how to use their site and their affiliate program.

Book Support Team

Key among them is my incredible summer assistant, Stephanie Bousley. This book would not have been finished this year without her invaluable help and support. Kazuha Torisawa came all the way from Japan to create the tools website!

Susan Graves who gave me the title to the book. Jennifer Hoche, copy editor, Justin Van Hoy, cover designer, and Will Hays, layout, who all turned around their excellent work with incredible speed to make the book happen.

My good friend Jon Kessler gave me invaluable counsel on the cover and design of the book. The incredible publisher Roger Gastman referred me to Justin and Justin referred me to Will. Thanks!

Book Readers

Scott Macauley, Liz Ogilvie, Gus Roxburgh, Orly Ravid, Darrin Holender, Kathleen McInnis, Stefan Forbes, Caitlin Boyle, Alice Elliot all read early versions of the book and gave me invaluable advice. The book is much better for their contribution.

Interviewees:

Thank you to the following people who allowed me to interview them and contribute their ideas to this book: Kate Christensen and Hung Nguyen, Cynthia Swartz, Matt Dentler, Jon Sloss, Chris Hyams,

Orly Ravid, Todd Sklar, Joe Swanberg, Ira Deutchman, Sara Pollack,

Mariana Palka, Jen Dubin, Cora Olson, Caitlin Boyle, Lisa Smithline, Kathleen McInnis, Liz Ogilvie, Christian Taylor, Richard Abramowitz, Jim Browne, Stephan Rafael, Darrin Holender, Meyer Shwartzstein, J. Todd Harris, Alice Elliot, John Hoskyns-Abrahall, Omer Nisar, Brad Balfour, Michael Medaglia, Ben Niles, Scott Kirsner, Steve Savage, Andrew Mer, Brian Chirls, Scilla Andreen, Lenny Magill, Adam Chapnick, Emily Abt and Marc Rosenbush. I didn't exactly interview Christy Dena, but via Facebook she gave me permission to use her Power to the Pixel presentation as a de facto interview.

Those who have guest taught on this subject in my classes:

John Di Minico, Kirby Dick, Arin Crumley, Mike Hedge, Steve Peters and Daniel Rappaport.

Filmmakers who completed my survey:

Curt Ellis, Ben Niles, Jim Tusty, Marty Ostrow and Brooks Elms.

If I forgot anyone or misspelled any names – I am very sorry!

Section 1
Getting Started

Whether or not you have made a film, it is important to take stock of your goals and resources. It is also important to consider who the audience or audiences for any film you make will be. These considerations are not static, but grow and develop as each project and your career evolves.

CHAPTER 1

YOUR FILM, YOUR NEEDS, YOUR AUDIENCE

Each film is unique and should have a unique distribution and marketing strategy (and should fit into your overall career/fan development path, if possible).

Before you can create a strategy for your film, you must take stock of:

1. What you want and/or need from the film.

2. The qualities of your film.

3. Your potential audience.

4. Your resources (I will cover this in chapter 2)

This is one of the most important steps in the process of distributing and marketing your film, and ideally should begin before you make your film, or at least during production.

WHAT DO YOU WANT FROM YOUR FILM?

This consideration is different for every filmmaker and every film, and could vary from year to year. You need to take stock of where you are in your career and what you need from your film. By getting your goals straight, it will help you make decisions about your film.

You can analyze this using the following categories, each of which needs to be weighed in relationship to one another:

1. Money

You either want to pay back your investors, make some money for yourself, make money for a charity, or some combination of all three.

2. A Career Launch, Help for Your Next Project, Reviews, and/or Fame

Many directors are not so concerned about making money from their current project (to the chagrin of their investors) and will choose a path that in some way furthers their career. For a filmmaker, this is often the rationale for losing money on a theatrical release. The release itself helps the filmmaker get the reviews and recognition needed for his or her next film that other forms of release do not garner as readily.

3. The Largest Audience for the Film

If having the largest audience possible for a film is the goal, a theatrical release may not be the best path. Television reaches millions more viewers than a theatrical release. This is one reason that some filmmakers have chosen a cable premiere for their film over a theatrical premiere. Just as a cable premiere has become a way to launch a film because of the number of eyeballs it offers, the digital realm is also being seen by many as a method for maximum exposure.

4. To Have an Impact on the World

You may choose to bypass the traditional film distribution structure and give the film away to groups that will screen the film to affect some kind of change — social or otherwise. While this more commonly applies to documentaries, there are narrative films that would fall into this category as well.

The above four goals (especially the first three) are generally what the old distribution model helped a filmmaker achieve. One of the benefits of the new approaches to distribution and marketing discussed in this book is the potential of reaching two additional goals:

5. A Long-Term, Sustainable Connection with a Fan Base

As opposed to trying for as large an audience as possible for one film, this goal is to develop deep connections with a committed fan base. These are fans who will return to your website and buy products from you or donate money to your films in order to sustain your artistic career. While the largest-audience-possible approach concentrates on breadth, this goal focuses on depth.

6. A Green/Sustainable Release.

Some filmmakers are starting to consider how the release of their films affects the environment. This is one argument for satellite/digital transmission of films to multiple theaters: it obviates the need for creating prints of your film and shipping them, both of which can have relatively high carbon footprints. In addition some filmmakers are choosing sustainable DVD packaging – or may choose not to release the film at all on DVD and instead only offer it digitally so it does not add to the flow of wasteful consumer products.

Your evaluation of the above desires will determine what a successful release will be for you and your team. Completing this evaluation will help when you have to make hard choices. This is especially true if your distribution alternatives do not allow you to receive all of these benefits without sacrifice.

YOUR FILM

When you have taken stock of your own and your team's desires, you need to make a close examination of your film.

1. How good is your film?

Will it hold up to the rigors of the ultra-competitive distribution marketplace? Perhaps this film is right for a full release, including some form of theatrical, perhaps not.

How has the film been received so far?

What have your immediate mentors and trusted allies told you?

Perhaps the film isn't really done and you need to take some time off and readdress it in a month or two, when you are fresh. Many film-makers are in such a rush to get their films done that they don't do them justice.

What has the feedback been from film festivals? (e.g., Have you gotten into any? How prestigious?) This, of course, should not be the only arbiter of value for your film. There are many films that don't fit the festival model. But for many independent films, festivals are a system of established gatekeepers, and if your film has not gotten into any of the 300 you have applied to, the universe might be telling you something.

How have the reviews been? (Note: same caveat as the festival question above.)

The point is to match the distribution path with the film, to balance your time releasing a film with the time needed to create new work.

2. Do you have any marketing hooks for your film?

Are their stars in the film? Do they have a core following?

Is there a compelling story in the making of your film?

Incredible reviews?

Major awards from major film festivals?

Is it shocking or controversial in any way?

Another way of looking at this question: What will motivate people to see or buy your film?

YOUR AUDIENCE

1. What is the market/audience for the film?

Audience identification should be a constant process of discovery during the production (and prep, post and distribution) of your film. Enlist your producers and close advisors to brainstorm. It is difficult to market to your audience if you don't know who that audience is.

There is rarely no one audience for a film. The audience is usually comprised of a number of different groups. The more targeted you are about this the better.

Audience analysis is much easier for documentaries than for narrative films, which is one reason why some documentaries have had an easier time utilizing the new models of distribution. Usually documentaries concern a specific niche topic, such as global warming, cross word puzzles, anti-war or any medical condition which will appeal to the family and friends of people afflicted with it, etc.

Unfortunately, for many narrative filmmakers, when asked about the audience for their film they don't get much further than "art-house audiences" or "young men from 18 to 35." Even if you have a multi-award winner from Sundance with piles of incredible reviews from the *New York Times, Boston Globe,* and the *New Yorker,* you need to be much more specific.

A narrative film that deals with any of the above topics (or a myriad of others) can also appeal to the same organized niche communities.

In addition, narrative films have niches that exist outside of those used by documentaries. Marc Rosenbush made a surreal Buddhist noir film, *Zen Noir,* so he took his film to David Lynch fans, Buddhists, and New Age communities.

2. Who Is Your Core Audience?

Your core audiences are those who are most likely to be drawn to your film and support it. Core and niche are two terms that are usually used interchangeably, but I think it is important to distinguish between them. A niche audience is a group of people with the a shared select interest or preference. The core audience(s) are the *strongest* niche audience(s) for the film. The core might be compsed of people from several niche communities. The core are the fans who will not only purchase your film but will be the most ardent promoters of it.

For *Bomb It* this was pretty easy: Our initial target core audiences were people who participated in graffiti and street art or were major fans of it.

For a documentary about food production in the United States, such as the awesome *King Corn*, which concerns food production

roxk

in the United States, the core audiences would be those people concerned about food policy, farm sustainability, treatment of farm animals. There are people organized around topics as specific as these.

3. Secondary and Tertiary Audiences - Concentric Circles

You should identify various layers of audiences that have varying levels of interest in your film. *Bomb It's* secondary layers of audiences would be fans of street culture/subversive culture (skaters, sneaker pimps), then lovers of hip-hop culture, or people interested in issues of public space. Further out are fans of modern art, lovers of documentary films about culture/subculture and finally lovers of documentary film generally.

For *King Corn,* the secondary and tertiary audiences would be people interested in treatment of all animals, public health policy, the environment, and the left wing blogosphere.

4. Reaching Your Audiences

Can you reach your various audiences? Are there active online communities for these audiences? Do groups and organizations exist that will support your film?

How do you reach the secondary and tertiary audiences?

As you expand outward from your core audience, you can see how it becomes relatively more difficult to reach the outer layers of your potential audience. That is why it is important to identify your niches' layers and consider how you might be able to access them.

Often it takes more resources to reach the secondary and tertiary layers of your audience. The more specific you can be, the more effectively you can utilize your resources.

5. What is the best delivery system for your audience?

Your film might be more naturally suited to one market than another. (e.g., It might have its best success in the educational market and may not be suited to theatrical release.)

How do your audiences consume media?

Do they go out to the movies, or watch television?

Your audience might live online and as a result you should be focused on getting your film out simultaneously to as many on-line outlets as possible at the beginning of the release.

By knowing what markets your audience uses to consume media it will make it easier for you to provide them to access to your content which hopefully will result in greater success toward your goals, whatever those may be.

The Next Step

Once you have taken stock of the film that you have made, the audiences for that film and what you want/need from the film, it is time to evaluate your resources, which is the subject of the next chapter.

This is not a hard-and-fast rule. Rather, it is a guide to changing your preconceptions

CHAPTER 2

YOUR RESOURCES: THE NEW 50/50

If you mention a 50/50 split to most film producers, they will commonly think of it as the last stop in an equity waterfall.

The *new* 50/50 does not concern net profits. It concerns a shift in thinking for filmmakers about the allocation of resources when making and distributing their films.

The new 50/50 is as follows:

50 percent of your time and resources should be devoted to creating the film. 50 percent of your time and resources should be devoted to getting the film out to its audience, aka distribution and marketing.

This is *not* a hard-and-fast rule. Rather, it is a guide to changing your preconceptions. Many if not most filmmakers still do not put aside any money or time for their distribution and marketing.

Each film will require a different set of resources. What you need to do is plan to put much more money and time into this process than you ever thought you would need.

Resources are broken down into **time** and **money**, which are equally precious. And there is an inverse relationship between the two, as most filmmakers know from making their movies. If you have money, you can buy yourself some time (more shoot days, larger crews to get more done, etc.). If you are handcrafting your own film, it will cost you less money but take a much longer time. It is the same with a release. If you have a lot of money you can hire someone to do your release for you. If you don't, they you will need to do much of it yourself.

In the second half of the chapter I give some ideas on ways that filmmakers can deal with this new reality.

TIME

Depending on what type of release you decide to pursue, you can expect to spend about a year releasing your film, especially if you choose to have a theatrical release and fully exploit all rights. While this could happen in as little as six months — or could expand to several years — a year seems to be a fair assessment based on my conversations with other filmmakers and distributors.

Framed within the new 50/50: If you spend a year making your film full-time (full prep, production, post), expect to spend a solid year releasing your film full-time.

Just as you spent years developing your script, you will spend years overseeing the ultimate disposition of the film. Fortunately however, just as your time in development is usually not spent full-time on one film, the same is true for distribution. After the initial intensive commitment, you can work on other projects, but your previous films will need some attention for some time.

The long tail is very long. This will be the case even if you assemble a great team to help you release the film.

Unfortunately, this is no joke. It is reality.

Todd Sklar, applied the band touring model to film in order to release his college comedy *Box Elder*. He has taken that experience to create the guerrilla distribution/marketing combine Range Life Entertainment. Sklar says that in any other industry, one half of the work is spent creating the product and the other half is getting it to the public. Think of a restaurant: half the work goes into making the food, the other half goes into running the restaurant business. He surmises that once filmmakers realize how much work it takes to release a film, perhaps they will decide to make: A) fewer films; and B) better films, ensuring that the films they make are as good as possible every step of the way in order to compete in a crowded marketplace.

The production team behind the Sundance-premiered, award-winning indie film *Good Dick* — writer/director Marianna Palka and producers Jen Dubin and Cora Olson — put it another way: Creating a film is like giving birth to a child. You don't abandon a child if parenthood isn't working out after a few months. Instead you work with that child and help it develop to its full potential. Whether you like it or not, that child is going to be with you for awhile.

> The more effort you put into your release, the better release you will have.

There is a bit of a myth that doing any work on your release is something new, that this new model of distribution places a new burden on independent filmmakers, who now have to be involved in their own releases. While I would agree that it is more work now than before, the truth is that for most independent films released by conventional distributors, the more effort they put into their releases, the better the releases were.

You might be exhausted from making your film, upset that you now have to take on this new burden yourself, which may prevent you from moving on to something new. I get it — it is a lot of work, and involves a skill set that is a struggle for many filmmakers. Being involved in distribution requires strong organizational and sales skills, qualities that may seem to be part of a producer's skill set as opposed to a writer/director's. But independent filmmakers have had to wear a lot of hats for a long time and have had to be their own producers for a long time. So this requirement that independents be more entrepreneurial is not new.

MONEY

Likewise, if you are spending $50,000 on a film's production, expect to spend $50,000 on the release. I have spoken to a number of filmmakers who spent the same on their release as they did on production: $200,000 and $200,000, $8 million and $8 million, $50,000 and $50,000.

This 50/50 "rule" is more prevalent in the studio system. It is not uncommon for a $100 million film to have $100 million or more spent on its P&A (prints and advertising — an inaccurate but traditional term for the total distribution and marketing costs).

What kind of release you can craft also depends on how much money you have. Traditional theatrical releases are very expensive, even when done in the most cost-effective manner. Theaters will be hesitant to book you if you are not spending some money on publicity and marketing. In New York and Los Angeles, the contracts often require you to spend a specific amount on the advertising for your movie (around $2,500 in each market, at the very bottom end); in some cases, you are required to hire a specific approved publicist (another $8,000, at least).

For a DIY theatrical release, at the very, very low end of funding, you should be setting aside $30,000 to $50,000. At the high end, for a small release, you could set aside $200,000 (and you'll be surprised at how fast that goes). You can readily spend more money and many people have.

There are ways to put your film out for free or nearly free and even earn a little income from it. However, putting some money into your release can improve the release dramatically, especially at the very low end of the budget range. The more time you have to plan, the further your money will go. In general, that eternal triangle of "good, cheap, fast" applies to releases as much as it does to production. You get to pick two, but not all three, and independents usually pick good and cheap.

Before and during the creation of your distribution and marketing strategy, you need to come up with two figures:

1. How much money do you have to release this film? This includes what you can set aside and what you can raise.

2. How much do you need? You get this figure from doing a budget for your release, just as you budget your production. You should do your production and distribution budgets at the same time, *before your shoot*. Specific budgeting instructions are in Chapter 19.

HELP FOR THE NEW THE 50/50

I wasn't going to outline a whole world of hurt for you without providing some thoughts on how media content creators can take some of the load off of the difficulty of marketing and distributing a film.

SOME IDEAS FOR TIME

1. Understand You Are Building for Your Future

The good news with the new paradigm is that the time spent on distribution and marketing for one film, helps build up your fan base and support for your future. This effort will build on itself and reap benefits that we can only begin to think about.

2. Take the Plunge

Some of the techniques that I hear filmmakers complaining about the most – social networking for instance - have a bit of a learning curve at first. But once you get into the swing of things – you can limit your time on Twitter, Facebook and your blog to a half hour a day (15 minutes in the morning and 15 mintues in the evening). You can of course spend more time if you enjoy it.

3. Crew: A Manifesto for a New Producer

Just like you most likely did not make the film on your own, you should not be distributing and marketing the film on your own. I would argue that from now on, every film needs one person devoted to the distribution and marketing of the film from inception, just as they have a line producer, assistant director, or DP. Since it always helps for a crew person to have a title I propose the following:

The Producer of Marketing and Distribution or PMD

I have given this position the title of producer because it is that important. (For someone learning the ropes start them at associate producer and move them up to producer).

This producer needs to be integrated into the film production team itself. They are not responsible for the physical production of the film (because if they are – you and I know they will never do their distribution and marketing work). During production this person would coordinate all of the work I outline in Section 2. During distribution and marketing, this person would coordinate the work of all of the other experts assembled for distribution and marketing as outlined in Chapter 5.

Having a PMD on your film would serve two important functions:

1. The PMD would be responsible for making sure that everything that needs to happen for distributing and marketing the film happens, from still photos to transmedia coordination and everything in between.

2. It would provide the necessary manpower to make it happen. As long as we push this work to the side, assign it to interns, believe that "we will get to it later", it won't get done. This person may need to bring on others to help, but one person needs to be responsible.

4. Distribution Co-Ops

Filmmakers might want to band together to share resources and knowledge in distributing and marketing their films.

There are a number of educational distribution co-ops that have been functioning for some time, the most prominent one being New Day Films (discussed in Chapter 27). These co-ops were started in part because a group of filmmakers decided to band together to share the intense amount of work that educational distribution involves. In addition these filmmakers did not want to reinvent the wheel each time and wanted a greater say in how their revenues were handled.

I feel that all filmmakers could use this model for all aspects of their distribution and marketing, not limiting distribution co-ops to the educational market. I look forward to hearing from the first collective formed by an enterprising group of filmmakers to release their films together, thus sharing the burden of those releases.

SOME IDEAS FOR MONEY

1.Sources of Money

Here is a quick summary of sources of funding for your release:

Your Investors

If you go back to your investors with a well-defined distribution plan, they might be convinced to put in some more money, especially if you've demonstrated some success on the festival circuit. "In for a penny, in for a pound" — in other words, how else are they going to get their money back?

Other Investors

Just as you raise finishing funds (depending on the financial structure of your film), you can raise money from other investors to pay for the distribution of your film.

Money Earned from the Sale of the Film

Perhaps you received a small advance from a DVD company or a cable sale. Do you allocate this to investors or do you put it back into the release? Or do you give a percentage to each? Or perhaps this decision has already been made for you in the investor agreement.

As you earn money from the film, you also need to decide how much will go into continuing the distribution of the film and how much can go toward paying back the investors.

Distributors used to make these monetary decisions for you. The upside is that you can now make these decisions yourself.

<u>Sponsors</u>

This takes lead time and effort, but it can pay off. The release of my film *Better Living Through Circuitry* was mainly financed through sponsorships. You can see sponsor logos all over the release materials for films these days.

<u>Non-Governmental Organizations (NGOs) & Community Organizations</u>

There might be an organization that will help fund your release, especially if it's a documentary. *King Corn* had the Kellogg Foundation fund their initial efforts.

<u>Your Supporters and Fans - Crowdfunding</u>

The goal of a career development model of filmmaking and distribution is that you create an active fan base and supporters who will help you in all phases of your work. Having your fans pay for your release is a form of crowdfunding which I will address more specifically in Chapter 10. I think crowdfunding is one of the most exciting new tools to come out of the new paradigm of distribution and production.

2. Keep Your Production Costs Low

Keeping your costs of production low allows you to put aside money for distribution and marketing. It is much better for the life of a film to have the production costs total $50,000 (with $50,000 for marketing and distribution) than to make a film for $100,000 and have no resources leftover to get the film seen.

The challenge is to make a great film with slim means and to have the discipline to *not* dip into the distribution kitty when times get tough in production and post. Having been in the production trenches myself, I know how hard this can be.

3. Fiscal Discipline

Filmmakers who often control all of the resources through their LLCs should consider these two steps for external discipline:

• Structure the LLC so that a certain percentage raised has to be set aside for distribution and marketing. It then becomes a legal requirement.

• Put the money for distribution and marketing into escrow. (Note that step 2 might be a way of ensuring step 1.)

A Caveat

If you only want to put your film out on the Internet for people to watch if they find it, you can still do this for next to nothing. But if that is all you want to do, you probably wouldn't have bought this book.

CHAPTER 3

OVERVIEW OF RIGHTS, MARKETS AND WINDOWS

Before you can contemplate the strategy for your film, you need to know what markets are available for you to monetize your film.

I am going to take a bold step and reclassify the rights that film-makers control for the exploitation of their films into three basic categories:

1. Live Event/Theatrical

2. Merchandise

3. Digital

I feel that this reclassification best helps filmmakers conceptualize how they can create a strategy that works for their film *and* helps them implement that strategy. This chapter will provide an initial survey of those rights. Much of the rest of the book will be spent exploring these in depth.

THE OVERALL DEAL

The new school of film distribution is based on the absence of an overall deal, also referred to as an all rights deal. An overall deal is when a distributor buys all the distribution rights to your film, either for the world or North America, for a long time — commonly 15-25 years. Normally they offer a cash advance against net returns of the film's distribution. Filmmakers have found that they rarely receive more than this advance. Hence, if you made your film for $300,000, a $2 million advance is going to make you very happy. However, a $25,000 advance for all rights is much less appealing for the same film.

An overall deal does not mean that your work is done once you turn over the film. You not only have to *deliver* the film — which can be relatively onerous and expensive if you need to satisfy a traditional distributor — but you will also be required to participate in the publicity of the film. If you are lucky, you will also be able to participate in the strategy of the release and marketing.

THE SPLIT RIGHTS SCENARIO

The rejection of (or failure to land) an overall deal leads you into the world of split rights. A split rights scenario is just as it sounds: The rights to each of the various revenue streams (theatrical, DVD, etc.) are split apart so that they can be sold individually. In general, you can make more money this way than with an overall deal. This is because nearly all overall deals cross-collateralize revenues. This means that if there are losses from one revenue stream, such as theatrical, the profits from another revenue stream, such as DVD, will be used to pay for those losses. However, in an overall deal, you as a filmmaker rarely have control over how much money is spent on the marketing and promotion of each revenue stream, and you have little control over the accounting of those expenses.

For *Bomb It* we were offered a number of DVD deals in which DVD distributors said they would do a theatrical release. However, we knew that by doing this, the cost of the theatrical release would likely eat up most of the profits from the DVD release, and hence we did not take these deals. A split rights scenario is the heart of a hybrid strategy to release your film.

A RE-CLASSIFICATION OF RIGHTS

There are several types of rights available to independent filmmakers today to get their films seen and to monetize their distribution.

1. LIVE EVENT/THEATRICAL

This includes all types of theatrical, non-theatrical, alternative theatrical, and grassroots screenings, as long as they are with an audience and the film is shown as the filmmaker intended (usually from beginning to end, in the dark).

This is a new category that I have created (reasoning explained in

Chapter 13) that includes the following traditional rights classifications:

Conventional Theatrical: Where films are screened in conventional movie theaters and admission is charged. Usually films begin with weeklong runs and receive reviews in the film section of newspapers.

Non-theatrical Screenings: Free viewings on school campuses, libraries, or any other venue where *admission is not charged*.

Semi-theatrical: All non-conventional theatrical venues in which a fee is charged for admission. This includes museums, cinematheques, and film festivals.

Grassroots/Community: An exploding field of individuals and organizations obtaining films to screen for their community. Overlaps with non-theatrical and semi-theatrical.

The lines between the above categories are dissolving every day. I consider the military screening market a part of this category, too.

2. CONSUMER PRODUCTS/MERCHANDISE

In which the consumer purchases an actual tactile product, whether it's a DVD, T-shirt, etc. While the actual DVD can be viewed in a variety of ways, the consumer interaction begins by purchasing a physical product.

Home Video/DVD: Home-use DVDs, boxed sets, signed sets, special editions, and collectors' editions. With the advent of digital delivery, the more filmmakers think about giving extra value in the packages they sell, the more likely they will retain these sales.

Merchandise: The old industry definition of merchandise is all consumer products that are not the film (e.g., not the DVD or VHS). This includes T-shirts, CD soundtracks, games, toys, books, mugs, stickers, posters — any non-film element that can be purchased and held in your hand, worn, put on a wall, or generally provides some use value other than viewing the film.

Educational: Educational sales are exactly what they sound like — sales to educational institutions. This is one of the rights whose categorization is blurry, since it involves selling both DVDs and tapes to institutions but also involves non-theatrical screenings. Since the bulk of this business is still oriented around physical products, I am placing it here.

3. DIGITAL

In which the content is delivered electronically, for viewing on a private screening device, whether it's a telephone or home theater. No physical product is purchased, no audience (outside of family and friends) is present, and often the viewing experience is broken up by time.

Television and Cable: Either free over-the-air broadcast (commonly referred to as television) or subscription and non-subscription channels delivered by means of a cable. Also included would be pay-over-the-air, such as satellite TV. It might be a bit of heresy to place television and cable in the same category as other digital rights, but I have a strong argument for it, which is discussed in Section 6.

Pay-Per-View/Video on Demand: Traditional video on demand or pay-per-view is sold over cable or satellite signals and not over the Internet.

Digital Rights and Mobile: These typically concern the distribution of your film through various Internet channels such as download to own, download to rent, and the various forms of streaming. However, mobile phone rights are beginning to be lumped into this category as the line between mobile phones and the Internet blurs.

FOREIGN SALES:

This is not one individual right but a grouping of all of the above rights outside of the home territory of the filmmaker or the film's origin. I am separating these rights out because of the different institutional structures that exist to sell these rights.

The advantage of categorizing distribution in the above manner is to focus on the audience experience as opposed to delivery. It also focuses on various established modes of distribution so as to make the process for independent filmmakers easier to organize their activities around. I will concede that some of these lines are blurry and that there are other ways to categorize rights. I'm sure I'll receive arguments for other methods. But for the purpose of this book, I feel this method is most helpful.

DISTRIBUTION WINDOWS

When discussed in terms of distribution, a window is the amount of time that rights are allowed to be exploited in one market before the film is made available for exploitation in another market. For example, a "theatrical window" of six months would mean that the film would only be available in the theatrical marketplace for six months before it would be made available on another platform, such as DVD.

Why Windows?

Windows were established so as to maximize the revenue for one rights category before allowing the film to be released in a second less expensive per-person rights category. This windowing structure allowed distributors to charge more to customers who wanted to see a film sooner than others. Seeing a movie in a theater has traditionally been the most expensive way to see a film, so it was given first priority. Traditionally studios would give a film as long as needed to collect theatrical revenue. If the only way people could see the film was in theaters and they really wanted to see the film, then they would have to see it in a theater.

The second traditional window is the rental or purchase of a DVD (or VHS or Laserdisc). Again, the studios would give a film three to six months to maximize home video revenue before it was given to pay TV (in which you pay a subscription per month for a variety of programming). Pay TV stations would require their own window, making their services and subscriptions more valuable to customers. The last window was free TV, for which you pay nothing. However, when a network bought a film for a high price to broadcast as an event, it would often go before the cable window. When video on demand (VOD) and pay-per-view were introduced, they were placed between theatrical and home video release. For documentary filmmakers, the lucrative educational market has traditionally gone between theatrical and home video.

Debra Zimmerman, executive director of the nonprofit Women Make Movies, which has grown into the largest distributor of media by and about women in North America, explains these windows (and the subsequent revenue from them) as a pyramid (the following is her order):

- Theatrical

- Semi-theatrical

- Television

- Educational

- DVD/Home Video

As you "descend" from market to market, it is very hard, if not impossible, to climb back up the pyramid and get people to pay more for a service that they can get for a lesser price or for free. Note: Others would put DVD/Home Video ahead of television. At this point it doesn't matter, since, as Debra notes, now there are many different pyramids.

The Collapse of Distribution Windows: The Emergence of "Day and Date"

Windows of distribution have been collapsing — becoming shorter and shorter (six months, down to two months, down to one month), to the point where there is no window whatsoever.

This lack of any window has been termed "day and date" and is the release pattern that has gotten the most press for the last year or two. Stephen Soderbergh's *Bubble* garnered a lot of press as one of the first "day and date" releases.

"Day and date" means that the film comes out in theaters on the same day and date as it does in one or more other markets. IFC Films and Magnolia have made a business out of releasing a film theatrically and on video on demand at the same time.

In this book we will explore a number of different release-pattern scenarios, but first, let's take a look at why release windows are collapsing and morphing for non-studio media products:

Independent Films Have One Best Opportunity for Press and Promotion

When we released *Better Living Through Circuitry*, we received an avalanche of press for the theatrical release, but when the DVD came out more than six months later, we were lucky to get a few reviews. For most independents, it is very hard to get a second review in a major publication for DVD or another ancillary. The studios, however, don't need to worry about this. They have enough resources to run as many marketing and publicity campaigns as they want. The high cost of theatrical marketing has caused filmmakers and independent distributors to take advantage of that marketing for their other revenue streams as effectively as possible. In order to do this, the ancillary releases need to be close to the theatrical release.

The reasons that filmmakers have one opportunity for press are:

- There are a ton of products on the market, all vying for attention from customers and from the press. Most journalists have, at best, one chance to give you attention.

- Because of the high-speed culture we live in, there is a constant demand for what is new. When you release your film six months to a year later on DVD, is often viewed as old news.

- You, the filmmaker, have limited resources in terms of time, energy, and money to promote your film. One concerted attack might be all that you can do.

The Internet and Internet Culture

The other major reason filmmakers are collapsing their release windows is that once you release a film, it is hard to keep it in the bottle. If people want to see your film, it will be up on a pirate site faster than you can blink. Therefore, if you want to try to maximize revenue, one theory is that you want to have your film up on as many platforms as possible at the same time.

Matt Dentler, who was the festival producer of the South by Southwest Film Festival and is now head of programming at Cinetic Rights Management notes that young consumers don't want to go back and be fed media one way. For better or worse, we are in a culture of "I want what I want right now and if you don't give it to me, I'll find something else." This puts incredible pressure on filmmakers (and all media creators) to day-and-date their entire release. I don't think that Dentler believes that filmmakers should dump their film into all markets at the same time, but filmmakers have to be aware of patterns of consumer demand and have to think strategically about how to meet that demand.

There is ongoing discussion as to how best to monetize content while also making sure you satisfy consumer demand. The music industry has been grappling with this for many years, and now the film industry is.

Creative Windowing

One of the opposing strategies to the "day and date" release is to keep some control over the release pattern (and windows) in order to more effectively monetize a film. Filmmakers and distributors are experimenting with new promotion and revenue-generating models to try to maximize their success, monetary or otherwise.

Creative windowing suggests that there is no one window pattern that will work for every film. Each film must find its own path and create its own window structure to achieve its form of success.

THE MOST IMPORTANT STEP

When you have taken stock of your film, your needs, your audience and your resources, you should examine what markets might be best for your film and what will be the best utilization of your resources to create the most successful distribution of your film. You have to decide what success means for you and your film. You then need to create a strategy comprised of a distribution and marketing plan that will enable you to achieve that success.

CHAPTER 4

CREATING YOUR STRATEGY

You need to create a distribution and marketing plan/ strategy that takes into consideration your film, your needs, your audience, and your resources, as well as the state of the distribution landscape.

You should create this as soon as possible, even before you have shot your film and perhaps before you write the film.

This strategy/plan is not set in stone. It is a living organism, just as your film is. It evolves as you learn more about your film and its relationship to the distribution landscape around it.

Distribution strategist Peter Broderick recently sat down with me to discuss distribution and marketing strategies. Peter has consulted with hundreds of filmmakers and has been a pioneer in helping filmmakers develop hybrid distribution strategies for their films. He was president of Next Wave Films, which launched many an indie's career, and was a key player in the growth of the ultra-low-budget feature film movement.

KNOW YOUR PRIORITIES

Broderick feels that this is one of the toughest aspects of maintaining a consistent distribution strategy for a film. Most filmmakers desire all six of the "wants" outlined in Chapter 1 in equal measure:

1. Money

2. Career Launch

3. Audience for the Film

4. An Impact on the World

5. Long-Term Fan Base

6. A Green/Sustainable Release

In other words, filmmakers want it all. Broderick notes that this is rarely possible. It is unrealistic to achieve all of these goals simultaneously. By not making hard choices about these priorities in advance, filmmakers hurt themselves when they have to choose between competing distribution options. Because the hybrid distribution world is fluid, it is that much more important that filmmakers have a framework within which to make decisions.

Broderick believes that filmmakers fear that if they don't pursue all their goals at once, they will limit their possibilities and lose out on opportunities.

Unfortunately, without a framework in which to make decisions, filmmakers are at risk of not achieving *any* of their goals.

Here are some examples that will illustrate some potential conflicts.

Example 1: You have a narrative film that has a large niche appeal to the spiritual community. The film has been endorsed by the makers of *The Secret*, a hugely successful spiritual documentary.

Rights Path A Sell all rights to a distribution company who is offering a $20,000 advance and is guaranteeing a theatrical release. The distributor also wants all rights for 20 years to cross-collateralize the theatrical losses.

Rights Path B A split rights scenario where the filmmaker could put together a no-advance home video deal with excellent terms, sell the DVD at personal appearances and off their website. The makers of *The Secret* are willing to help you create a grassroots screening campaign and share their email list with you. But there is not enough money for a theatrical release.

If your goal is a potential "career launch," then you might be jumping at Path A. In conventional terms, a screening at a conventional theater means you have arrived, or it means this to your ego, your parents, and perhaps your friends. Maybe you'll get a few reviews, if the New York/L.A. papers don't fire any more reviewers before your release.

Path B gives not only a greater chance of monetary return, but of a larger audience experiencing the film. Granted, you don't have a conventional distribution apparatus behind you, but you do have a very strong, active niche with a very successful sponsoring organization. Based on the success of *The Secret* you have an almost guaranteed chance of making more than $20,000 on your film through DVD sales alone. You won't have conventional reviews of your film, and even though there might be screenings in community settings (probably a lot of them), there is no theater that you can point to and say, "See, my film is playing there."

You can see how in this circumstance the conventional career launch goal directly conflicts with monetary recoupment, since it is unlikely that the investor will get any additional money beyond the advance. In addition, this approach most likely conflicts with a goal of attaining a broad audience, because conventional releases are generally not the best way to reach the widest audience possible.

Example 2 comes courtesy of Broderick: You have a global environmental documentary on a pressing issue. You have already partnered with an environmental organization to help promote the film.

Rights Path A An online platform has offered to do an incredible amount of viral media to create awareness around the film in exchange for the exclusive streaming rights to the film. However, they are not going to pay for these rights. They will work with your partner organization to create fundraising events in a number of cities to not only raise money for the cause, but to create awareness for the film. This online site has a global audience. In addition, you are able to get the film on PBS, but PBS is not paying. Instead they give you two minutes of national sponsorship airtime. During this airtime they will indicate that the DVD is available online for a donation, at whatever the customer wants to pay.

Rights Path B An innovative distributor wants to create a hybrid theatrical/grassroots release of the film, but wants to sell DVDs through their DVD distributor at $24.95. An up-and coming-cable outfit has offered $30,000 for the television rights. They also want to window the digital rights of the film, holding off on free streaming for at least a year.

Both paths represent good split rights scenarios. However, Path A represents a clear choice that supports the goal of having an impact on the world, and secondarily reaching the broadest audience possible. All of the effort is put into raising awareness of the problem, fundraising to seek a solution, and getting the film out to as many people as possible, as soon as possible.

Path B does a fair amount of audience awareness, but by selling the DVDs at a higher price point in an attempt to recoup production funds, as well as choosing a smaller cable company because a sale is involved, and creating a free streaming holdback, this path represents one of greater financial reward, but with less audience and cause outreach.

In both of these relatively extreme examples, if the filmmakers did not have their priorities straight, they might not have made the best decision for their goals/needs, simply because they did not have a clear idea as to what their goals/needs were.

EVALUATING YOUR PROGRESS

You must set your goals so that you can evaluate whether your chosen strategy is successful in meeting those goals.

If you have not chosen your priorities, it is impossible to evaluate your level of success.

Stages

As mentioned above, the advantage of this new model, is that you are able to change the direction of your release.   Broderick indicates that it is a matter of stages:

> **Stage 1:** After you have decided what your priorities are, you decide on a course of action that best fits those priorities.   You put that plan of action into practice.

> **Evaluate Stage1:** Using your priorities as a guide, how successful was Stage 1? To evaluate the strategy and implementation, you should ask:

> - How have sales been?
>
> - How has attendance been?
>
> - How has the core audience responded?
>
> - How have distribution partners responded? For instance, some environmental groups like the film, others did not like it. From this evaluation, you would put more resources into the first group.
>
> - Have you reached any of your secondary audiences?

- Have your priorities changed?

- Do you need to adjust the strategy and implementation to accommodate changing goals and/or changing market circumstances?

From this evaluation you move on to:

Stage 2: Enhancing or reinforcing the old plan, or putting a new plan into practice. Perhaps it is as simple as broadening the markets in which the film is available.

You then proceed to evaluate this stage as you did Stage 1, and continue to do so for the commercial life of the film in various successive stages.

I would argue that the stages need to be relatively short in the beginning of the release, so that you can monitor the effectiveness during the most critical stage of the release and react appropriately.

As the film's release matures, you can lengthen these stages and modify them less frequently. This should be an organic process, because as the film is in release, it should eventually find some comfortable best path of distribution and marketing. After all, at some point you might want to move on to a new project.

YOUR BEST TIME FOR RELEASE

Here are some factors to consider when determining when you should release your film. More in-depth discussion of each of these points will occur later in the book. However, these are overall guidelines to keep in mind.

1. You should release your film when it is ready. Make sure your film is the best it can be before you release it into the market. A caveat to this would be if you are going to crowdsource feedback for your film online, which could be an interesting way to engage your audience.

2. Release your film when you have had proper time to prepare for the release. Do you have enough lead time to handle your publicity properly? This takes three to six months.

3. Release your film when you have the first stage of your distribution ready to go, all materials, all markets lined up. Things happen

so fast during a release that it is best to have all your ducks in a row before you start. If you are having some form of live event/theatrical release, are you poised to take advantage of the publicity — for example, are your DVD and/or digital rights ready to go within an intelligent windowing strategy?

4. Consider the sequencing of your various rights. For instance, will the film be broadcast? Do you need to get the film into theaters before that? If the film is going to be on television, you want to make sure you have the DVD ready to go, since television is becoming another avenue of promotion for DVDs. How do you sequence the VOD and television release? Is your educational release important to your strategy? If so, how do you sequence that with your DVD?

5. Release your film when you have the ability to organize promotion around some live event. Whether this is a festival, conventional theatrical, grassroots, etc., having a live event helps.

6. In terms of booking your film as a live event, here are some additional factors to keep in mind:

- The availability of the theaters you want to book. Fall is crowded territory for art houses, as is from late fall to the Oscar voting deadline, when studios four-wall theaters in New York and Los Angeles to keep their films in front of voters' faces. Study the changing landscape of releases.

- Are there any community events that you can organize around? National months or weeks concerning your topic around which you can coordinate press and community screenings in support of your release?

- Weather (especially if you are doing regional releases). If the Northeast is a critical territory for your film, it might be tough to get people out in the dead of winter.

In summary, Broderick points out how the new distribution paradigm allows independent filmmakers to be more nimble in the current swirling pool of markets and rights. Large distribution companies are used to doing business one way, the way that has worked for them. A hybrid approach allows filmmakers to change their strategy not only as their project develops, but as they encounter market forces during the distribution of their film. Dentler observes that the ability of filmmakers to experiment with different release patterns and strategies allows them to tap into audiences they never would have found before.

You have incredible choices available to you in determining how you will release your film. Get your priorities set first, and then determine a plan of action to achieve those priorities.

every film needs one person devoted to the distribution and marketing of the film from inception.

CHAPTER 5

BUILDING YOUR TEAM

A classic distribution company is full of people — bookers, publicists, marketing experts, graphic designers, etc.

Without a distributor, filmmakers need to do their best to re-create this setup. The reasons are obvious: Distribution is a lot of work and it is nearly impossible to release a film yourself (although some intrepid souls have done it). I suggest that you assemble as many people around you as possible to help in specific areas. What I want to layout in this chapter is a best practice guideline to the people that you would want to assemble for a release in the digital era.

Having a team usually requires paying people, so if you are on a budget, you may not be able to hire as many people as you would like. However, with a bit of ingenuity you can get some people on board without a lot of money.

If you can't assemble anyone to help you, I do feel that you can release your film and encourage you to do so. The shape and scope of that release will be different than if you had help. As I have indicated before, depending on how extensive of a release you desire, doing it purely on your own can be a tremendous amount of work, so be prepared.

Besides having someone on your team solely responsible for distribution and marketing (your Producer of Marketing and Distribution), you need:

THE BARE MINIMUM:

DISTRIBUTION CONSULTANTS

Bringing in a good, qualified distribution consultant early in the process (preferably while in production) can save you a lot of time, money, and heartache. You can get advice from other filmmakers, but unless they are good friends, you will need to be respectful of their time. In addition, there are very few filmmakers, and very few people at all, who understand how all of the rights in a split rights scenario fit together. Hiring good distribution consultants is probably one of the best ways to spend your money — especially if you are new to the process. The best consultants have connections to DVD distributors, television outlets, etc. They also have connections to the companies who are familiar with the new distribution paradigm. They will help you create a distribution strategy for your film and connect you with publicists, bookers, and others in the field. They have generally replaced, or supplemented, the sales rep in this new model for many films. In the old model it was unusual not to have a sales rep, in the new model is unusual not to have a consultant. Consultations start at $500 to $1,000 and go up from there. After the initial consultation, your consultant will work with you on a per-hour basis or on a monthly retainer. Depending on your film, some consultants might take a percentage against a base flat minimum.

LAWYER

A good lawyer who is familiar with split rights scenarios and the vagaries of new distribution models is essential, although hard to find. If you cannot find one, I suggest using a consultant in tandem with a lawyer. The consultant negotiates, the lawyer goes over the language. Find someone who is open to working in new ways. Lawyers will either work on a per-hour fee ($175 and up) or for a percentage of the deal(s) (5 to 7 percent). Since the field is changing so rapidly, you may have to train your lawyer regarding certain terms that you will want in your deals.

Note: It is important that you or someone on your team keep track of who has the rights to what. A lawyer will never have the time to do this for you. You should create a grid and track it, because it can get confusing.

WEBMASTER

If you are not a technically-oriented person, you need an IT person to set up your website. Chances are, they will know a lot more about search engine optimization (SEO) than you do. Ask them to set up a site that you can regularly modify on your own, so that you are not spending thousands of dollars over the course of your film's life. If you can get a qualified person to do it for free, great — but you should be able to find someone to set up a simple site for $500 to $2,000. Maintain your relationship with this person so you can ask them to come back from to time to time to tweak your site (like when you want to sell DVDs, merchandise, etc.).

If you are lucky, you will find someone who will not only design and program your website but actually develop tools and techniques for you to distribute your film on the web. Brian Chirls was the tech genius behind *Four Eyed Monsters'* groundbreaking distribution strategy and execution. Many of the film's techniques, such as the Heart Map, were invented by him. If you can find someone like this to work on your film, you are golden. You will be well on your way to not only creating a website, but to developing innovative distribution and marketing techniques that you can share with the world, thereby getting even more attention.

NOTE: Oftentimes the best designer is not the best programmer, and vice versa. You may need two separate people: one for the look of the site (which hopefully is integrated with your key art), another to do the actual programming. If you have to choose to pay one or the other, go for the programmer. It is easier to find good designers for free (i.e., someone needing to build their portfolio) than programmers. You might need a third person to do the SEO, or search engine optimization (although the person doing the coding should really do SEO as well).

GRAPHIC DESIGNER

You will probably need two graphic designers: one person (who will be more expensive) to do your initial key art and a second, less expensive up-and-comer who can modify this key art for the print ads, banner ads, postcards, etc., that you will need.

AN ASSISTANT

Not having one during the theatrical release of *Bomb It* nearly drove me crazy. I strongly, strongly recommend finding an assistant. You will need one to do the following:

- Handle the prints and promotional deliveries.

- Help with your social networking and other web-based marketing — for instance, posting to your blog.

- Do basic accounting and pay bills.

- Research community organizations and interact with them.

- Help organize community screenings.

- Research and perform outreach to press.

- If they are good on the phone, they can help book theaters, especially in smaller markets.

- Handle T-shirt and other merchandise creation.

- If they know Photoshop, they can do small graphics jobs like adjusting banners, creating print ads, and changing the information on the back of postcards.

- If they know Final Cut Pro, they can create promo reels, recut trailers, etc.

SALES REPRESENTATIVES/ SALES AGENTS

There is some discussion about the role of sales reps in the new distribution world. There are several types of sales representatives/ sales agents. A classic sales representative or producer's represen- tative, as has been known to the independent film world for the past 15 years, is someone who will broker your film to the various distribution entities, generally in search of an overall deal. The main advantage of sales reps is their relationships with the various com- panies that buy films, from full-service distributors to DVD compa- nies to cable companies, etc. In exchange for a percentage of the profits, a good sales rep will get your film seen by most or nearly all the potential buyers for your film. This can be a benefit if you don't have those capabilities yourself. Many sales reps are also lawyers who include the legal fees in their commission (from 7 percent to 15 percent of any sales). Other sales reps work in tandem with lawyers. In the past (and this will probably change), most sales reps were generally only interested in you if they felt that your film could be sold for significant advances, preferably in an overall deal.

In the old model, it was almost taken for granted that an unsold independent film would engage a sales rep. Not anymore. Whether or not to engage a sales rep is one of the first decisions you need to make in the execution of your overall distribution strategy. If you have one or more sales representatives interested in your film, certainly talk to them. Have your distribution and marketing strategy before even talking to sales reps, so that you can put their recommendations into context for *your* film. Remember, your strategy will evolve, so at least have the first draft before you take these meetings. In general you should go to *any* meeting knowing:

1. What you want from the meeting or person.

2. What they want, or can provide for you. You learn this by doing research.

It will be interesting to see what happens to sales reps in the new paradigm. Since there are fewer advances, sales reps will most likely take on fewer films. I also feel that, by necessity, sales agents will begin to specialize in certain ancillary markets to accommodate the new split rights world. The money is in split rights, not overall deals. Sales reps will most likely accommodate this scenario. Cinetic, one of the premiere sales agencies in the independent world, has already set up separate ancillary and digital divisions. Since sales reps generally work on commission, they will be choosier about the films that they select. Hence more and more films will end up not being represented by a sales rep or will not have a sales rep for each right. Other sales reps might become consultants or might be sales reps for some films and consultants for others. So don't despair if you don't have one. If a sales rep is helping you obtain and negotiate split rights deals, they are helpful, but you can function without them.

I believe that because of the current economics, some sales reps will try to start charging fees and/or request retainers. I *strongly* recommend doing your research before agreeing to this arrangement. You *must* talk to filmmakers the rep has worked with to make sure that it was worth it. All of the sales reps I know do not ask for advances or retainers. If you are paying money, it should be for a specific service that can be performed by the person, not for a *potential* service.

While a select few sale reps are good split rights strategists, I believe there is a need for cooperation and collaboration between sales reps who have contacts with distribution entities and consultants who can create a unique strategy for each individual film and have a greater understanding of the nuances and opportunities of the hybrid world.

Television Sales Reps/Foreign Sales Reps

These are reps/agents that are relatively established in the split rights world. Generally they take a higher percentage (25 percent) than sales reps and many of them charge expenses as well. I feel that a good television sales representative is extremely valuable, especially if they can handle both foreign and domestic. In Section 7, I will discuss foreign sales agents in more detail.

Digital Rights Aggregator

This is a new form of company/representative who will handle and broker your digital rights to the larger digital platforms. I will discuss these in depth in Section 6. Generally they take from 15 to 25 percent.

BEYOND THE MINIMUM

The five components outlined at the beginning of this chapter comprise the barest of minimums for building a distribution team, assuming you have the personality and inclination to hustle and work the phone for bookings, publicity, and anything else you need to organize. If not, you will also need the following:

ON-PHONE HUSTLER (OPH)

This is Sklar's term and it fits. For *Bomb It*, I was the OPH. If you're not good at hustling, get someone who is. Hopefully that is your PMD. This person not only books screenings but also helps organize events, assists with networking, helps the publicist with smaller markets, tries to get swag, etc. You do not need this person if you are going to hire a conventional theatrical booker *and* an alternative theatrical booker *and* a national publicist and a regional publicist and a promotions person.

PUBLICIST

You can DIY your publicity or you can hire someone. I strongly recommend taking the time to find someone who will make a deal with you. There are film publicists who handle national press campaigns (these normally also handle your New York or L.A. release) as well as regional/local publicists.

Traditional publicity is based on relationships (hence it's difficult to DIY) and much of what you are paying a publicist for is his or her relationships and strategic expertise. As print media threatens to become obsolete, space in newspapers and magazines is vanishing by the month, even though projects to write about are exploding. It is good to get a leg up if you can afford it. On a bigger release, you will have a combination of people handling different markets. The more publicists you have, the more relationships you can count on. Unfortunately, this can cost you.

The going rate is $8,000 to $15,000, just to open in New York *or* Los Angeles (although a couple of people suggested to me that you can get someone for $5,000 each for L.A. and New York). Smaller cities cost much less. Since so much of the foundation for publicity is created during production, it would be great to bring this person on board as soon as possible unless your PMD has publicist chops in which case they can handle it.

Traditionally, publicists get paid up front because they don't want to wait and see how successful the reviews/release is before getting paid. Most tend not to negotiate their rates, although this is beginning to change.

You will find unexpected benefits of having publicists throughout your career. My relationship with Karen Larsen, a fabled San Francisco publicist, led to *Bomb It* being in the San Francisco Indie Fest, which led to our booking at that city's Red Vic Movie House, which was a linchpin for booking *Bomb It* in eight other markets.

AFFINITY PUBLICIST

There are also publicists who cater to particular markets and niches. If you have an environmental film, it might make sense to have a publicist who knows the environmental community, in addition to a traditional film publicist. If you have limited resources, you might end up choosing the niche/affinity publicist and hope that they can cover some of your general film press as well. Or this niche publicist might hire someone who can work for a short time and target a few specific film reviewers in a particular market. For *Bomb It* and *Better Living Through Circuitry*, we hired Lynn Hasty and Green Galactic, who normally handle alternative culture, music, and art. Because of the subject matter of these films, Lynn was a natural choice. For *Bomb It*, Lynn in turn hired someone to provide some extra traditional film press for our New York release.

MARKETING TEAM

While someone in film marketing would be ideal, someone who knows or does any kind of marketing is a plus — especially since filmmakers don't tend to think like marketers. These people include copywriters, creative directors, or other types of advertising executives. Trailers and print ads are only one aspect of marketing. I had a friend in advertising who gave me a number of great ideas for *Bomb It*, most of which were too expensive or required too much lead time.

WEB MARKETING TEAM

At the very least, either you, your PMD, or someone else needs to hit the social networks to promote your film. You might not be an eternal Tweeter or Facebooker, but someone you know is. Get them to spend some of that time online to promote your film in exchange for a credit.

There is so much more to web marketing than social networks (in terms of relationships as well as specific tools and tricks), and there are people who specialize in this. Talk to them and consider hiring one for a specific task or two. You can get people to develop a web campaign starting at around $2,000. You can spend much more if you want — an average for independent films is $5,000 to $20,000. This can also turn out to be some of the best money you spend.

THEATRICAL BOOKER

There are a number of freelance bookers whom you can hire for short periods of time to book your film for you, usually with a three-month minimum. This is an intermediate step between total DIY and hiring a distributor, and can be much more cost-effective. You can pay anywhere from $1,000 to $5,000 a month (and higher) for this service, so you're looking at a bare minimum of $3,000 to $5,000 for three months.

Booking is similar to publicity in that it is about relationships. Established theater chains tend to only work with established bookers. Hiring a booker for a few months for a few thousand could save you a lot of grief if you don't have a track record as a filmmaker and/or your film does not have a pedigree. In reality, it will save you grief even if your film has a track record and a pedigree.

GRASSROOTS COMMNITY-SCREENING CONSULTANT/BOOKER

A community consultant/booker will help identify and target the audiences for your film. Because they are relatively inexpensive, in my mind they are a requirement for issue-oriented documentaries. Even if you don't hire a community booker for screening, you should hire one to consult as early in the process as possible. They will help you with your community outreach, specifically with brainstorming what kinds of groups you can target and market the film to. Since this is a relatively new arena for indie filmmaking, the few good community-screening consultants get busy fast, so try to hire one as soon as possible. Rates start at $500 for a consultation and go up to $6,000 a month for full-service booking. Sometimes they will work on a combo salary/percentage basis.

UNIT PUBLICIST

Unit publicists are publicists whom you engage in production (and potentially some prep and post). I actually think that many unit publicists are a natural fit for the PMD position. Here is what a unit publicist can do for you or your PMD can do:

> 1. Position the film in the film press and blogosphere, as well as within any niche audience you have, such as nonprofits. Make connections with journalists and bloggers, letting them know about your project. Use a combination of press release and direct emails.

> 2. Position your film in the independent distribution and festival world. This involves the creation of your press kit and other distribution and sales materials. It is basically the initial marketing — creating a campaign for the film that takes into consideration *both* the film that the director and producers think they are making, as well as the film that is actually being shot. They are not necessarily the same film (and the director and producers often have diverging ideas on this).

Kathleen McInnis, a festival strategist for independent filmmakers, as well as publicist and festival director/programmer whose previous festival work has included Seattle Int'l Film Festival, Slamdance Film Festival (she is currently at the Palm Springs International Shorts Fest), points out that you are creating the language of the film that will be used to sell the film.

3. Take good production stills, i.e., photographs of the action on set. Many festivals and distribution contracts will require a large amount of photos.

4. Ensure you are getting a proper electronic press kit (EPK) and other promotional materials. Often the unit publicist will produce the EPK, so if you can't hire someone, make sure you, a producer, or a production assistant is getting it done on set.

While you can readily take care of steps 3 and 4 on your own, it would be good to have help with 1 and 2. Good publicists have relationships with distributors as well as festivals. In a unit publicist you often have someone who can get all of the above taken care of.

NOTES ON HIRING

You hire any of the people above as you would any very important member of your crew. Start by asking around. Do your research. Ask fellow filmmakers about people they do and don't recommend. Talk to the filmmakers these potential team members have worked with and ask about their experience working with them. As a general rule, I check at least two references of *everyone* who works for me, whether it be an intern or a sales agent.

Make use of online hiring resources. For interns, assistants, editors, and producers, I find mandy.com, shootingpeople.com, and entertainmentcareers.net the best. Craigslist is good for graphic designers. There are more hiring resources on the website.

When interviewing anyone, you should be pitching *them* on your project as well as asking what they feel they can bring to your project. People who are good at what they do are busy, so you will need to sell them on your film to even get them to watch it.

For publicists and marketing people, you should be asking about what strategy they feel is best for your film and why; how they would position your film; their ideas for promotion, marketing, and publicity; what reviewers, blogs, and interest groups they would feel are right for your film. You should ask consultants, lawyers, and reps about what markets and buyers they feel are the best suited for your film, as well as their release strategy.

NOTES ON LOW-BUDGET HIRING

Assistants

There are two ways to hire an assistant: Hire someone for $15 to $25 an hour, or get an "intern." Here is how they have both panned out for me.

I have had amazing luck with interns. There are great people who want to get started in film, and if you convince them that distribution is a key component of filmmaking these days, that's a good sell. However, they usually only last three months, and after five years of having people come and go on *Bomb It*, I was looking for a little consistency. There is a fair amount of training, after all, and if someone is on board for only a few months, the training and retraining can wear on you.

I thought paying someone $15 an hour for 10 hours a week would get me that consistency. I was wrong. (Perhaps if I had paid $25, that would have helped.) In late 2008, early 2009, I had two different people whom I paid to be assistants last three months and two months, respectively. They each realized that they couldn't afford to live on $150 a week and it was difficult to find another part-time job that worked with their existing free time.

There are two ways to get around this.

> 1. Hire someone full-time. This gets expensive — it will cost at least $2,400 a month. An alternative use of this money would be to pay for a booker and do the deliveries and other not-so-fun work yourself.

> 2. Hire an assistant with several other filmmakers and split the full-time cost. In essence you each are only paying a portion of the assistant's salary, but you can hopefully keep the person afloat and in turn from looking for other jobs. Plus, if the person is doing similar work on multiple projects, there will be some economies of scale. This is yet another argument for starting more distribution cooperatives.

SECTION ONE SUMMARY

The most important thing that you can do for your film is to create a distribution and marketing strategy. This strategy is unique to your film, due to:

1. Its unique qualities.

2. Its unique audience.

3. Your unique needs and goals.

4. Your resources.

It is impossible now to rely on old distribution patterns created by the studios to service their films. To not strike a new bold path that is suited to your film and situation is to incur pain, disappointment, and impaired financial gain (or heightened losses). Fortunately, by thinking ahead and assembling a good team, you can now avoid the pitfalls that have befallen many a filmmaker before you.

By looking at the markets before you in terms of live events, merchandise, and digital rights, you can begin to conceptualize a path that will allow you to monetize your film to the greatest degree possible.

The next paradigm shift that filmmakers must embrace is that they must integrate the distribution and marketing process into the production and pre-production of their films. Doing so will give you, the filmmaker, the greatest advantage in making your film a success — whatever you have determined that success to be.

Section 2

Preparing For Distribution & Marketing Before You Finish Your Film

Marketing and distribution are intertwined. You cannot plan for or engage one without the other. In this section, we will discuss not only laying the groundwork for marketing and distribution during prep and production, but we will also examine the importance of marketing your film as early as possible, even before you have started to make it, and the techniques involved therein.

CHAPTER 6

RETHINKING MARKETING

While people will read this book at different stages after they have finished their film, I feel that it is important for filmmakers to shift their mindsets to consider the distribution and marketing of the film as early as possible, before they finish their films or even before they raise the money for their films.

Film studios have been doing this for some time — and the indie world has criticized them for this, often with good reason. The studios regularly consult their marketing department before committing to a film. But when the studios think this way, they are thinking of what they can market and sell to a mass audience. Independent filmmakers should take the methodology from the studios, but not necessarily the studios' conclusions.

After you identify the audiences for your project, the next step is to get those audiences to want to see your film. This is the realm of marketing and it is as important as distribution.

You will most likely not have a single or multifaceted marketing strategy for your film at its inception, but it is an important goal to work toward. I strongly recommend that you start planning this strategy as soon as possible, even at the inception/script stage, for the following reasons:

1. If you integrate the marketing and web life of your film into the film itself, the marketing of your film will be much more organic as a result.

2. It allows your audience to be involved in the creation of your film, in aspects such as funding, subject matter, and promotion.

3. With actors and crew accessible, you can create the marketing materials you need while you are making your film.

4. You have the largest support staff during production to create these materials.

5. It is never too early to start a dialogue with your audience.

Omer Nisar worked as a digital marketer at Island Def Jam, Wired-Set Digital, Penton Media and Sony BMG Music and is the Social Media Strategist at B-Side Entertainment. Omer says that it takes time to get the online community around you, so you need to start as early as possible.

Cynthia Swartz, previously executive vice president of publicity for Miramax, is currently partner at 42West and co-head of their Entertainment Marketing Division, overseeing film release campaigns and publicity initiatives for filmmakers. She points out that if you have built a tremendous fan base before you finish your film, it will help you garner deals from distribution entities that still provide advances: DVD companies, some digital rights concerns, VOD, etc.

Caitlin Boyle, who is the founder of Film Sprout and the architect of grassroots and community screenings campaigns for numerous documentaries, including the award-winning *King Corn*, *Pray the Devil Back to Hell*, and *The End of the Line*, says, "Proactively reach out to the audiences for whom the film is most resonant. Consider five main groups to whom it is most appealing." You won't know these people right away — but you will develop this knowledge over time.

MARKETING TO YOUR AUDIENCE

In marketing you are trying to engage with your audience and get them to support you financially in some way, so that you can continue your career as an artist and filmmaker.

I feel it is important to introduce some basic marketing advice now so that you can consider this as you develop the strategy for distributing and marketing your film. My good friend from film school, John Di Minico, is a branding strategist and creative director in digital, interactive and integrated media who consults on projects for television networks (FX, ABC/Disney/ESPN, Fox, E!, CBS, AMC) and works with independent filmmakers as well. He suggests that you consider the following as soon as possible:

- Who are you in the media landscape? Look around. Be objective.

- What makes your brand (you and the content) unique? Is there a point of view or experience you can own? As an example many incredible filmmakers have the qualities of a brand: Quentin Tarantino, Woody Allen, David Lynch, Alfred Hitch cock, Jane Campion, Michael Moore, Martin Scorsese. With each of these filmmakers, you know it is their film when you watch it. In general, you know the experience that you are going to get when you see one of their films.

- How will you build equity and a community around your content and brand?

- Determine the full spectrum of your audience - from core to casual. How and where do you reach them? What drives them to view, refer/tag, and return to your content/site?

- What organizations and social networks exist in the world to ally yourself with? Can you integrate or partner on some level and extend your reach?

Meyer Shwarzstein started selling TV rights when he was hired in 1980 by MGM. Since 1995 at Brainstorm Media he has sold TV and VOD rights for Blockbuster, Lions Gate, Samuel Goldwyn Company, Magnolia, Image, BMG, HD Net and is an independent consultant who works with filmmakers to construct marketing and distribution strategies. He offers the following advice:

- We have the biggest entertainment dessert buffet ever created — but dessert buffets are overwhelming — so what do people do? They take a few things they know well and perhaps they will take a bite of something that looks interesting, and then they are done. Somehow you have to be the one thing that they haven't tried that looks especially inviting, and then taste so good that the customer will eat all of you (and then tell their friends about you and go out and buy more of you).

- People are much more discriminating than they have ever been. The valuation used to be whether you will spend your money on a product. Now the valuation is whether you will spend your *time*. You have to produce a really excellent experience and product to make it worth people's time.

- People don't buy what they want anymore, they only buy what they need, or what their friends tell them that they need.

- Filmmakers should look at the psychology of buying. For example, something will be missing in you if you don't buy that product or film. How do you create that sense in a consumer?

(As a former punk rock/anarchist/neo-Marxist economist, I can't believe I am writing this — even if it is someone else's opinion!)

- Think of the kind of need or want you as a filmmaker can fulfill. People need to cross a threshold in their purchasing decisions. You need to help put them across that threshold. Examples of such desires would be:

  - I'm supporting a cause.

  - I'm making a statement.

  - I want to support the passion of the filmmaker.

  - I'd watch that movie 10 times.

  - I want all my friends to watch that movie.

  - My friends will think I'm hip, smart, whatever if I watch that movie.

  - Everyone else is watching that movie, so I'd better just see it so I have something to talk about.

In the next few chapters we will begin to examine the marketing of your film and the ways in which you can connect with your audience during prep, production, and post.

ART VS. COMMERCE

Many filmmakers fear that if they consider the marketing of their film early in the process of the film's creation, it will interfere with their creativity.

In other words, thinking about the market will interrupt the very process that will help them create a groundbreaking work that will crack through the media landscape.

The most successful films are often the most creative and innovative, the ones that do not look to past successes but boldly blaze a trail forward. By chasing the market, a filmmaker runs the risk making work that feels dated and/or unoriginal. Originality of vision should be one of your strongest selling points.

However, just because you are making a singular artistic vision does not mean that you can't consider who the audience for your vision might be.

Many if not most of the marketing tools that filmmakers can use to reach their audience should not hamper their creativity, and might even enhance it.

In addition, filmmakers may want to have at least some heads-up as to what is happening in the market so that they can avoid spending several years and thousands of dollars making a film that has limited chances of recouping its investment in time and money.

You have to decide what works for you and your own process. However, the film distribution world is a very tough place — too many filmmakers have gone out to make films without a possibility of return, nearly bankrupting themselves in the process. Revisit your motivations to make a film — perhaps distribution and marketing do not matter to you. You just need to make a film for whatever reason. I'll be the first to defend your right to self-expression. That said, the market may or may not support your desire to get your self-expression seen by others.

Assuming you want your film to be seen and purchased by as many people as possible, read on.

SUGGESTIONS TO HELP YOU IN THE MARKET:

Choose a Good Title

Along with the key art and the trailer, this is another one of your film's main selling points. A good title can help where nothing else can.

Make Your Film As Good As It Can Be

I know this seems obvious, but in talking to people in the film industry, there was a consensus that many filmmakers didn't take the time and effort to make their films as good as possible before bringing them to market.

Some truly brilliant filmmakers don't need comments or criticism from the creative community to produce wonderful films. But most filmmakers could be served by some advice.

Making Better Films, Part 1: Make sure your film is ready to shoot before you shoot. I recommend that you assemble some trusted advisors to help you work and rework your script. Your job as a creative person is to trust your gut as to what feedback will improve your film and what won't. A caveat to this is that sometimes over-writing can suck the life out of a project. Again, you need to find balance.

Making Better Films, Part 2: Learn the art of directing. Do you have a sense of why you put the camera where you do? Is there a reason that you have chosen a particular style? It might make some sense to practice a bit before jumping into a feature. Study films, study how films are made, what makes them good or not in your opinion. Develop your own vision.

Making Better Films, Part 3: Be ruthless in the cutting room. Another cliché: There are three times when you write your film. First at the script stage, second during production, and most critically when you are editing. Don't let your preconceived notion of the film force it into what it is not. Let the film live as it wants to live.

Do your own test screenings. Get opinions, but don't show your film to everyone at once. Keep some trusted fresh eyes for the fifth, seventh, or tenth screening. *Listen* to what people are telling you, but again, filter it through your inner guide and vision.

CONSIDERING DISTRIBUTION AND MARKETING OF YOUR FILM IN CHOOSING THE CONTENT OF YOUR FILM

I will now discuss those aspects of distribution and marketing that might affect your creative process (so for those of you who don't want to be poisoned by these thoughts, skip to the next chapter).

It is no surprise that certain choices that you make during the course of writing and creating your film will affect the commercial viability of your film. I reiterate that what will help your film and career the most is having a unique, fresh, singular vision, brilliantly executed. If your film has these qualities, it has a chance of succeeding without any thought given to more commercial considerations. However, the film world is filled with brilliantly conceived and executed films that have had trouble finding an audience.

Some of what I am going to outline is relatively obvious and has been written about before — in such cases I will attempt not to dwell on it.

1. Stars help sell films.

Having a big name doesn't guarantee success, but all things being equal, it provides a marketing hook for you to sell your film, as long as the presence of that star is not detrimental (e.g., a poor performance or wildly inappropriate casting).

Stars help sell documentaries, hence the profusion of stars as narrators.

2. Have a marketing hook or sellable story about the creation of the film.

Stars are an easy marketing hook because they are promoted via a name or a photo. However, you should strive to find a compelling hook about your film that reviewers and bloggers can write about. Morgan Spurlock eating nothing but McDonalds for 30 days to see the effect on his body (*Super Size Me*) is a great marketing hook.

3. Consider niche audiences for your film.

Or think of niche audiences that need films created for them. There is a huge market for Christian films for Christian audiences, which some filmmakers are mining to great affect. I don't necessarily agree that this is the best motive to make a film, but you wouldn't be the first filmmaker to do this.

Documentaries usually have at least one built- in niche audience.

4. Consider genres that sell.

There are certain genres that don't need stars or incredible production values to attract an audience. Two of these are horror and broad comedy. All I need to say is "*Saw*" (the short premiered at Sundance) and "*Napoleon Dynamite.*"

Ira Deutchman has been making, marketing, and distributing films for 27 years, having worked on more than 130 films as well as creating Fine Line Features. He is now a managing partner of Emerging Pictures, a leading distributor exploring hybrid strategies. Deutchman believes that the narrative genres that consistently do well with art-house audiences are Jewish, gay, French language, and spirituality.

Ira also notes that documentaries that are star-driven and/or about cute animals, environmental issues, or competitions also consistently do well. He made these statements with "tongue slightly in cheek." A film about cute animals facing environmental collapse framed in a competition narrated by a star might do very well.

If you are interested in generating a YouTube fan base, Sara Pollack, the Entertainment Marketing Manager at YouTube, suggests looking at what genres appeal to the YouTube audience.

For features: horror, animation/anime, documentary, and comedy.

For shorts: animation, comedy, something titillating — Sara references crackle.com's *Mommy XXX* about a porn star raising her kids in Los Angeles.

5. Avoid genres that require elements your film will not possess...

...such as a specific cast that will sell that genre. The classic example is romantic comedies that are almost always driven by existing romantic comedy actors. It is difficult to compete with the romantic comedies that the studio produces with stars.

6. Add a new twist to a genre or a stylistic innovation.

These are my personal favorites — so please make more! *Brick* reinvented the noir thriller by bringing it to high school. *Memento* told a story backwards, *13 Conversations About One Thing* followed multiple story lines. It usually helps to be the first one doing whatever you are doing.

7. For documentaries, consider focusing on one character.

I overheard documentarian Kirby Dick's advice to two young enterprising filmmakers who were making a doc with three main characters. Kirby was suggesting that they cut two of the characters out of the film because it is much easier to sell a documentary that focuses on one character — as long as that character embodies everything that you are trying to say.

Chapter 7 Conclusion

How much you pay attention to the marketability of your film before or during the production of your film is ultimately a creative decision that only you can make. However, if you want your film to have the best release possible, in most cases it makes sense to start the marketing of the film as soon as possible.

Start your mailing list and collect email addresses from everyone you encounter at the very beginning

PREPARING CONVENTIONAL DISTRIBUTION AND MARKETING MATERIALS DURING PREP, PRODUCTION, AND POST

In this chapter we will address the types of conventional marketing and publicity materials that you should be creating during production and postproduction. We will also address what delivery elements you should be creating before you finish postproduction. Doing so will save you a lot of heartache.

But first...

YOUR MAILING LIST

START YOUR MAILING LIST AND COLLECT EMAIL ADDRESSES FROM EVERYONE YOU ENCOUNTER AT THE VERY BEGINNING.

Whenever you have a group of people gathered in relationship to your film, pass around a pad of paper to collect names, emails, and ZIP codes.

CONVENTIONAL PUBLICITY AND MARKETING MATERIALS

These are materials that any publicist is going to require to sell your film.

1. Good Production Stills

This cannot be stressed enough. Photos are still one of the key ways to sell your film, and filmmakers continue to neglect them.

Look at any film festival catalog — how many photos make you want to see the film?

You need three types of stills:

Of the Film This is a still of the film as if the still camera is the movie camera. Rent a blimp and put your still photographer as close to the lens as possible (squeezed between the DP and the set). Don't just take the shots from the side while you are filming. The lighting is not the same, the shot is not set up for the side angle, etc. Film stills are essential. You need hundreds for delivery and hence you need to take thousands of photos. Really.

You will need even more raw photos if your actors have a kill clause. This is an actor's right to veto a percentage of pictures you take of them. If an actor has a 50 percent kill clause and you have to deliver 200 photos, you'd better have 400 photos for them to approve. If you have 3 actors with 50 percent kill clauses, you'd better have 600 photos for them to collectively kill.

Don't tell anyone I told you this: Do not give your actors pre-selected photos, give them everything — so they use their kill clause on out-of-focus shots, bad angles, etc.

Tip from McInnis: If you can't afford a unit publicist, sit down in advance and figure out which scenes will be most effective for stills. What are the scenes that will sell your film? Have a photographer on those days. Pick the high-traffic days that have lots of talent.

Of the Crew (especially the director) You need a shot of the director next to the camera, pointing at something. Get some shots of the director talking to the actors. Get some of the rest of the cast and crew. Assume that one out of every 30 to 40 shots will be good, so take hundreds.

Specials These are shots of your actors individually and together in front of a plain cyclorama or neutral background in a variety of looks and poses. Get these on set in case you can't get your actors later. You will most likely need these for key art.

⭐ **DON'T SKIMP ON PRODUCTION STILLS! THEY ARE ONE OF YOUR MOST EFFECTIVE MARKETING TOOLS.**

2. Press Kit

Create this while you are in post or earlier. Traditionally, publicists create these, but you can save a lot of money doing it yourself and then have a publicist rewrite portions.

Our *Bomb It* press kit started with many of the elements of the business plan that we used to raise funds. Much of this material you will need for your website, so the earlier you start with this, the better.

If you don't have a publicist but know someone who is good with copy (the written text of any promotional material, whether it be a press kit, trailer, or ad), have him or her take a pass.

A standard press kit includes at minimum:

- Short Synopsis

- Long Synopsis

- Crew Bios

- Cast Bios - Leave time for them to be approved if necessary.

- Selected Production Stills

- Production Story - Think of what can sell your film — what makes it unique, especially in the making of.

- Director's Statement (no more than a page) A compelling pithy essay on why you had to make your film and what it means to you. Publicists seem to prefer production stories. Festivals seem to prefer director's statements.

- Final End Credits

- Technical Specs: Original format, final format, final audio format (you can only list and screen Dolby if you buy the license), total running time (TRT), black and white or color, aspect ratio (native 16:9 or 4:3 letterbox, which has the black bars at top and bottom, etc.)

A quick and easy way to do create a production story is to have someone interview the director and/or team. If you film this, you have an element of your EPK (electronic press kit, described below) as well.

Industry standard photo credits include:

- Photo File Name

- Title of Photo

- What is in the frame, indicating actors/subject from left to right

- Photographer Credit

EXAMPLE

"REISS FILMS RASTY AT WORK IN CAPETOWN, SOUTH AFRICA" – L-R: DIRECTOR JON REISS, RASTY CREDIT: TRACY WARES

3. Electronic Press Kit (EPK) Material Shot During Prep, Production and Post

Interview your actors. Have a crew shooting "behind the scenes" and "making-of" footage. The publicist will need the EPK, but you need this material to create clips that will generate interest in your film during production and can be posted on your website. You will also need the EPK or similar for your DVD extras.

Don't just interview the director and producer during production; make sure you get an interview later so it includes reflection on the process as well.

Kirby Dick taught me a good trick: Film all your festival question-and-answer sessions for DVD EPK material, but you can also use it for web clips.

4. A Good Trailer

You need a trailer.

Don't put a trailer up on your site until it is good.

You absolutely need at least one trailer by the time of your festival premiere.

Regarding the trailer and EPK, Swartz advises not to cut a trailer unless you have a trailer editor. I agree that this is a specialized field and that if you spend money on copy and a trailer editor, you might end up with a better trailer. But it depends on your resources.

If you have time with your editor, have them cut your EPK and take a turn at your trailer, but if this isn't possible, give the material to the assistant/apprentice editors who are slaving away on your film. It's something creative for them to do and a great break from logging footage. All of our trailers, EPK, and extra features for *Bomb It* were cut by up-and-comers, and they did a great job. They can work on their Final Cut Pro systems at home and bring in their cuts. Also, some assistants are commercial/trailer editors trying to make the transition to long form, so they might be better than your editor in cutting this material.

Keep in mind that if all your non-pro resources fail to produce a good trailer, you should pay someone to create a great trailer, because, other than photos, it is the one item that will sell your film above everything else. I cannot stress this enough.

One last thought on trailers — if you shot on film, there are two ways to go: One is to go back to the original negative; the other is to use your HD or other tape master. If you have a high enough quality tape master, you might want to avoid going back to the negative if you are on limited means. Take a look at tape-to-film trailer transfers. They can be quite good and save you a lot of money. The film conform can cost an extra $5,000, which could buy you a lot of web promotion instead.

DELIVERY ELEMENTS/ REQUIREMENTS

Prepare for your delivery requirements while you still have a production team.

Delivery elements are those items that distribution entities require you to provide them before they consider the contract complete. Too often filmmakers are in a rush to finish their films for a festival and do not begin to think about their delivery requirements until after their festival premiere.

Some filmmakers are lucky enough to have producers who will stay all the way through delivery, no matter when it happens. But because budgets are low and people need jobs — often right after the glamour of the world premiere — your support staff will start to move on. This is why it is critical to start the delivery of your film as soon as possible, so that you have as much help as possible in completing it. Even if you have a PMD, the more you can do before distribution, the more time you will have to actually distribute the film. Anyone who has delivered a film knows it is one of the most tedious and time-consuming aspects of filmmaking. It requires:

All of the conventional press materials mentioned above:
- Stills
- EPK
- Trailer
- Press Kit including synopsis, bios, production story.

Proper chain of title and copyright registration for the film
This can happen before picture lock (or the bulk of it can be done before picture lock). This should be scanned for delivery.

Copies of all cast and crew releases
The first part is to make sure you have all the cast and crew releases. The second part is to scan and organize them so that you can quickly copy the files onto CD-ROM for any distributor. I recommend scanning every release as you obtain it to avoid an avalanche at the end.

Music licenses and composer agreements
Same as cast and crew releases. You should, of course, have the final payment to your music supervisor be due when all agreements and the music cue sheet are finalized. Don't forget that you need sync and master licenses for each track, as well as the performing rights society for each publisher.

Stock footage releases

You need still photo and stock footage license agreements with any footage or photo that you did not take yourself. Warn your editors in advance not to pull just anything off the web and assume it is okay, even for background plates for animation or motion graphics.

Music cue sheet

As you lock sections of your film and secure licenses, you should be putting the information into a proper industry standard delivery format. This is something that your music supervisor should create for you before you give him or her the final check.

Stock footage cue sheet

Same as the music cue sheet.

Dialogue list

As soon as you have a locked video transfer or output, you should have interns creating your dialogue list. The bulk of this work is the transcribing.

As soon as you have your final time code on your delivery masters, you should convert this dialogue list into a subtitle list. A subtitle list provides time code for every time the image changes and/or for every line of the film. This is much more work, but it will enable you take advantage of foreign film festival translations (more on this later).

Final credits

You should start this early and update it over time. It is much easier than trying to remember everyone who helped on your film, especially if your records are spotty. You should be done with it by the time you lock picture (or nearly done).

Key art

Have your producers find and vet graphic artists for your poster, website, etc. If you are on a budget, getting good key art will take time.

International television version for documentaries

After picture lock, have your editor cut the film down to 52 to 54 minutes for international television sales. It is much easier to do this with your principal editor, or associate editors supervised by the editor, while it is fresh. It also allows you to include the sound mix for this version in the overall sound mix package of your film.

You will need a separate music cue sheet, stock cue sheet, and dialogue list for this edit. Have your assistant/apprentice editors begin work on this as soon as possible.

Online delivery elements

In addition to the output of your original film, don't forget to output a tape of textless backgrounds for any part of your film that you have your native language text over. This is a foreign sales delivery requirement. However, if you have a film with a lot of native language text (subtitles, for instance) you need to consider two options:

1. It might be cheaper to output an entire textless film than to have your online house configure an entirely new textless edit list.

2. If this is the case and you are planning to DIY a foreign language version of your DVD, you will want to produce a hybrid texted/textless version. This would include those titles you are going to retain in English — main and end titles, for instance — and then let the sections that you are going to subtitle remain textless. I wish I had done this for *Bomb It*.

You will also need PAL versions of your film and your EPK/trailer (or NTSC if you are PAL native).

You might also need a 4x3 full frame extraction of the film. This is similar to a pan-and-scan and unfortunately is still used for a lot of foreign sales. To facilitate the cheapest way of doing this, which is a tape-to-tape transfer, you need to keep the titles in your film placed within 4x3 title safe, not just 16x9. An alternative is to have your online house include a separate 4x3 version as part of your package. Because of the placement of my lower thirds and subtitles, my 4x3 extraction will be more complicated than most. However, I have not as yet needed said 4x3 extraction.

And there are even more delivery elements on a standard foreign sales contract. You should really go over these elements one by one and determine if they make sense for your film. This is something that you can negotiate with your foreign or television sales agent.

After looking at the list, it should be apparent that you need to start all of this as early as possible. So get going!

CHAPTER 9

YOUR WEBSITE

The web is the most cost-effective way for you to promote your film, and your website is the frontline in your sales to the outside world.

I recommend that you maintain a dynamic website with continually updated content. Everything you do on the web in relation to your film should be directed at engaging your audience to get them *involved* in your film. This can be as simple as getting people to give you their email address in exchange for a coupon, or enticing them to return to your website to see your film's progress. Better yet, you might be able to have them pass along your website and trailer to their friends and post them to their Facebook pages.

THE WEBSITE AND WEB 2.0

We live in a world of Web 2.0, on our way into Web 3.0. The numbers 1.0 and 2.0 do not designate software versions, but overall approaches to using the internet, overriding philosophies about how we relate to the content we find on the web. Most film websites fall into the category of Web 1.0 — that is, a monologue from creator to audience. Web 2.0 is a dialogue. The problem with Web 1.0 websites is that, once people have seen the trailer, read the synopsis, and perhaps seen where the film is playing, there is no reason for them to return. Nor is there a reason for them to tell anyone about your site. Hence, not only will people stay on a 1.0 site for a shorter period of time, fewer people will come to the site in the first place.

Fortunately it is relatively easy and is becoming less and less expensive to set up a dynamic 2.0 website. While ideally your website should be created with an eye to the overall marketing and distribution of your film, your presence on the web is too essential to put off just because these strategies aren't in place. Get the website up. You can make adjustments and relaunch it later if necessary.

CREATE A WEBSITE THAT YOU OR YOUR ASSISTANT CAN UPDATE

I encourage you to set up a site that can be altered by any person with minimal training. To do this, you need to have your webmaster set up your site with a user-friendly content management system (CMS) such as Wordpress, Joomla, or Drupal — with Wordpress being the easiest to modify on your own and Drupal the most difficult. Both Joomla and Drupal are relatively complicated for the novice. Many people are not aware that Wordpress can be used as a CMS, but go check out the websites for the B-Side films on the B-Side website — not only are they designed for audience action, but they are done in Wordpress.

The user-friendliness of Wordpress, however, does not necessarily mean that you should set up the initial architecture of your site on your own. There are tricks to setting up your site that will not only allow it to run much more smoothly, but will also aid in your search engine optimization (SEO). Have a web programmer create your site with the idea that you will do all the day-to-day operations.

Register Your Domain and Get a Hosting Service

While you can host a blog on a service like Blogspot, and while you can set up a page on Facebook and MySpace, only hosting your own website gives you the control you need over your mailing list and content. Doing this is a must. Ask your IT person to recommend a hosting service. We have been using Site 5 for the last few years for *Bomb It* and have not had a problem. For those of you who don't have an IT person yet, here are some tips from mine, Michael Medaglia, a consultant and programmer who specializes in strategy and development for film-related sites such as those for *Bomb It*, *Asylum* (*Snakes on a Plane*), and *Filmmaker* magazine.

Michael Medaglia's 10 Items to Check for in a Hosting Service:

1. Low monthly fee that comprises the services you will require, including bandwidth.[1]

2. Reputation of reliability (research online and look for reviews).

3. Ability to run Wordpress, Joomla, or Drupal for free, as well as a free mailing-list application, such as phplist.

4. An FTP site available to you to share files, with the ability to create different FTP accounts for different users.

5. Enough email accounts to handle your film.

6. Enough disk space (online storage) for your files and trailers.

7. Timely about updating its technology and software to release new versions.

8. Provides statistics to analyze your website traffic.

9. Reliable customer service/technical support.

10. Ability to set up automatic nightly backups.

Michael Medaglia on the right way to research a web host company: "Get recommendations from a friend or from your webmaster. Look at the forums on hosting sites."

Michael Medaglia on the wrong way to research a web host company: "If you Google for reviews on web host companies, you'll see lots of sites that review and rate hosting companies. Check out the sites: You'll probably see the same 10 to 15 companies listed on all of them. That's because these review sites are total bullshit — they're actually marketing sites that make a commission if you purchase after visiting their site. That's not to say the hosting sites they promote are bad. Just know that the review sites are actually advertisements."

YOUR SITE ARCHITECTURE AND ITS ESSENTIAL COMPONENTS

The Web 1.0 components of your site:

- **Media** Trailer(s) and stills

- **About: The Film, The Filmmakers, The Cast** While this won't drive traffic to your site, it will help potential co-laborators and the audience understand what you are trying to accomplish

- **Reviews** Lend credibility to your film

- **Upcoming and Past Screenings**

---

1 DO I NEED "'DEDICATED HOSTING'"? I"D SAY 95 PERCENT % OF INDIE FILMMAKERS DO NOTNOT NEED TO SHELL OUT THE BIG BUCKS FOR DEDICATED HOSTING. THEY SHOULD INSTEAD OPT FOR THE CHEAPER "'SHARED'" HOSTING. THIS URLURL EXPLAINS THE DIFFERENCE between the two way better than I could: http://www.netmechanic.com/news/vol7/hosting_no3.htm

- *Mailing List Sign-Up* (this is borderline Web 2.0)

The Web 2.0 components of your site:

- *Your Blog* with comments section

- *Links* to your film's pages on social networks

- *Your Own Social Network* (possible through several plug-ins)

- *Feeds* from Web 2.0 social media sites such as Flickr, YouTube, etc.

- *Links to Sites You Are Partnering With* or cool sites that relate to your film

- *Widgets* that your audience can spread around on their own sites

This is just a basic list. More components like these are being developed every day. You should have an idea of what you want your website to look and feel like before you hire your designer/programmer. The clearer you are, the cheaper your site will be to design.

I also recommend that you discuss your needs and desires with your designer/programmer and see what they recommend. But make sure that you are able to handle the day-to-day of everything they recommend.

OPTIMIZE YOUR SITE FOR SEARCH ENGINES

Search engine optimization (SEO) is a multi-step process. Whole books and websites are devoted to it. But there are some basics you should incorporate into your site architecture, and this is best done by your IT person.

Make The Most Out of Search

Brad Balfour is film writer who has learned so much about SEO the hard way (programming his own site) that he now writes and speaks about it. He contributed the following essay on SEO:

"Search engine optimization (SEO) has evolved in order to make your web efforts effective not only as a tool for users directed to your site, but as a vehicle to gain eyeballs from the vast wilderness of the web. This is a set of techniques and strategies you can use to, in effect, game the system — or rather, best present your site to the eyes of the web, the algorithms called "crawlers" or "spiders" that troll the internet and its myriad websites for evidence of your site's existence.

The traffic your site generates (whether it occurs through organic, contextual, or paid search) and the rankings that come as a result are determined by a set of rules or options that you can exercise or manipulate in order to increase your search ranking and your traffic.

The key is to get Google or the other search engines to index your site and as many of its pages as possible. Once that is done, your site is in the vast directory of data run by Google, et al., which allows for your site to register in a search and for pages to be found, and hopefully meets the needs of data seekers.

Here are several concepts you have to keep in mind to effectively optimize your site:

1. To get your pages indexed properly with search engines, your web designer can do some things internally, such as making sure there are many interlinked pages throughout the site. That means when someone's name is mentioned in one place or on one page, it should link to where that person is mentioned elsewhere. For example, when you mention an actor's name in the plot outline, it should link to that person's bio within the site.

2. Another thing you or your designer can do is place lots of photos that are properly named so that image searches can provide further traffic. Remember, your site can be found through your visuals as well; still images and videos are as keyword-friendly as text.

3. Make sure the URL for each page of your site is effectively, efficiently, and succinctly written. Web sites are found by their address, a URL (Uniform Resource Locator). Every website and page within it is assigned a URL with a set of instructions that catalog the site, the pages, and information on the pages

according to a set of prioritized words. Sometimes CMS systems will create less-than-useful URLs, and you may have to ask your webmaster/programmer to manually modify your URLs to be effective.

4. Use well-conceived meta tags, meta descriptions, or meta keywords. Meta tags are the words that lie behind the text and images you see. They are part of the stuff (text, images, layout, designs, databases, links to videos, etc.) that's described in the HTML (the language that makes the internet run) that makes up your site. They can be seen through the programs that construct your site.

5. Most important of these are meta descriptions — those sets of words under the URLs found through a web search. You can actually go in and write or change the ones that appear when a search engine finds your site or some subject that is related to it. Those descriptions not only define your site, they can direct people to look at your site over others that have related content.

6. Understand and exploit the best practices for keywords and key phrases. You need to think, "What 10 or 15 words or phrases is this page *most* about?" Consider this question throughout your site, whether it's the page that lists the film's plot, the cast and crew bios, or business information.

7. Remember, your site doesn't just exist within the context of itself. Use the subject of your film to have as many links as possible between your site and other relevant sites; and by relevant, that means everything possible! From what the film is about, who is involved, what influenced it, etc., you should forge links with everything related to your film in any way. You should have the sites you link to link back to you in turn. You can often do this by simply emailing the other sites, their administrators, webmasters, designers, or owners and ask them to create links back to your site.

8. Make sure that when you post anything — a blog about the film, a fully realized press kit, the director's statement — you intelligently situate keywords and key phrases that you want search engines to pick in the first paragraph or headline that accompanies the text. That goes for captions and the underlying names of photos or videos that are integrated into the site, too.

9. Of course, the richer the content of your site, the greater chance search engines will find keywords in the range of subjects your site covers. If your film is about a certain subject, include related articles or stories and images about that subject.

10. Though often overlooked, two other important elements can improve your ranking in searches. One is "duration" — how long do people stay on your site, either by reading or watching it? The other is "click-throughs" — how much do users jump around the site? Getting a hit or, as the term has been updated, a page view, demonstrates user activity. The diversity of page views is more important than just someone hitting the site, because hits can be rigged. Most important is that someone is really moving through the site, not just clicking at one point."

★ *LEARN HOW TO USE WORDPRESS*

In order to work with your designer/programmer on your site, you will need to understand some basic Wordpress concepts. My assistant informed me that anyone under 30 should know everything in this step and that I should cut it out. So if you know how to use Wordpress, skip to the next step.

Some explanation of terms:

Website: A collection of web pages.

Page: A web page is an individual HTML document that is viewable and accessible on the Internet. Pages can be static or dynamic.

Post: An essay that you write. It is information that changes with time as opposed to information that is relatively more static. Think of it as a column for news as opposed to reference information.

Tag: A word that you are using to identify or label a post, page, or piece of information. Tags form metadata that is used by the web to identify information for people performing searches.

Metadata: Data about other data of any sort in any media. It can include time/date, size of file, or — more importantly — tags.

Category: A hierarchical way to organize information for your website viewers. A page generally only has one category, while it can have many tags.

The Wordpress Dashboard

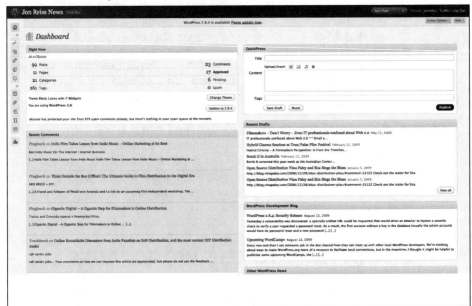

The far left column is your menu. In the middle column you have a summary of your site/blog. Below that are recent comments. On the top right is a handy place to post a blog quickly. Note: The dashboard will change over time. Check the Wordpress Codex for developments, but the principles outlined here should remain relatively stable.

For configuring your site/blog, you will be using the column on the far left. It is broken into three sections:

Dashboard Icon The dashboard is the "home" page of your site/blog administration.

Posts/Media/Links/Pages/Comments

 Posts are your blog entries.

 Media is where the media that you import to your site is stored, whether it's used in a page or a post.

 Links is where you connect to other sites. You post their website into a link, give it a name, and then this name appears on your Blogroll (a list of your links).

Pages are very basic, but I found this definition from the Wordpress Codex useful: "Pages live outside of the normal blog chronology, and are often used to present information about yourself or your site that is somehow timeless — information that is always applicable. You can use Pages to organize and manage any amount of content."

 Comments You should respond to comments as soon as possible to create a dialogue with your audience. You should also add these people to your email list.

Appearance/Plugins/Users/Tools/Settings

These controls adjust the look and content of your website/blog.

 Appearance

Theme is a pre-designed format, layout, and coding that serves as a basis for a web page or blog main page.

Widgets "A widget is anything that can be embedded within a page of HTML, i.e. a web page. A widget adds some content to that page that is not static."[2] Their code is similar to embed code, but they include a player or other tools offering specific opportunities, such as "buy now" or "join the mailing list." For the purposes of your website/blog, this is where you can add Widgets to your blog. Wordpress gives you a variety of available widgets such as a Blog Archive, Blogroll of Links, a search function, etc. You can also use the text widget to add embeddable text, such as your YouTube trailer, Box Office Widget for your mailing list, a link from Flickr, etc.

You adjust the placement of widgets on your page by dragging them in relative position to each other.

Editor I would leave this section to your webmaster unless you know HTML.

 Plugin A plugin is a computer program that interacts with the main program and adds functionality to it. Flash, for example, is a plugin. One very useful plugin is Askimet, which is a spam filter for your blog (for comment spam). Another use-

[2] Wikipedia

ful plugin is "AddThisSocialBookmarkingWidget," which "allows any visitor to bookmark your site easily with many popular services."

Tip from Michael Medaglia: Don't add too many plugins — they are made by third parties and can interfere with each other. Only add items that will really make a difference. Poorly written plugins can introduce bugs and security holes, so before adding them, check with your webmaster.

 Users People allowed to access and change your blog/site. Here is where you would allow crew people or cast to blog on your site — and only set them up as contributors. Here is a quick list and explanation of the various levels:

> <u>Administrator</u> Somebody who has access to all the administrative features of the blog
>
> <u>Editor</u> Somebody who can publish and manage all the posts.
>
> <u>Author</u> Somebody who can publish and manage his or her own posts
>
> <u>Contributor</u> Somebody who can write and manage their posts but not publish them
>
> <u>Subscriber</u> Somebody who can read comments/comment/ receive newsletters, etc.[3]

 Tools You don't need this too often, except to export and import a complete blog which serves as a poor man's blog backup. You can also update Wordpress here.

 Settings It is not necessary to go into all of these. I just want to point out one feature under Writing:

Post Via Email This is where you can set up posting to your blog via email. This has somewhat been replaced by Twitter, but is a cool option if you want to post blogs from the road.

Using Pages

Use pages for any content that won't change on a daily basis. This includes: About the Film, Cast and Crew Bios, Reviews, Screenings, Mailing List Sign-Up Forms, and Screening Sign-Up

You will be able to edit these pages simply by selecting Pages, then Edit, and using it like a word processor.

Page Hierarchy Each page can have several subpages. For instance, "About Crew" might have clickable links to pages for individual crew biographies. When you are writing a subpage, you can select a "page parent" for that page — your new page will then be a child of that parent page. To make the parent page look nicer, do the following: Copy the URL for the child page. Go to the parent page and type whatever text you want to be the link to the child page. Select the text. Click Link and paste the URL into the box. This is the way you will connect URLs to links in your blogs as well.

UTILIZE EMBEDDABLE SOCIAL NETWORKS TO KEEP YOUR SITE DYNAMIC

Take advantage of social networks that allow you to embed changing information on your blog. If you look at Picture 3, you will see a Flickr sidebar on the mid/lower left that updates photos from our Flickr site. (Our Flickr site allows people who are interested in graffiti and street art to participate in the project by posting their own pictures.) You can also embed your Twitter feed into your blog.

[3] Wordpress Codex Summary of Roles

[o}[ox

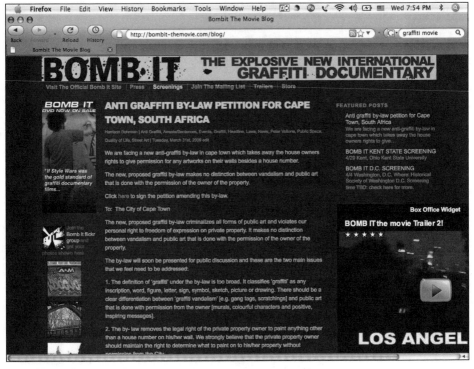

PICTURE 3

SETTING UP YOUR MAILING LIST

The mailing list is essential to the distribution and marketing of your film. It is the basis for selling your film directly to your long-term fan base. It is essential that you establish a way for people to join your mailing list and to motivate them to do so. Having a mailing list management system is one of the key criteria in choosing your hosting site.

Here is a list of suggestions for your mailing list acquisition:

1. Keep it simple, with as few clicks as possible. Best to have the entry fields right on the blog or homepage.

2. Keep the number of fields to be filled as minimal as possible — just name, email address and zip/country is fine.

3. Make sure you get the ZIP code at least, and perhaps country. This is so that you can target your emails when you have live events.

4. There is some debate as to whether you ask permission for various email list marketing attributes. I feel that the fewer the check boxes, the better. If you indicate that the email list is to keep them informed about news about the film and promotions related to the film, I believe you are safe in terms of sending subscribers emails regarding this. However, this will not allow you to sell their email addresses to someone else. I don't think selling your email list is a good idea; in fact, it's a way to alienate your audience.

Box Office Widget

The fulfillment service Neoflix offers something pretty cool called *Box Office Widget.* This service allows you to set up a mailing list widget with or without your trailer embedded. To put it on your site, you just cut and paste the code into the appropriate place. The widget with the embedded trailer comes with clickable links for people to do the following:

1. Join your mailing list

2. Promote your film (it gives people code so they can embed your widget on their sites)

3. See a map of your fan base

4. Soon to come is a "Buy DVD" link that will take people directly to your store

Neoflix does charge for the emails that you send your fans from Box Office Widget, but it does not charge a monthly fee like many services. It charges based on the number of emails sent. There are some other established email client services such as *Constant Contact*; however, some of these can be relatively expensive. A number of free services seem to be cropping up on a weekly basis.

CAVEAT: WHEN YOU DON'T WANT TO BE ON THE WEB BEFORE THE FILM IS IN THE CAN

There are going to be some cases when you do not want to be on the web before your film is finished. This concerns documentaries about sensitive subjects, where information about your film might prevent some people from participating. Examples might be films that investigate abuse or cover a controversial topic.

Even for *Bomb It* we ran into trouble when we posted our full artist list on our website. Not from any anti-graffiti enforcement agencies or officials, but from graffiti artists themselves who we were approaching to be in the film. We were in Japan, our last location, and we were told by a couple of artists that they didn't want to be in the film if so-and-so and so-and-so were in the film — even if we had not cut the film and had merely identified that we had interviewed those people. Sometimes you need to be careful about the timing of full disclosure.

Chapter 9 Conclusion

You need a dynamic website for your film — a home base in addition to your social networks. You should consider getting a programmer and/or designer to set one up for you, but make sure it is one that you can make basic changes to on your own.

CHAPTER 10

INCREASING, CULTIVATING, AND PARTNERING WITH YOUR AUDIENCE

So you have your site set up. Now what?

How do you get people to come? This is done partly through optimizing your site architecture for search engines; through outreach to people via social networks, which is covered in the next chapter; and through organizational outreach and making your site attractive to search engines and people on the web. These latter elements are the subject of this chapter.

WHAT DO YOU HAVE TO OFFER?

It is important to have the proper attitude toward your audience and supporters. You need to think, "What can I give them?" instead of "What can they do for me?" If you think of the former, the latter will flow. People are very busy. You need to give them an incentive to be involved with you. The film is not enough. How will the film service their organization, their lives?

ORGANIZATIONAL OUTREACH

As founding partner of Brave New Films and director of alternative marketing at Focus Features, Lisa Smithline pioneered a new model of community-based distribution while working on films as diverse as *Wal-Mart: The High Cost of Low Price, Trouble the Water, Crips and Bloods, Crude*, and many more. As a top-notch grassroots, community marketing strategist, she has a catchphrase for working with organizations: DIFY, or Do It for You. Engage organizations who will, in turn, do a lot of marketing and outreach for you.

★ Research

Recognize the organizational and institutional structures that exist around your film's topic or theme. This is much easier with films that deal with an issue that has an organized base (e.g., environment, women's issues, etc.). Many organizations exist now for so many issues — and even for types of films. Organizations also include fan communities around a subject, blogs, or press. Find them! Many of these groups will be eager partners. They might help fund your film or generate audience awareness. For docs, they might also help you connect with people to interview. A consultant can help brainstorm ideas for various types of groups and niches.

★ Outreach

You might consider hiring a researcher or grassroots consultant to do the organizational research and outreach (which I think could cover some of your Internet press outreach). It is best to hire someone interested in the subject of the film. They will be more enthusiastic, and enthusiasm is important. It is not a stretch to give an associate producer credit to someone whose sole role is audience/community outreach. This is a perfect task for the PMD.

Boyle suggests contacting organizations in a conversational, non-pitchy way via a personal email. Some tips:

- The email should be personal, not a blast.

- The email address (from you) and the subject lines must be used effectively, so the reader actually opens the email (it is all they will see initially).

- The outreach person should use an email address that incorporates the title and/or subject of the film.

- If you have been referred to the organization or person being contacted by someone else, put the name of the recommender in the subject line.

- Research the person you are emailing and direct the contents of your email to their interests. Engage them from *their* point of view.

- Keep your email very short.

- Phone calls: While Boyle does not recommend cold calling, I think it depends. There are still many people who will respond to a phone call faster than an email. Some people get too many emails.

- Remember that outreach is about relationships. You will have many of these relationships for a long time. They are valuable. Treat them as such.

USING YOUR WEBSITE

Blogging and Tagging

Search engines like activity on your site that has substance. One of the easiest ways to regularly change and update your site with new content is with blog posts. Use blogs to chronicle the progress of your film, to write about other organizations that you are partnering with, news related to your film, the people in your film, and whatever else might be of interest to your audience. While Twitter has begun to take the place of the instant short blog, I do feel that there still is space for more in-depth writing about your film.

I feel it is important to blog from your website and not a blogging site — it creates activity for *your* website, and that is what you need.

If you don't like to blog, you should think about getting someone who does. Perhaps it's the same person doing your organizational outreach and/or your PMD. One of our producers, Tracy Wares, handled *Bomb It*'s blogging for the first three years of the project's existence. She then had to move on and get a life, so I enlisted Harrison Bohrman, who earned his co-producer credit through a two-year commitment to blogging and tagging on the *Bomb It* site almost every day, while also running our street teams and handling some bookings. Whoever blogs should have a real connection to the film.

Benefits of Blogging

Blogging drives traffic to your site as you link to new and interesting stories that are related to the subject of your film. (For *Bomb It*, we post news about graffiti around the world, in addition to news about the film.) Blogging activity will result in higher search rankings for your film in relevant categories: For us, it was "graffiti movie," "graffiti documentary," etc.

Tagging

Tagging is marking your posts with key words that you want associated with the post. You need to tag your posts in two ways:

First, search engines pick up on keywords in the words you tag. We tag every post with the following words and then we add more tags based on what the post is specifically about: *Bomb It*, Graffiti Film, Graffiti Documentary, Global Graffiti Documentary, Street Art Film, Street Art Documentary, Graffiti, Street Art.

Second, search engines also pick up the keywords in *the title of the blog post*.

Frequency of Blogging

You should be posting at least once a week if possible. Don't let time go by so that when people look at your website and your posts, they are months old. Try to develop a manageable rate that you can maintain to get your audience accustomed to a regular flow. You need to consider your time for blogging and your other social network activity, such as Twitter and Facebook, as discussed in the next chapter. Obviously your activity will depend on where you are at in your film's process as well.

Blogging About the Subject of Your Film

Of course you should blog about your film and your screenings, but you should also consider blogging about subjects that relate to your film. This will make your film relevant to your audience on a broader level and keep them coming back to your site. It will also make your site relevant to a broader audience interested in the subject of your film. One simple way to come up with information to blog about is to use Google Alerts. Sign up for some keywords of interest and then Google Alerts will email you related articles on a weekly or daily basis. We receive a weekly Google Alert about "graffiti" and "street art" and select a few top articles to blog about. You should, of course, also receive Google Alerts for the name of your film and your name. This will also give you information to tweet about.

CULTIVATE YOUR RELATIONSHIPS

Blogging and linking are two easy ways to cultivate and expand the relationships between your film and other people who should be interested in your film, organizations, and other blogs. In addition, search engines will improve your rankings, not only by other sites linking to you, but also by them writing about you. So it is best to create a dynamic relationship with other sites and organizations:

- Blog about their sites and link to them.

- Request that they link back to you.

- Have the other sites write about your film during production, post, and distribution. Have them review it and post about screenings. When other sites write about you, they surround your website with relevant text, and this improves your search engine rankings. Reviews will do this as well. Make sure they list your website when writing about you.

- You can create an affiliate relationship with those sites or organizations (discussed in Chapter 23, on direct marketing).

- Use this relationship to generate community screenings (discussed in Chapter 18).

These suggestions are just the beginning of your relationship with these organizations, groups, and blogs.

INCENTIVIZE PEOPLE TO JOIN YOUR MAILING LIST

The best way to get people to join your mailing list is to give them something. Why should they give you their valued email address for free? When we got our website online, we offered people free stickers. It became a little cumbersome and cost a few hundred dollars, but it did help us get 2,000 people to join our mailing list before the film was released. Here are some easier-to-implement items to offer exclusively to people on your mailing list:

- A discount coupon for when the film is released

- An ability to buy the film before anyone else

- A signed copy

- A special combo package (e.g., DVD and poster combo)

- Email updates about the film

- Access to behind-the-scenes footage

CROWDFUNDING

Crowdfunding is crowdsourcing applied to film finance. The opportunity for your fans and supporters to invest in your projects and career is one of the next steps of participation beyond signing up for the mailing list. I would also argue it will become a significant source of fundraising for media content creators in the future. Instead of giving away any of the benefits listed above for the price of an email address, you can charge incrementally for different levels of participation.

You might post something like this on the donations page of your website:

> With a $10 donation, you get access to behind-the-scenes footage and updates.
>
> A $25 donation gets you a free copy of the film two weeks before anyone else (perhaps even before the festival release).
>
> A $50 donation gets you all that, plus a "special thanks" credit in the film.
>
> A $100 donation: All that, plus the ability to make suggestions on the final cut of the film.
>
> A $500 donation: All that, plus an invitation to the set.
>
> A $1,000 donation gets you an Associate Producer credit.

And so on.

You can do this from your site via PayPal or any number of online tip-collection services. But you can also do it on a number of emerging financing sites on the web: IndieGoGo.com is strictly devoted to film. IndieGogo has about 2000 projects currently in progress on their site. IndieGogo takes 9% of funds raised. Slava Rubin, one of the founders of IndieGoGo, views crowdfunding as one step in developing a relationship with an audience. He reports a one to five ratio of funds raised on the site to funds raised *due* to their site. E.g.

if a project has raised $20,000 on IndiGoGo their studies indicate that the film usually raises five times that ($100,000) because of the film's existence on the service. According to Rubin, contributors see that the film is crowdfunding, but the contributor does not want to go through the web to make their donation and instead gives the money directly to the filmmaker.

In addition, IndieGoGo just announced an alliance with the San Francisco Film Society for fiscal sponsorship. Fiscal sponsorship is when your non-profit worthy project is covered through a larger non-profit entity allowing people to take a tax writeoff for donations to your film (usually a documentary). This allows you to collect tax deductible donations without achieving non-profit status yourself. You can apply to SFFS for fiscal sponsorship and if accepted, any funds raised through IndieGoGo will only be subject to a 7% fee which includes both IndieGoGo's fee and SFFS's fee for fiscal sponsorship. Note that it is indeed less than the 9% for non-fiscally sponsored projects.

An excellent example of how to crowdfund your film can be found on the site for the *The Age of Stupid*, a U.K.-based documentary about climate change that is pioneering a grassroots screening model as well. Go to ageofstupid.net.

One caveat: You should consult with a lawyer about this type of fundraising, especially if you are also raising funds through an LLC or other financial tools.

INVOLVING YOUR AUDIENCE: CROWDSOURCING

According to Jeff Howe who is one of the people credited for creating the term, "crowdsourcing is the act of taking a job traditionally performed by a designated agent (usually an employee) and outsourcing it to an undefined, generally large group of people in the form of an open call."[4] In other words, to use the talent available throughout the world to provide content and resources for your film. Crowdsourcing can also be a new way to create films completely generated by audience content. *Lost Zombies*, "the community generated zombie documentary,"[5] is a great example of this. Check them out at lostzombies.com. The team behind the crowdsourced film *Star Wreck* have set up a site to help other filmmakers make their film using these techniques. Go to wreckamovie.com.

4 CROWDSOURCING.TYPEPAD.COM
5 LOSTZOMBIES.COM

Crowdsourcing is also a great way to involve your audience and get them engaged and excited about your film. Since they are a part of your film, they will be your advocates. Think of all the new friends you'll have all over the world.

In a sense, nearly all of *Bomb It* was crowdsourced. Almost all the crew — except for the music supervisor, webmaster, several of the animators, and one of the editors — came from the web, virtually all from mandy.com.

We crowdsourced *Bomb It* music, stock footage, and animation through the web. We found one of our key pieces of animation from Kriss Salmanis, an animator in Latvia. Nearly all of the photos of the graffiti writer Rev's work were obtained through Flickr (and many photos of other artists as well). Much of our music was obtained by reaching out through MySpace and other music blogs and sites on the web.

Don't forget: In order to deliver your film, you will need contracts with each of these content providers, which can take a fair amount of cajoling. However, a lot of people are putting their work up online as "creative commons - attribution." This means that they are putting up their work for use by others but are requesting credit in the piece. I print out the photographer's web link with the photo and the creative commons license and put it in my stock footage file (and save PDFs of the same).

Chapter 10 Conclusion

Community outreach, crowdsourcing, crowd-funding, and other ways of engaging your audience and collaborators is one of the most exciting aspects of this new model of filmmaking, distribution, and marketing. The surface has only been scratched as to the creative potential of these new techniques, with more techniques to come.

CHAPTER 11

UTILIZING SOCIAL NETWORKS

It is equally important (perhaps more important as time goes on) to set up your social networks as it is to blog.

Search engines are only one way that people get information. In the referral economy, much of the information and advice concerning media comes through their friends or "friends" on the Internet. These referrals increasingly come through social networks, which wall themselves off from the greater web and search engines. This is the source of the brewing battle between Facebook and Google, between search engines and social networks.

At the bare minimum, you should consider a Twitter account and film pages on Facebook and YouTube. Other sites to consider are other video and photo sites and MySpace (although MySpace is mostly thought of for music and certain niche audiences, it is still one of the most popular and most trafficked websites). While on these sites, spend time going to other groups or people with similar interests, joining them, and encouraging them to become friends with you. By the time we released our film, we had 4,500 MySpace friends. Our audience at the time lived on MySpace, as opposed to Facebook.

> Swartz: "People are more likely to friend you on Facebook than they are to give you an email address."

But having a Facebook or MySpace page is not enough, since it does not allow you to own or directly access your email list or the emails of your "friends." In fact, you can be kicked off of these sites and have no access to your fan data. On social networks, you should offer people incentives to go to your website and join your email list or buy the DVD.

SOME SOCIAL NETWORKING TIPS

1. If possible, personalize the page. Facebook gives you limited choices, but MySpace and YouTube give you more options, especially for filmmaker pages.

2. Use the bulletins feature or email to your group to communicate with your fans.

3. Answer fan comments quickly.

4. Focus on one, two, or three social networks — whatever you can handle comfortably without it taking over your life. If you have a team, you can assign one social network to each. Don't set up networks and let them die on the vine.

5. However, you should blast your trailer and clips to as many sites as possible. Tubemogul is one of the free video publishing and analytics sites that will launch your trailer out to all the usual suspects, and later tell you what kind of viewership you received.

6. Embed your trailer from YouTube so that when people watch your trailer, it registers as a view on YouTube — helping your total views.

7. Connect all your sites and network links to all your sites and networks.

10 TIPS FOR MAKING THE MOST OF FACEBOOK

1. Create a Page/Group for the Film

There is some dispute as to which function is preferable, since you are creating yourself as a brand in addition to your film. I recommend creating a page for yourself as well as one for each of your films, so you have multiple ways to appear in a search result. With the group function, you can invite friends to become members and once they accept, you can send them messages related to something in the group. This is an easy way of being able to get information across to a lot of people quickly (better than the email function, which only allows you to message a certain number of people at a time). With groups, you can also post on the discussion board and share pictures. People may not know you, but once you turn off the privacy settings, they can see your group and choose to become a member with one click. Categorize your group accurately and fill out as many fields as possible to maximize searching potential. Again, watch the settings, because the standard setting for groups requires you to approve members; turn these off so people can quickly join and start exploring the page.

With the "page" function, you have "fans" instead of "members." When someone becomes a fan of your page, the graphic for your page displays as a larger picture (instead of just a title, as with groups). Your page will stand out more than your group will on other people's profiles and is naturally more attention-grabbing on their sites. The page also acts as a completely secondary site, which is especially great for films. You can input release date, cast and crew info, awards, and plot; and best of all, you can put a big link to your website at the very top. As usual, fill everything out so you have maximum search potential.

2. Fill Out Everything in the Profile Box

Unlike MySpace, which is more about customization of your page's look, Facebook has a clear, unchangeable visual layout and is more about content. Since you can't express your individuality by designing your page, you have to do it with writing. Fill out every available box in the profile to come across as a unique, interesting person with a film and something to say. People will read it. Another reason to do this is because Facebook organizes users by interest, and everything is searchable/clickable. If you write that your favorite movie is *Bomb It*, someone else with the same favorite movie can click or search *Bomb It* and find you. Create as many avenues as possible for people to connect with you.

3. Change Your Privacy Settings

One of the reasons Facebook is so popular is that users like its elaborate privacy features. These allow users to control who can see them, write to them, post on their page, etc. The standard setting for Facebook only allows people who are already your friends to view your page. Unless you change them to "allow all" for each facet of Facebook, the settings will remain this way and people who may be interested in simply viewing your profile can't. You should still save certain benefits for friends (as incentive for people to become your friend), like the ability to see your pictures and contact information, but as a bare minimum you should allow "everyone" to be able to view your general profile. After logging in, you can change these settings by going to the top right corner of your profile page, and click on "Settings," then "Privacy Settings."

4. Update Your Profile Constantly

Every time you log into Facebook, you are first presented with a "Mini-Feed" page that lists all of your friends' recently updated profile statuses. When you update your status, you show up on theirs. Update a lot to stay extra visible, and be creative! If you write something funny/intriguing, your friends are more likely to visit your profile, and then also join your groups, visit your pages, etc. You can also post links in the "Profile Status" box; do it sometimes to drive traffic to your blog or website, but don't go overboard.

5. Join Other People's Groups and Post on Them

Groups and pages are a great way to meet people who are not in any of your networks and whom you would probably never meet. If you are a member of a lot of groups, you can also promote your page or group to those members. Again, don't go overboard with this, either, as no one likes someone self-promoting on his or her group all the time. This tip applies to most social networks.

6. Download the YouTube Application and Post Your Trailer on Your Profile Page

This is a great feature of Facebook and one that all filmmakers should use. A simple search in the Facebook search engine will get you the application; you then just click to add it to your page. Now you can start uploading trailers and short films to your page. It plays in your page, rather than opening YouTube in a new window. You may also want to keep a link to this in the "Links" section as well; because again, the more ways to find things on Facebook, the better. Promote your film by asking other friends to post your trailer's link on their pages for maximum visibility.

7. Develop an Application

Think of an application you can develop that would garner interest from your fans, and then interest them in your film as a result.

8. Blog in the Notes Section

"Notes" is basically Facebook's version of a blog. Like MySpace, it alerts all of your friends when you write something, so try to keep it fresh, updated, and interesting. If this means just doing a copy-and-paste from your actual blog, so be it.

9. Use Mini-Feed, Publisher, and Events

This way, your information will show up three times on people's pages. Again, similar to MySpace, you can create events with Facebook and invite all of your friends. It's a great tool for notifying people of screenings, release dates, etc.

10. Advertise on Facebook

Use www.facebook.com/advertising (or Facebook search "advertising") to create a customized ad with a specific target market. You can target people by virtually any of their profile qualities, in any age, located anywhere. Facebook will actually spit out a number of how many people fit into those qualities, so start specific and work your way out. Cost is based on your budget, which can be as little as $1 per day, and you can select to be charged per click or per ad runtime. Before you spend too much money on this, however, make sure you can track the results back in some manner. Try to have the Facebook ad go through an affiliate link on your web store so that you can see if anyone is buying from the ad. (Affiliates are explained in Chapter 23.)

10 TIPS FOR MAKING THE MOST OF TWITTER

1. Post a variety of topics

Twitter users tend become less active on Twitter sites that constantly ring the same bell. Similar to blogging, don't just blog about your film, blog about what is of interest to people who might be interested in your film. Twitter about what interests you, especially as you begin to be to become your own brand. Come across as a human being with important things to say. Also, post items that don't contain links at all. You can use a URL-shortening service such as tinyurl, bit.ly, or xrl.us for your links.

2. Follow Important People

This includes colleagues in related companies and in your industry, brands and journalists and pundits in your market, and your competitors. Find them and don't expect them to find you.

3. Tweet on Controversial Subjects

Twitter's entire model is based on talking; and the best way to get people to notice you is to create arenas that get people talking. It will grow your followers and make people more likely to then retweet you.

4. Don't Try to "Sell" Things Over Twitter

Use Twitter to drive traffic to your website and sell there. Folks are more likely to make money off Twitter if they view Twitter as a "talking" site and use their own blogs/websites for selling. The model should be: Make followers first, Tweet about your blog or website and hope that you get Tweeted back, then drive people to the site, where they will hopefully buy the product. Most retailers report a low level of success from just getting a lot of followers and blasting them with advertisements on Twitter; this typically does not convert into dollars coming in. If you're writing about something that interests people and gets them talking, they're more likely to go back to your website and potentially buy from you.

5. Don't Automate

Products that "automatically" update your blog posts into Twitter posts or automatically gain followers quickly make you come across as a promotion machine, and do not engage people or drive them to your site. There are several other products that promise to grow your followers at a rapid pace — this may sound good, but if no one feels that they know you and there is no personal, human connection, it also will not necessarily translate to DVDs sold and money flowing in.

6. Get Everyone You Know on Twitter

I think this is pretty self-explanatory. You may think coworkers or family members won't like your film or buy your products, but some of their followers might.

7. Reply to Tweets That Mention You

Try to keep track of people who Tweet about you and post responses. It makes you come across as a living person instead of a faceless brand. People will be more likely to mention you again, and this snowballs into more people reading your blog, seeing your film, etc.

8. Routinely Conduct Searches on Your Name

A lot of businesses are currently doing this to find customers who have had negative experiences with their company in order to remedy them. Knowledge of what other people are saying about you and your film will only serve as tools for your decision-making processes in the future. You can use Twitter's search features from the website, or a Mac-based Twitter client program such TweetDeck or Tweetie that supports saved searches.

9. Ask Your Followers Questions and Listen to Their Answers

Is there something you're doing wrong to market your film, or something you could be doing better? Are there other avenues of getting your work out there that you are unaware of? Is there something related to your film people want to see more or less of? Twitter users love to talk, and in a very short amount of time, you can get a better idea of what you're dealing with in the marketplace.

10. Don't Underestimate the Power of Twitter

Even if you're not the type of person who uses social networking sites yourself, there's no denying that these new forms of connection and communication are powerful and becoming increasingly important. It can work for or against you. If you offer incentives for your followers to Tweet about you, you may get more traffic/followers initially, but you may also get your followers' followers Tweeting negative content. Remember, word on Twitter travels quickly, so try not to do anything that will hurt your reputation down the road.

10 TIPS FOR MAKING THE MOST OF YOUTUBE

1. Post Your Trailer or Short Film; Make Friends

YouTube is a great way to generate interest for a feature film or film-maker by showing trailers. You can invite people to be your friends by using their email or user IDs, and when they watch your film it will broadcast as a "video being watched now" when other YouTube members log in. This is a great way to generate interest and promote your film to countless audiences around the world.

2. Subscribe to Other Members; Ask Them to Subscribe to You

When members subscribe to you, they are automatically notified when you post a new video. If you don't have a lot of things to post, try posting links to videos you like. This makes you appear more active on the site, thus increasing visibility.

3. Post Comments and Video Comments

Post comments on other people's related YouTube videos. More importantly, post your trailer as a comment on popular videos that relate to your film or any viral video.

4. Ask Friends to "Favorite" Your Video and Add Favorites to Your Profile

The "Favorites" function is another tool for building visibility and buzz around your film. The more favorites you have, the more likely other people will want to add your links to their favorites page. Don't forget to favorite your own videos.

5. Have a Link to Your Website and Store

You want to drive traffic to your website or store, where people can buy the DVD.

6. Regularly Change Your Tags

From Sklar: On YouTube, switch your tags on your trailer every week during your release. Don't just tag it with items related to your film, tag it with whatever is popular that week, in the news.

7. Create Playlists and Share Them With Other Users

Playlists are a great way to organize your videos by whatever criteria you deem appropriate. Users can play videos from a playlist individually or as a group. This is a way to share different bodies of work with other users, and again, increase visibility to your profile.

8. Share Your Videos Via Email

When you post your video, you should see a link that says "Share" somewhere by the picture. By clicking on it, you can send an email to anyone and it will include the direct, active link to your video. Drive traffic to your video posts with this feature. You can also share videos from your Favorites list.

9. Remind People That They Can Also Watch Your YouTube Video via Their Mobile Phone

See m.youtube.com for more information on this.

10. Post Your YouTube Videos on Your Blog And Other Sites.

I've already discussed the Facebook video posting in the previous section. In addition, if you have your own personal blog, YouTube makes it easy to send any public YouTube video to your blog as a new blog posting. First, however, you have to tell YouTube about your blog so that it knows where to send the post. Start by clicking the "My Account" link at the top of any YouTube page. On the My Account page, scroll down to the Account Settings section and click the "Video Posting Settings" link. When the next page appears, click the "Add a Blog/Site" button. YouTube now displays the Add a Blog/Site page. Pull down the Blog Service list and select your blog host. YouTube supports automatic posting to Blogger, Friendster, LiveJournal, Piczo, WordPress.com, and WordPress self-hosted blogs. Now enter your blog username and password, click the "Add Blog" button, and you're finished with this preliminary setup. Once configured, it's a snap to send any public YouTube video to your blog. Just open the video's viewing page and click the "Share" link.

10 TIPS FOR MAKING THE MOST OF MYSPACE

1. Set Up Separate Accounts for Your Film/Business and Yourself

There are many reasons for doing this. First off, you will come up in two searches. In addition, you will have one site where you come across as a filmmaker (or film), and one where you come across as a real person with likes and dislikes, a face, and a name. Link these two profiles to one another, and to your website. Keep in mind that having two accounts will take up more time. It is more important to have a film site on MySpace.

2. Customize, Customize, Customize

There are hundreds of websites that can help you create a customized, interesting-looking MySpace page that reflects your personality and the personality of your film. Use them. Google "MySpace Layouts" and take your pick. Many of these layouts are free and can give your page a big boost aesthetically.

3. Acquire as Many Friends as Possible and Don't Spam

More friends obviously equals more publicity for you, as you will show up on their pages. Don't just stick to your own country of residence, as the power of the web can connect you to fans in other countries whom you may never meet, and if you have the resources available for them to buy/view your film online, they could easily translate into customers. MySpace users are starting to become more and more inundated with advertising, so pick the messages that are most important to you and go from there.

4. Create Eye-Catching Flyers to Send Out as Bulletins

You can use sites like wix.com to create Flash e-flyers, which can then attach to bulletin posts. Flash bulletins are much more exciting and eye-catching than MySpace's simple text ones. Templates are available and they're easy to use; otherwise you can start from scratch. Title the bulletin with something simple, informative, and attention-getting. Subjects of the posts could involve screenings, new merchandise available on your site, awards won in festivals, etc.

5. Use the Gigs Tool on Artist Pages and the Event Tool on Personal Pages to Promote Screenings and Other Events

The "Gigs" tool helps your film come across as successful and out in the world (and advertises your events); with the "Event" tool, you can send personal invitations to all of your friends.

6. Keep Your Page Current and Interesting

This should be said of all social networking sites, but because MySpace has more options for customization and does not consist of simple posting, try to freshen up your page with different looks and styles to keep friends checking back in. These changes should report as "recent activity" on all of your friends' pages, which is like free advertising that drives more people to the site. MySpace also posts a large listing of when you were "last logged on," so make people think you are aware of their visits to your site. And, of course, make sure your screenings and everything else are up-to-date.

7. Search for Widgets and Applications That Can Enhance Your MySpace Page

MySpace has been around longer than the other "big" social networking sites, so there are more of these tools available as quick, easy, free downloads: banners, advertising tools, decorations, etc. Find ones that drive people to your website, advertise DVDs and merchandise for sale, etc. Since they simply appear on your page, these can help you cut down on spamming your friends with email messages, but still get the word out that you have things to sell and announce.

8. Post on Other People's Pages

Posting on friends' pages increases your visibility to other users and is a quick and easy way to drive traffic to your page. If you post something interesting/clever on someone else's page, it is likely that their friends will at least click to see who you are, and will find themselves on your MySpace page. More clicks to your name equals more friends, which equals a larger fan base.

9. Use MySpace to Find Music for Your Film or Trailer

Although sites like Facebook have bypassed MySpace in terms of user activity, MySpace is still the number-one site for start-up musicians and bands who want to self-promote. Many of them are not attached to any labels or publishing companies yet, and might be up for collaborating with you for low to no cost. You can listen to their songs for free via their pages.

10. Use the Blog Feature

MySpace has a blog feature and announces to all your friends when you've posted something new on it. Keep your blog fresh, updated, and interesting to keep people coming back. If you already have another blog, at least copy-and-paste it into your MySpace one so you can benefit from the announcements.

Chapter 11 Conclusion

This is not a comprehensive list of tips, but it's a start. We will post more social networking tips for filmmakers on our site — and you can post your tips there as well.

Utilizing social networks to tell people about your film and give them updates about your film is fine, but they have so much more potential. One of those avenues of potential is in the realm of transmedia/crossmedia storytelling. The idea is to use social networks as just one of many storytelling platforms available to you as a creative person. Our next chapter is a basic introduction to transmedia and the simple things that you can do in prep to enable you to create a cross platform strategy for your film.

CHAPTER 12

AN INTRODUCTION TO TRANSMEDIA

Transmedia, also referred to as cross media, multiplatform, or enhanced storytelling, is a when a narrative takes places over a number of various media platforms.

Christy Dena, who speaks and writes about the subject (see christydena.com), says that cross media is where you desire to fuse two or more media together, creating multiple story channels.

A classic example is *The Matrix*, for which there was a unified narrative that was carried out over several films, an animated series called *The Animatrix*, several video games, comic books, and various merchandise.

Henry Jenkins is the Provost's Professor of Communications, Journalism, and Cinematic Art at the University of Southern California. Until recently, he served as the co-founder of the Comparative Media Studies Program at the Massachusetts Institute of Technology. In his recent book *Convergence Culture: Where Old and New Media Collide*, he writes that the "the Wachowski brothers played the transmedia game very well, putting out the original film to stimulate interest, offering up a few web comics to sustain the hard-core fan's hunger for more information, launching the anime in anticipation of the second film, releasing the video game alongside it to surf the publicity, bringing the whole cycle to conclusion with *The Matrix Revolutions*, turning the whole mythology over to the players of the massively multiplayer online game. Each step along the way built on what has come before, while offering new points of entry."[1]

While graphic novelizations of films or filmed versions of comic books qualify as transmedia, since they are utilizing more than one medium to tell a narrative about a set of characters, there are many more interesting possibilities that have been created by the explosion of media platforms over the past few years. Think of a story that takes place via a feature film, but extends out over mobile devices, gaming consoles, social networks, through websites, text messages, downloadable clips, or iPhone apps. An exciting amount of creative potential awaits adventurous filmmakers.

[1] Henry Jenkins, Convergence Culture: Where Old and New Media Collide. NYU Press; 2006

MULTIPLE POINTS OF ENTRY

One of the key phrases in the Jenkins quote above is "offering new points of entry." As we have discussed and will continue to discuss in the book, media consumers don't consume in one unified pattern anymore. Each person has his or her own way of encountering and engaging with a piece of media. Transmedia accommodates that new fragmented consumer marketplace by providing multiple ways for audience members to experience and engage with content.

More Work?

For independent filmmakers who are struggling to get a film made, taking on more work to fulfill a transmedia strategy might seem overwhelming.

However, just look back on the media that I have outlined in this section: websites, blogs, social networks, YouTube, and electronic press kits. Each of these is a media platform with which to engage your audience. Seen individually or chapter by chapter, they can appear to be fragmented. However, if you can envision them in the context of an overall narrative and strategy for your film, you can begin to see their greater potential. Hence, by coordinating the work you would probably already do to distribute and market your film, you can begin to engage a transmedia strategy.

It depends on how you plan to use the tools available to you.

CREATING MATERIALS FOR TRANSMEDIA

Filmmaker and DIY visionary Lance Weiler sat down with me to explain some of the relatively easy things that you can do in production to give yourself some options later to create a variety of media. Lance also runs workbookproject.com, which is a fount of information not only about DIY distribution and marketing, but also about these new forms of storytelling.

The following are every bit as important to create as your standard EPK, and can be done concurrently, by the same crew:

- 360-degree still photo views of each set. You need these to create any kind of potential gaming environment for the film.

Whoever is shooting your stills should capture these as well. Games should not just be thought of as first-person shooters; they can be any kind of interactive experience between viewer and media.

- Photos and detailed reference of any props. For the same reason as the above.

- Wild sounds that might fit the narrative of the film.

EXPANDING THE NARRATIVE

Think creatively about how the characters of your film might live beyond the confines of your film's world. Don't just think in terms of deleted scenes (although those are fine) — think of creating new, stand-alone scenes or storylines that can live on the web as an alternative life for your film and its characters. Studios and TV shows have been doing this for a number of years now. But there is no reason that independents cannot embrace this opportunity and use it for methods of storytelling that we have not seen yet. Weiler is actually surprised at how independents are lagging behind the studios in a field with such creative potential.

Some obvious possibilities are the backstory of characters and their relationships. Directors will often do improvised exercises with their actors in rehearsal as a way to create relationship. Think about writing these scenes out after the improv (or filming another improv with your actors, in wardrobe, on location) and using these bits for the web.

Consider the lives and world of your characters during the film but not seen on screen. Perhaps there is an actor in a small role who is incredible, whom you want to see more of but you can't fit them into the narrative. Shoot the material and use it for the web. Think of how you can create an alternate reality for your characters that you can explore via short pieces on the web, which will interest your audience and draw them to your film. You may release these shorts into the festival circuit as separate entities to create anticipation for your feature in the conventional film world.

This material is called "extra-diegetic" and includes all content that is not part of the final released film, especially material that is created but never intended to be part of the final released film. However, as our understanding of film expands, there will not need to be a separate classification between diegetic and extra-diegetic; it will all be part of a seamless whole.

It is important to keep this material authentic. Nisar states, "Don't try to fake out your audience. News travels instantly on the web, and web denizens are particularly sensitive to deception."

Four Eyed Monsters is an excellent example of a transmedia experience. The film works seamlessly across the film and its podcasts. Check it out at: foureyedmonsters.com

Documentaries are usually blessed with lots of extra footage that does not find its way into the film. The web provides a home for that material. When we were shooting *Bomb It*, we knew all along that we would have enough material for at least four more films (we are actually cutting those now), but this material is actually finding an equal place on the web. We are cutting a number of short episodes that provide a deeper look into each of the characters who were in the film or even cut out of the final film. We struck a deal with Babelgum to create a *Bomb It* channel and "super landing page" as a home for this content. Not only are they putting the material on the web, but they are sponsoring screenings of *Bomb It* at graffiti festivals to promote the channel providing additional points of entry.

Issues with SAG

Currently there is a problem with the SAG contracts concerning this material and the actors you use for your film. It is my understanding and I could be wrong that any "promotional material" that is created for the film with the actors under the current SAG agreement may only be used within the first six months of the release of the film. After that, it must come off the web. Lance Weiler got around this for his transmedia work for *Head Trauma* by using different actors. I am hoping that we as a community can talk to SAG and come to some agreement to solve this potential issue.

★ Be Creative About Your Behind-the-Scenes Footage

This material does not involve the characters or story of the film itself, but the real human beings behind the film. Do something different from the norm. Involve your actors: Do they have quirks or hobbies to explore? I'm sure you can think of 10 things no one has done before. Come on, I know you can.

Its Not Just Promotion

Do not think that you are creating this material solely for promotion or to monetize your film. Think of it as a creative opportunity that expands the boundaries of what we consider film to be. We have only begun to tap the potential of how these techniques can expand storytelling. This is one of the areas of independent film that I am most excited about.

SECTION 2 CONCLUSION

My hope is that you have a good understanding of not only very basic marketing for independent film, but also a grasp of the following essential concepts for taking a hybrid/split rights distribution path:

- Develop an evolving knowledge of who your audience is.

- Engage with your audience as soon as possible.

- Find allies who can help you engage with your audience.

- The earlier you engage allies and your audience, the sooner they can help you with making your film.

- Be active on a dynamic website to attract new audience members.

- Use social networks to do the same.

- Prepare your marketing tools as early in the process as possible, certainly before you have finished your film.

- Think outside the box in terms of what kind of materials you can create for expanding the world of your narrative and the points of entry to it.

It is time now to examine that holy grail of film distribution: theatrical. Contrary to popular belief, I believe that a theatrical release is now more possible than ever.

Section 3

Live Events/ Theatrical

I am going to redefine the entire rights category of public screenings of films. My argument is that all types of public performance, wherever they take place, either in a theater or in a bar, whether paid or unpaid, are theatrical screenings. To avoid confusion, I am going to call these screenings "live event/theatrical."

Live because it happens in front of or with an audience.

Events not only because it happens at a specific place and time, but because I feel that the future of the theatrical model for independents are screenings that feel like happenings or special occasions, aka an event.

Theatrical because independent filmmakers like to say that they had a theatrical release. It's a term that has been in use for decades; let's not throw it out yet, let's take it back.

CHAPTER 13

REDEFINING THE THEATRICAL EXPERIENCE

What is a "theatrical" screening/release?

Here are some of the conventions that have arisen over the last century to define a theatrical release:

A film (delivered on celluloid of at least 35 millimeters in width and at least 70 minutes long) is screened in a traditional movie theater outfitted with film projectors and sound systems.

The film is only available to be seen in theaters, so people must come to the theater if they want to see the film.

With few exceptions, these theaters are owned by chains and programmed by people who have established relationships with distributors.

With a few exceptions, releases begin on Friday and run for at least one week (with everyone hoping for more).

These movies are reviewed in print media that usually runs on Thursdays and Fridays, preceding the release.

Any booking of a film into a projected environment that does not meet the conventions outlined above falls into a category of "non-theatrical" or "semi-theatrical". These include screenings in colleges, churches, cultural centers, museums, etc. Given that these screenings are defined primarily in negative terms (non-, semi-) it is not surprising that they receive a second-class status.

Equally responsible for establishing this second-class status is the lack of attention the press has traditionally given to non- and semi-theatrical releases. Considering the glut of theatrical screenings supported by large publicity and marketing budgets, this is not surprising.

Finally, the prestige that filmmakers themselves have conferred on traditional theatrical releases has also had an effect on the ghettoization of the non- and semi-theatrical market.

This classification of theatrical markets wasn't always the case. In the earliest days of motion picture films, screenings occurred in a variety of spaces: storefronts, tents, public parks, churches. Films often toured with vaudeville acts or circuses or on their own.

Over time an official distribution system developed as a controllable, reliable delivery system for studios. Even after the vertical integration of the studios was broken up in the 1950s, the delivery system remained intact, just not under the direct control of the studios.

> It is time for filmmakers to reclaim the meaning of a theatrical release so that it is inclusive of a multitude of live-screening event scenarios. The theatrical experience needs to be redefined as people watching *"films"* with other people. Any place. Any time. Any media.

 Live Event/Theatrical should be defined as any exhibition of a film to a live audience, following whatever formal guidelines are intended by the filmmaker.

With "live," I am emphasizing the *communal* nature of the filmgoing experience.

I also want to emphasize the "event" nature of the screenings: Something special is conveyed by going to a screening at a specific time at a specific place. The more specific that time and place is, the more it will take on the qualities of an event. It also encourages filmmakers to think of ways to turn their screenings into events.

Venues can and should be as diverse as:

- Conventional film theaters
- Community centers
- Bars, cafes, and nightclubs
- College auditoriums
- Churches
- Parking lots

- Parks

- Galleries

Home theaters and living rooms that allow for an audience and provide for a coherent, shared experience can be theatrical in nature. However, the film must be screened as the filmmaker intended, usually in the dark, from beginning to end without interruptions and preferably with at least some people outside of those who live at the residence, so as to create a communal as opposed to a familial experience. In my view, "theatrical" does not include watching a film with one's immediate family as the sole audience. Nor does it allow for interruption of the screening by phone calls, bathroom breaks, or food breaks — which, unlike communal viewing, familial viewing usually permits.

FOUR INDELIBLE ASPECTS OF THE LIVE EVENT/ THEATRICAL EXPERIENCE

1. A live event retains the magic of viewing a film in the dark with other people.

2. A live event provides filmmakers with a way to have their film experienced in the manner in which they intended it to be experienced.

3. A live event provides the opportunity for direct personal connections between filmmakers and audiences.

4. A live event provides a platform around which to organize publicity. For most independents, the theatrical release is where they will garner the most critical and public attention.

I would argue an additional emerging aspect to live events:

Live events provide filmmakers with the opportunity to experiment with the form of film in the live experience.

We will examine the forms of public screenings in the ways that have emerged to experience them.

- Film Festivals

- Conventional Theatrical

- DIY Theatrical

- Event Screenings

- Non-theatrical / Semi-theatrical / Alternative theatrical / Grassroots / Community

Currently, each of these markets has its own specific ways of booking and delivery. As a result, to give you advice on accessing these individual markets, it is still easier for me to address them in turn.

How you organize screenings for your specific film may vary. Perhaps you will start with grassroots screenings in order to build up to conventional theatrical screenings. For most filmmakers, however, I believe it makes sense to book these various live event markets simultaneously, so as to take advantage of your one big publicity push.

You may find, as some filmmakers have, that your screenings will not only continue after this first run, but that you might also have a second large push of screenings if you can reformulate those screenings in some manner. For example, a first run might consist of the film with occasional appearances with the filmmaker, a second run could be the film and a live band touring together — in each of these runs, the venues would be agnostic. In essence, it is the content of what is being presented that creates a potential window, not any previously known market classification of the specific venue.

CHAPTER 14

FILM FESTIVALS AND YOUR DISTRIBUTION STRATEGY

The festival world has exploded and morphed. These days, it is not only a way to screen films to hungry filmgoers or a marketplace for getting a distributor. Festivals are your next opportunity to develop your fan base and usually your first opportunity to engage your fans in a live event/theatrical context.

This chapter is not meant to replace books that have been written about film festivals or film festival strategies, such as Chris Gore's *Ultimate Film Festival Survival Guide* or Christopher Holland's *Film Festival Secrets*, which I suggest you take a look at for traditional festival advice. (I will give my top 11 traditional festival suggestions at the end of the chapter.) The intention of this chapter is to talk about film festivals from a distribution and marketing perspective.

THE HIDDEN POTENTIAL OF FILM FESTIVALS

While a number of people have disparaged the explosion of film festivals around the world in the last 10 years, I think this surge is extremely healthy for independent film and filmmakers.

Festivals love film and gather film lovers. Festivals have spent years gathering audience data from their attendees. This is an invaluable resource for filmmakers. Some festivals are starting to create year-round screening relationships with their audiences. These qualities allow filmmakers an opportunity to collaborate with the one organization that cares the most about filmmakers in any particular town

— the film festival. For all the film festival programmers and directors out there: Please continue this expansion of the concept of film festivals. It will benefit the film community in innumerable ways.

THE OLD MODEL

As outlined briefly in the introduction, the old relationship between festivals and distribution for independent films was for producers to use festivals as a way to sell their films. A few U.S. festivals became de facto independent film markets for the specialized distribution business: Sundance/Slamdance, Tribeca, Los Angeles Film Festival, South by Southwest, and a few others. (This is in addition to the already traditional international film festival/markets Toronto, Berlin, and Cannes.)

If accepted into a major film festival, most filmmakers had been advised to:

• Get a sales rep (often best before acceptance into festivals, so that the rep could help get your film into said prominent festival).

• Keep your film a secret so that distributors would be forced to see it in a theatrical environment with an unbiased audience of film lovers, without interruptions.

• Pack festival screenings to indicate audience potential.

• Spend money on publicists ($8,000 to $15,000 at Sundance and Tribeca alone), parties, promotion, and travel costs for stars to promote the film. All this was to build up hype to aid a potential bidding war. Many films would spend well over $30,000 on their festival premiere.

Since the deals that filmmakers used to occasionally get because of this strategy don't exist as they once did, doesn't it make sense to reevaluate this strategy? Of course it does.

RETHINKING THE ROLE OF FESTIVALS

Following this traditional sales path in lock step, without creating a strategy for your film before your festival premiere, can possibly hurt your best route to distribution. Perhaps your film should start its distribution at that world premiere festival. Holding it back for a potential sale might delay it from getting a release at the most propitious time.

One prominent independent director indicated that he wished he had had his theatrical release right after his Sundance debut, because it was nearly impossible to re-create the buzz the film received at Sundance. However, he was still thinking that a distributor would pick up his film.

Festivals are one of the best event generators that independent filmmakers have access to. They are often unprecedented at creating a level of hype and promotion that is difficult for independents to create on their own. Filmmakers need to be aware of this, and utilize this strategically in their distribution plans.

DETERMINING WHETHER OR NOT TO USE YOUR FESTIVAL PREMIERE AS A SALES PLATFORM

How do you take advantage of the buzz and promotion of festivals to help monetize your film? First off, you need to determine if you are going to try to be one of the few lucky films in this market that might be able to make a sensible sale to a distributor at a premiere festival.

If you are trying for an acquisition, a good sales rep should be able to help you determine whether there is a market for it in advance of the festival. If no respectable sales rep feels that a sale of this kind is possible for your film, you should consider this a form of collective advice. However, don't despair, you are in the same boat as at least 95% of the other films being made that year.

Even if a premiere sales oriented festival accepts you, it might make sense for your film to pre screen for distributors in advance of your premiere festival. Discuss this with your sales rep.

Here are a couple of potential alternative scenarios for most filmmakers:

FESTIVALS AS THE PREMIERE EVENT(S) FOR YOUR THEATRICAL RELEASE

Larger independent distributors have known for some time that festivals are a cost-effective way to premiere a film on the verge of a release. In essence, they use the festival(s) as a premiere screening and party.

Utilizing the festival in this manner creates an event for the film to organize publicity around. The relative prestige of the festival gives the film some heat. The stars are out on the red carpet and bring the press to the party (literally and figuratively). The reportage of the event gives another level of press coverage for the film — not just reviews, but coverage on entertainment news shows such as *Extra, Access Hollywood*, etc.

The festival premiere provides a lot of exposure with much less expense for a distributor or you. This is why an increasingly large proportion of festival slots are taken up with premieres a week before a film's conventional theatrical release with a conventional distributor.

There is no reason that filmmakers without a conventional distributor cannot use festivals in the same way, but they need to plan accordingly. If your film is prominent enough, or the festival is small enough, or a combination of those two factors, you might be able to get the festival to create an event for you. If not, then this premiere creation needs to be done by you. Although festivals will usually try to support your event, they will generally only take an active part if it is one of their official events.

Having the party at a festival makes it easier to attract sponsors or to use the festival's sponsors. Because of the festival, you might get your whole party for free, like we did with our premiere party at Tribeca (we used the festival's liquor and a bar gave us three hours of free door because we were a Tribeca film). The festival is also, of course, providing the theater, as well as using their PR resources. Ultimately this can help promote the theatrical release in a town. Or if it is a national festival, it can help the national release.

Some cautions if you are going to transition to a conventional theatrical release in the same city of your festival premiere: you have to coordinate it with the local theater, since many theaters are loathe to share their audiences with a festival. Some theaters, though, will realize the promotional value of the festival and be happy for the rollover audience.

You can negotiate with the festival to reduce the number of times the festival plays your film. You can also restrict the size of the venue. This will give you the promotional benefit of the festival, but will cut down on the number of ticket buyers taken away from your theatrical release.

An alternative is to make the festival be your sole theatrical event in that town (but still function to launch the rest of your nationwide release).

With *Bomb It*, we went all out promoting our New York premiere at Tribeca (to create buzz to sell the film). It was then hard to re-create that buzz and hype for our actual theatrical opening. Had I known then what I know now, it would have been smart for us to have had the Tribeca Film Festival be our NY theatrical run and let all of the press come out at that time. This way we would only have had to "open" NY once, and we would have done it with the most support from all sides.

Note: Doing festival "premieres" in cities doesn't have to be restricted to your world premiere. You can use festivals in this way at any time in the life of your film's release.

FESTIVAL PREMIERES TO PROMOTE AN ANCILLARY MARKET RELEASE

For many films that have not been able to obtain a theatrical release, a new phrase has popped up: the festival release is the theatrical release. This may still be the case for filmmakers who don't have the resources to pull off any other types of live event/theatrical screenings in conjunction with their festival release.

For these filmmakers, just as they would use a theatrical release to promote their ancillaries (DVD and VOD, for instance), they should prepare in advance to use their festival release in this manner.

Thought of in another way: They want to have the buzz of a theatrical release but do not have the time or money to conduct one. Hence, the festival run will be their theatrical release and they will monetize it as such.

FESTIVAL PREMIERES AS A CORNER-STONE TO A LIVE EVENTS/THEATRI-CAL RELEASE WITH ANCILLARIES

My recommendation would be to use the festival release as a basis for booking other types of live events in order to create a combined live event/theatrical release during your festival run. I believe this is ultimately the future for many independent filmmakers.

FESTIVAL DIRECT

IFC is a pioneer in these strategies with their Festival Direct program. With Festival Direct, IFC uses a festival premiere and the festival run of the film to promote the film's video on demand (VOD) release. The VOD is released at the same time as the festival premiere. This day-and-date release allows the VOD to take advantage of the film festival hype and press. (See Chapter 30 for an explanation of VOD.)

IFC released Joe Swanberg's film *Alexander the Last* with Festival Direct at the 2009 South by Southwest film festival. Joe decided to go with IFC in releasing the film in this manner for the following reasons:

- IFC had spent a lot of money on the theatrical release of Swanberg's film *Hannah Takes The Stairs* and they are still recouping. He felt they could get similar exposure with Festival Direct without the outlay of money that then must be cross-collateralized against other revenues.

- Swanberg wanted to capitalize on the attention that the festival premiere provides. In his previous releases, Swanberg felt that the six- to nine-month lag time between a festival premiere and a theatrical release killed the promotional momentum of his small films.

- Swanberg and IFC coordinated the festival premiere with a number of other theatrical releases in New York, Chicago, and Cleveland, creating a live event/theatrical release.

- Having a film on VOD day-and-date with the festival premiere allows people from across the country to see the film (as long as they have access to the VOD system releasing the film). This allows people who either missed the local screenings or were not in the cities of the local screenings to see the film in some manner.

• It allowed Swanberg to do one concerted press push for the film, saving him from having to do separate press for the festival, theatrical, and VOD releases.

Because of this last point, Swanberg would have preferred to have done all markets day-and-date with the festival release: VOD, iTunes, DVD, and theatrical. Unfortunately, due to contract obligations, IFC is currently only set up to do VOD day-and-date with their Festival Direct program.

DIY LIVE EVENT/THEATRCIAL DAY AND DATE WITH A FESTIVAL LAUNCH

If you do not want to be part of IFC's Festival Direct program (or weren't asked), you can set it up for yourself. You also have the advantage of not being fettered by pre-existing contractual requirements that a distributor might have.

Once you commit to this approach, you need to get as many of your revenue streams established to run concurrently with (or within a creative windowing strategy following) your festival premiere as possible.

Not only does your film need to be finished, but you need deals and materials prepped for any or all of the following releases: live event/ theatrical, DVD, VOD, digital, etc.

COUNTERPOINT/CAVEAT

The above approaches require filmmakers to have a distribution and marketing plan in place before their festival premiere. The preparation necessary might be overwhelming for first-time filmmakers, or ones just struggling to get their film to the festival.

Other times, just being in a premiere festival might not be enough ammunition to book the film into theaters, especially if it is a first time filmmaker. Filmmakers with a track record should have an easier time booking theaters without advance press (although it depends on the track record).

In these cases Swartz indicates that filmmakers might be able to participate in a premiere festival to determine if a sale can be made and to gather reviews for use later in a release. If a sale isn't made, you can then regroup and at least know where the reviews for the film will be positive. You can then use the buzz of the festival to help book your film. McInnis notes that in this scenario, you can still use the festival to build buzz and connections with online press that you can utilize later.

You might get into a second prominent festival and can then launch from that, as was the case with *Weather Girl* (premiered at Slamdance, launched theatrical at Los Angeles Film Festival five months later.)

In my opinion, this can be a more difficult route. Any time you need to do additional media pushes, it's more difficult. If you are the beneficiary of a lot of hype, the sooner you can roll out your theatrical, the better.

One alternative is to focus on just a few cities for conventional theatrical following your festival premiere (perhaps just NY and LA) and then flush out the rest of the release with grassroots/community screenings that can be mobilized much more quickly than conventional theatrical. This grassroots approach is especially wise if you have worked with some organizations throughout your production and post. They can help you organize these screenings.

It is still the wild west in utilizing these new distribution strategies. It is important for your team to determine what makes sense for your film.

I would recommend doing a full evaluation of your film and its distribution prospects and creating your strategy for your film's release well in advance of your festival premiere, so that you can best take advantage of what festivals have to offer you. Having a PMD on board who is preparing for different scenarios will go a long way to helping you tackle this new world.

OTHER WAYS TO MONETIZE FILM FESTIVALS

1. Festival Screening Fees

Just because your film is in a festival doesn't mean that you have to give it to them for free. No top festival will pay for a film (although I can imagine this changing over time). However, many smaller festivals are accustomed to paying for films, anywhere from $200 to $1,000 (the latter is mostly foreign festivals). In fact, foreign festival fees can be rather lucrative, especially for a popular film. Smaller U.S. festivals will often pay $200 to $300 if they want your film. We've made about $1,500 from domestic film festivals on *Bomb It*.

2. Convert Festival Screenings to Theatrical Screenings

As indicated above, a number of farsighted festivals are using their relationship with their audience to exhibit films year-round. Several, such as the incredible True/False Festival in Missouri and the Denver International Film Festival, actually have theaters that they program. If you are planning and/or booking a theatrical release for your film, you might consider trying to convert a festival screening to a theatrical booking (especially if the festival does not run during the time of your live event/theatrical release). That way, you can also get a share of the box office. You also add another city as part of your release, making your release appear more substantial.

3. Incorporate Festival Screenings Into Your Live Event/Theatrical Release

In the spirit of the new live event/theatrical model, if a festival can't be converted into a theatrical booking, incorporate that festival into the fabric of your overall release. If you are looking for promotion instead of box office, this approach makes more sense since you are likely to get more exposure being in a festival than being out on your own, especially for a smaller film. Not only does having another screening/city as part of your national release give it more gravitas but it also broadens the national appeal of your film.

JON'S CONVENTIONAL TIPS FOR FILM FESTIVALS

Since we are talking about film festivals, I might as well provide my advice on having a successful festival run:

1. Make sure your film is finished before submitting. You normally have one shot. Put your best foot forward. As I mentioned before, use preview screenings, listen to comments, and then filter.

2. Apply strategically to fests that make sense for your film both in terms of genre and quality.

3. Research the festivals you're applying to, especially if they charge submission fees. Talk to other filmmakers. Read online reviews of the fests. See how many years they have been around and what they have programmed before.

4. If you feel a festival is critically important to you, don't be afraid to call ahead and talk to the coordinator. You don't need to talk to the programmer. Just don't be a pain.

5. Apply simultaneously to top, mid-level, and smaller festivals. Don't just hold out for top fests and let your film get stale.

6. From Thomas Harris, a film festival programmer and consultant: Submit your film one-third of the way into a festival's submissions window/cycle (between the opening and closing dates). This gives the programmers time to digest the films they have on their shelf but still gets you in before the crush of submissions during the final submission deadline, which you should avoid at all costs.

7. Follow instructions. If the festival wants information in a certain way, give it to them. Fill out all forms as requested.

8. Keep your cover letter short, direct, and infused with your personality.

9. Always send backup media, either two DVDs or a DVD and a VHS or DV tape. Most fests will reject anything that won't play without a backup. They simply don't have time.

10. Go to prominent festivals to meet people, even if you don't have a film in the festival. Use these relationships for when you have your next film done.

11. Consider saving yourself time by automating the film festival submission process through withoutabox.com

FESTIVALS AS DISTRIBUTORS

A few savvy fests, such as Cinequest, are using their brands as a way to create a distribution label. Sundance also has an iTunes deal for its shorts. It won't be long before festivals start their own online streaming channels. However, a few people I mentioned this to argued that festivals won't want to compete with the distributors they need to get their premiere films from.

Perhaps echoing this view, a former prominent festival director confided in me that a number of theatrical chains had approached him, stating that they wanted to program independent films and that they had lots of available slots, but didn't know outside of the usual suspects how to connect with independent filmmakers. They also didn't want to be inundated with requests from thousands of filmmakers. They wanted a gatekeeper who already reviewed content and would provide a conduit for them. The theater chains felt that this major festival was a perfect candidate. I was aghast when this former festival director said, "But I don't think we should be in the distribution business, do you?" I replied that festivals should do anything they can to help their filmmakers and their festivals. Acting as a gatekeeper for unreleased films (much like digital aggregators) seemed like a win-win situation for both. Unfortunately, he was unconvinced.

I feel that because the distribution landscape is changing so rapidly and many people are looking for solutions to help independent films, companies will stop looking at these issues of distribution in a black-and-white, win-or-lose way and instead will start looking at what works and what doesn't work.

Many festivals are respected, known, qualified gatekeepers of certain kinds of content. Their programming staffs are very similar to a distributor's acquisition staff. I think it makes total sense for festivals to be in the distribution business. There are plenty of films that festivals champion that won't receive conventional distribution. Festivals have proven branded curatorial power that can be monetized both for festivals and filmmakers. One problem that might arise is a potential conflict between some festival's non-profit status and the for-profit business of distribution. However, considering how difficult the independent film distribution business is, perhaps all distributors who handle independent film should be allowed to take on non-profit status. I'm only half kidding.

There are several paths for independent filmmakers to release their films to conventional theaters without conventional distribution or an overall deal.

CONVENTIONAL THEATRICAL

Conventional theatrical (formerly known as theatrical) can still be an important part of your live events/theatrical release.

There are several paths for independent filmmakers to release their films to conventional theaters without conventional distribution or an overall deal:

1. Hire a Distributor

In the old days, this would be considered a service deal. A full-service theatrical distributor for hire will handle everything for you, including:

- Book your film in theaters.

- Develop your marketing campaign (e.g., creating your key art, trailers, log line, etc.).

- Hire or use in-house publicists.

- Book all advertising and any promotional events for your film.

- Coordinate the creation of your prints.

- Deliver your prints and promotional elements.

- Collect your receipts from the theaters.

- Pay you.

- Some will even help you get your ancillary deals, such as DVD and digital.

However, a release such as this can cost you anywhere from $100,000 to $500,000, or into the millions.

You still must be involved in your campaign, but the distributor handles the bulk of the specialized work. There are many advantages to this:

1. You are in control. The distributor works for you and, within reason, they will release the film the way you want.

2. You are not reinventing the wheel. These companies have been releasing films for some time and do their job very well.

3. You keep all receipts, less the service fee. If you think you have a blockbuster, this allows you to keep all the revenue from your film minus the expense. Not bad if you've made the next *Harry Potter.*

4. You get your theatrical release without the stress of doing everything yourself.

2. Do It Yourself

This is what I did. It involves doing everything that distributors do — but you are doing it on your own — and reinventing the wheel with no economies of scale.

- You book the film.

- You create the marketing plan and key art and any other promotional materials.

- You hire a publicist or do your own publicity.

- You create and book all advertising and any promotional events for your film.

- You deliver the prints and promotional materials.

- You collect the money owed from the theaters.

- You get your own ancillary deals.

3. Hybrid Approach

This is where you act as the distributor but hire various elements to help you distribute the film. Normally this would involve hiring a booker, a publicist, graphic designers, marketing consultants, assistants, and still collecting revenues yourself. In this approach, you are much more involved in supervising, coordinating, and even doing the above activities.

This is more cost-effective than hiring a distributor and saves you from completely reinventing the wheel. However, it will still cost you much more than a total DIY approach.

IMPORTANT NOTES REGARDING A THEATRICAL RELEASE, NO MATTER HOW YOU DO IT

The following are lessons learned from my experiences with releasing *Bomb It* and from talking to other filmmakers who have done pure DIY releases or hired distributors.

1. Overestimate the Time That It Will Take

Here are some of the reasons why it takes so long:

- Many conventional theaters book approximately three months in advance.

- Calendar houses, those theaters that publish a calendar such as the Nuart in LA, book up to six months in advance!

- If you are booking it yourself, it will take even longer because you need to get the programmer's attention.

- Sponsorships take time. Corporations, who are the ones who have the money to sponsor, move slowly and have very long lead times for their sponsorship seasons.

So here is a conundrum that faces independent films wanting to take advantage of the heat from festivals: You have to book your film six months ahead of the festival release. How do you know anyone will be interested in the film when it hasn't gotten any festival buzz or press yet?

However, depending on the prestige of the festival you were accepted into, and the kinds of theaters you wish to book into, I believe getting late bookings to coincide with your festival premiere is still possible.

2. Expect to Lose Money

Conventional theatrical is a classic loss leader. One of the principle reasons that distribution company B-Side's business model for theatrical is to give the screenings for their films away for free is because Chris Hyams (the head of B-Side) did the research and found that *all* films (studio and independent), on average, lose money from theatrical.

We lost money on our theatrical, too. Even in Los Angeles, where we grossed $10,000 for the week, we still lost money after we factored in all the promotion we did. However, our DVD distributor is convinced that the promotion helped their DVD sales tremendously.

3. Know What You Want

Gear your release to your goals of the release. If all you are after are large market reviews and don't have a ton of time, it may make sense to go after only New York and L.A. If you want to screen your films to as many audiences as possible, you will want to book more cities and plan for it accordingly. Once you are booking a few theaters, it is not that difficult to start adding others. But each additional city does add time to execute the release properly.

4. Consider the Two-Month Window

I like to think of this as my own invention, or reinvention. (It is has been used by studios to dump films for which they have a contractual obligation for a theatrical release but know the film will do poorly at the box office).

A two-month window is where you release the movie into theaters on a specific date and two months after this release, you officially release your DVD.

A two-month window splits the difference between day and date and a conventional theatrical window of four to six months.

It is most useful when you are working with a conventional DVD distributor. You may still be able to day-and-date your VOD with the theatrical and then have a two-month window for DVD in this scenario.

There are three major reasons for the success of the two-month window:

1. Conventional theater owners still will not book your film if your DVD has been released commercially (or is even within two weeks of its DVD release – so you really have six weeks to be in theaters).

2. Very important: The two-month window allows your theatrical publicity to roll over to the DVD and any other ancillaries you release two months later. You also engage your publicist to get

reviews for all your releases (theatrical, DVD, VOD) that are oc-curring within this window. This is crucial.

The theatrical release is the live event that drives your publicity. It is difficult to create this event just on a DVD release.

Based on my experiences with *Better Living Through Circuitry* and *Cleopatra's Second Husband*, I learned that a long window between your theatrical and your DVD release was the kiss of death for DVD publicity. While today there are more press avenues for DVD-only releases, nothing beats a theatrical release for press. It is not just mainstream press and mainstream marketing (e.g., print ads); it is all the work you do to promote your film, such as parties, web mar-keting, street teams, and email blasts. If you think you have the energy to do this twice, think again.

By having the strength of a theatrical and DVD release within two months of each other, the media will take you more seriously and you will get more reviews and larger reviews than you otherwise would have. It is a *very* crowded entertainment landscape and you need all the help you can get to make your film stand out.

3. When you DIY your theatrical, it is almost physically impos-sible to release your film in all cities simultaneously. So you need to roll out your film week after week in different markets. Two months was just enough time to roll out *Bomb It* and give me enough time to focus on individual markets.

5. Start Publicity Early

Long lead press, which is possible for independent films that have a strong hook or star, needs at least six months' lead time to book, sometimes eight.

You can, however, save yourself some money if, after consulting with your publicist, you don't feel that you will get long lead press. In this case, you can work out a part-time deal to hire your publicist for a number of months and only bring him or her on full-time for two or three months.

Further benefits from the two-month window: The publicist for Do-curama, our DVD distributor, saw how our short window was going to benefit the press for the DVD, so he came on board to help with the theatrical publicity. I had engaged my publicist for both the the-atrical and DVD — hence I got the best of both worlds.

6. Create Your Pitch for Distribution

You pitch your film when you're looking for actors, crew, and investors, so get ready to do the same for distribution. Instead of convincing and inspiring DPs and actors, you need to inspire bookers, programmers, and publicists.

You need to be able to convey two essential elements:

1. Who your target audience is.

2. How you will sell your film to that audience.

Like your strategy, your pitch will evolve over time, but knowing these two simple things will show people that you have thought about your film not just from a marketing perspective, but also from the perspective of people who need to take a risk on your film.

Follow the guidelines of any good pitch:

- Keep it short.

- Have backup — prepare to answer questions about details related to the above points, as well as your budget for the release.

With the cost of developing, making, and distributing movies going up and the fierce competition for jobs in the industry, Daniel Rappaport, a founding partner of Management 360, gives this boiled-down advice to young filmmakers who are trying to get hired in Hollywood: "Your job is to allay fears and inspire greed."

I feel that you can apply these two maxims to booking theaters (and any type of pitch you need to make for distribution):

1. Inspire greed. You do this by telling the theater, DVD company, how big your audience is and how you are going to connect with them.

2. Alleviate fear. Be confident and assure the theater that you have a staff and a system for deliveries and execution. One of programmers' biggest fears with DIY independents is that they won't follow through properly and deliver materials. Don't screw this up for everyone else — have your shit together.

7. Automate the Process

Your promotional materials (such as photos, press kit, trailer) should be online and downloadable for anyone who needs them, not just viewable on your website.

Have your webmaster put them on an FTP (file transfer protocol) site for you and make them accessible from a URL so that people don't need a program like Fetch to obtain them. Dropio.com can also do this for you.

HIRING A DISTRIBUTOR

If you have the resources for hiring a distributor to handle your theatrical release, here are some tips:

1. Get someone with experience and a track record. Much of what you are paying for is the person's relationships with exhibitors. Get references. Talk to other filmmakers who have used them. Ask other filmmakers if they've been paid.

2. Get someone who "gets" your film. Even though you are hiring them, they need to believe in your film and be able to sell it.

3. See what kind of marketing ideas they have for your film, and see if these ideas make sense to you.

4. See what they can bring to the table. What kind of key art/ graphic designers do they work with? Do you like their work? Talk to their in-house publicist, if they have one. Find out if the publicist is a fan of your film.

5. Can you work with them? Do you click and are they likable to you? You will be dealing with them for a long time, so it should be enjoyable.

6. Will they work a deal with you — are they negotiable?

7. Are they open to working with you and receiving input from you? They should be willing to collaborate with you.

I feel that the best way to illustrate working with a distributor is to look at two examples, each at a different budget range.

1. Good Dick

Director Mariana Palka and producers Jen Dubin and Cora Olson made *Good Dick* for $200,000. It was a hit at Sundance in 2008 and they received offers for the distribution of their film, but nothing made financial sense. The offers were in the now standard range of $20,000 to $50,000 for all rights for 20 years, with no guarantee of a theatrical release. So they decided to do it themselves.

They decided that they needed $200,000 to release the film on all platforms, although the largest chunk went to theatrical. Fortunately, their investor believed in them and gave them the whole distribution budget. They released in seven markets for one week each, grossing on average $5,000 per market — which is respectable for an independent theatrical release. While the $35,000 gross puts them in a bit of a hole to recoup the $200,000 in expenses, they feel that they would not have gotten their subsequent DVD, VOD, and cable deals without this theatrical release.

Here are their lessons and advice:

1. To be an artist, you need to be a cultural warrior. It's going to be a battle a lot, if not all, of the time. You need to mentally prepare yourself for this battle and accept that it is part of the process.

2. Don't keep your film under wraps when you are looking for distribution. Get it out to distributors, under guidance, and see the lay of the land. This will help you prepare for what to do for your festival premiere.

3. You don't need a sales agent, but you do want advisors. *Good Dick* hired Richard Abramowitz to consult, who ended up releasing the film through his company Abramorama. 42West handled publicity and Peter Broderick supervised all of their strategy and rights.

4. Have your DVD and VOD ready to go close to your theatrical (note the two-month window discussion above). Landmark Theaters (where most of *Good Dick*'s dates were booked) was still averse to DVD day and date. The *Good Dick* team wishes in retrospect that their DVD and VOD came out much closer to their theatrical, but they were still learning. In their words: "Our film was a baby at Sundance — it's a toddler now."

5. Sell your DVDs from your website, even if you don't have permission. Some theaters would get mad and the *Good Dick*

team would apologize. They learned from Broderick that it is better to ask for forgiveness than permission. They sold the DVD on their website in advance of a home video deal and it did not hinder their HV or VOD deal.

6. They really feel the child metaphor is apt for distribution. Like a child's parent, nobody will care about your film more than you. Like raising a child, you really have to nurture a film through the various stages of its life including distribution.

7. Think about who the audience is for the film. (As you can see, this is a very common theme.)

8. Teach yourself web programming and do your website your-self. The *Good Dick* crew learned *RapidWeaver* and have their office assistant do the web upkeep.

9. Remember that strategies for release depend on the specific year and film.

2. Bottle Shock

The second example we will look at is the film *Bottle Shock*, which is at the high end of release budgets for independents. I had a chance to interview one of the producers of the film, J. Todd Harris, who has produced quite a number of independent films.

Bottle Shock (about the early days of Napa Valley wine, starring Alan Rickman) was made for $5.5 million (still an independent, no studio involvement) and all the money was raised as equity. It pre-miered at Sundance in 2008 (same as *Good Dick*), a year in which only three films sold for significant sums: *Hamlet 2* for about $10 million; *Choke* for about $5 million, and *Henry Poole Was Here* for about $3 million. *Bottle Shock* received an offer from Magnolia for $500,000 in prints and advertising (P&A) and a tinier advance for all U.S. rights. The filmmakers rejected this offer.

Simultaneously they met someone who had $12 million worth of ad buys to unload in the summer of 2008. This person was offering that $12 million of advertising at a cost of $8 million, but would re-coup on a 2-to-1 split to the investors up until recoupment of the ad costs. What this means is, from each $3 the filmmakers earned from the release (all revenues), $2 would go to the provider of the ad buys and $1 to the investors. In the world of P&A financing, this is not a bad deal. Because of the availability of this media buy, their concern about a competitive film that was on the brink of release, and the fall crush of art-house films, they decided to release in summer '08.

However, media buys are not the only expense in a release. All in, Harris figures that they spent $8 million in cash — around $5 million for the media buys after adjustments and $3 million for everything else (booking services, prints, publicity, etc.).

Harris' two biggest regrets are that they spent too much on their release and that they rushed their release. According to him, the rule of thumb for releases (on the studio side) is that to make money on your release, you should gross theatrically what you spend on P&A. So if you are spending $8 million on the release, you should gross $8 million at the box office, to be safe.

Now, of course you don't get to keep all of that theatrical gross.

- First, the theaters take anywhere from 50 to 65 percent (usually the latter).

- Then the distributor takes off their expenses.

- Then the distributor takes off 25 to 40 percent of the gross as a distribution fee.

You begin to see the math. Unless the film is a hit, it is very difficult to make money theatrically. The idea of this previously mentioned "rule" is that whatever the loss is on the theatrical, it is made up on the ancillaries. With *Bottle Shock* they grossed $4 million theatrically (not bad at all — most indies would jump for joy). Of that, they received $1.6 million. So on an $8 million release, they lost $6.4 million. Quite a large sum to make up for with ancillaries.

Here is the money as J. Todd Harris laid it out to me:

MARKET	HOPED FOR REVENUE	ACTUAL REVENUE
Theatrical box office	$10 million	$1.6 million
DVD	$10 million	$2 million
Foreign	$3 million	$3 million
All other ancillaries	$2 million	$2 million
Total	**$25 million**	**$8.6 Million**

Since the P&A money ($8 million) needs to come off the top, there is then $1.6 million leftover of the $8.6 earned to cover the original $5.5 million investment. Thus they are at about a $5 million shortfall.

Regarding DVD, the producers were hoping that Fox Home Video would up their advance if they spent more on P&A, as this had been normal behavior in the past. Unfortunately, due to the changing DVD sales landscape, Fox did not.

The producers did make $1 million on airline fees, which is high for this specialized ancillary.

Let's look at a couple of the numbers a little more closely.

P&A Finance: Like most filmmakers, the producers of *Bottle Shock* had not raised P&A in advance of making the film. So when they were left without a distributor, they had to raise the P&A money to release the film. As usually happens with film finance, the last money in wants to be the first out. Even though the person with the media buy was willing to cut the investors in for one-third of the money before full recoupment of the media buy, the others who contributed to the P&A wanted to be out before the investors (even though some of the P&A investors were, in fact, the original investors).

Distributor for Hire: The *Bottle Shock* producers hired Freestyle Releasing, who have been doing these types of releases for many years. The producers spent between $200,000 and $300,000 for Freestyle's services, which included booking the film, handling prints and deliveries, publicity, and marketing. They also spent a fair amount of money on a premiere party in Napa, and flew in the cast for that (although the flights were sponsored by American Airlines).

Based on this experience, Harris says he has learned the following lessons:

1. Keep your release costs low. He uses the example of *Elegy*, which was able to gross $3 million at the box office but only spent $2.5 million on the release.

2. Don't rush your release. With more time, Harris figures they could have gotten more sponsorships and have been more targeted about their media buys — all of which would have reduced the cost of the release and made it more successful.

3. Give yourself time and pay attention to your niche. While the

niche for *Bottleshock* might be hard to target and motivate to the theater, he feels that a core niche of wine lovers never got targeted properly.

4. Raise money for your P&A while you are financing your film.

Harris is applying these lessons to his next film, *Crooked Arrows*, slated for a 2010 release. It is an "inspiring sports film" centered around the world of lacrosse. This is what he has done differently:

1. He has identified a rapidly growing, relatively large niche audience: Lacrosse players (and the film has a Native American lead — another niche). He has calculated that there are approximately 500,000 living lacrosse players, and if you include their family and friends, he estimates that there are about 8 million people who care about lacrosse. He figures that if he gets only a percentage of people to buy the film in some way, he is doing well.

2. He has already obtained endorsements from national lacrosse associations, as well as major players and coaches.

3. He is financing the film by holding house parties ("Tupperware parties" is his term), where he pitches the financing LLC for the film directly to the wealthier elements of the niche audience.

4. He has already begun sponsorship relationships with Gatorade and Reebok.

5. He is raising P&A money in advance and is guaranteeing a 250-screen theatrical release as part of the finance package.

Chapter 15 Conclusion

Of the three potential paths for a conventional theatrical release, hiring a distributor is clearly the most expensive. However, it does allow you to go on with your life more than either a DIY approach or a hybrid approach will.

Remember to keep in mind the lead time necessary to book a conventional theatrical release, probably the longest lead time necessary of any of the available markets for your film. Don't expect to make money. Most of all, integrate this release into the release dates for all of your other rights, or at least as many as you can. Doing so will allow you to take best advantage of the publicity that you can mobilize around your release.

CHAPTER 16

DIY THEATRICAL

If you decide to handle your theatrical release yourself, hopefully you will have some people helping you. Here is what you need to keep in mind when taking this route:

FIVE STEPS TO DIY CONVENTIONAL THEATRICAL BOOKING

Step 1: Research.

Most of the information you'll need to book your film is readily available online. There are lists of theaters at places like arthouseproject.org and the theatrical mapping project at workbookproject.com (Lance Weiler's wonderful DIY site). It is surprisingly easy to find the phone numbers of most independent theater programmers. Research venues where films with a similar audience to yours have played. Most theaters have websites, and the office number is usually located somewhere if you look hard enough.   I recommend going for the independent art house theaters.   The chains are generally much more difficult to work with on your own.

Step 2: Make the call.

Bookers are generally nice people who love film. Why else would they be involved with small theaters that struggle to stay in business? Therefore, if you have a compelling reason for them to look at the film, chances are they will at least listen.

Call first. An email cannot express your passion for the film, nor will an email exchange allow you to address their concerns about your film in a direct and instantaneous fashion. I would always follow up my phone calls with an email (not the other way around). You can find one of my standard email pitches on the website.

Step 3: Be persistent but not a pain.

Don't leave more than one or two messages. If the person isn't there, just hang up — it's as if you didn't call. If you get a live person who isn't the booker, ask when that person is likely to be there and call back then. (Always ask for "the person in charge of programming _____ theater.")

Don't listen to naysayers. When I was booking *Bomb It*, many people said that the Nuart programmer never returns phone calls and wouldn't talk to me. When things looked desperate, I finally just called him. Turns out he loved *Better Living Through Circuitry*, he remembered we did $21K the opening weekend, and he said he would have loved to have booked *Bomb It* had we just called earlier.

Step 4: Get that first booking.

I can't stress enough how much getting that first respectable booking helps. Bookers are not unlike most people; if they see that someone else already made the plunge, they're more likely to take a look themselves. After we set up the Red Vic booking in San Francisco, the first thing out of my mouth when talking to new potential bookers was, "Our Red Vic booking is scheduled for..." This led to bookings in Seattle, Portland, Chicago, and New Mexico.

Unexpected Festival Benefits Having premiered at Tribeca was enough to have people at least listen to me. But surprisingly, it was the SF Indie Fest that was most crucial for our theatrical release. Our press from this festival in February 2008 helped convince the Red Vic to book us in April 2008.

Step 5: Have programmers help you.

Programmers know each other and often form loose partnerships. If one of them is excited about your film, have that person recommend you to other programmers. Many programmers are responsible for booking several theaters.

A HYBRID APPROACH: WORKING WITH A BOOKER

While it's certainly possible, booking theaters on your own takes a lot of work. If you have a little bit of money, you might consider hiring a booker. This is an approach in between hiring a full-service distributor and total DIY.

Most bookers charge per month and some have a minimum number of months. Some also charge per screening booked, although I have heard this deal is on its way out. However, savvy filmmakers might make a low monthly fee deal with bonuses per screening booked — an incentivized system that might make it affordable for you.

I considered hiring a booker initially, but the costs at the time were too high, about $5,000 a month with a three-month minimum. It appears to be less expensive as of the writing of this book.

One filmmaker recounted to me that he and his staff tried on their own for months to approach the programmers of a prominent theater chain that caters to independents. They didn't get a response. One day after they hired their booker (a top booker, at $6,000 a month), they were booked into several theaters in that chain and eventually were booked into more.

No booker can guarantee that you will get bookings. Bookers are also choosy about working with you, just like any top talent you want to hire.

WORKING WITH THEATERS

1. Theater Terms

There are three basic deals that you can make with theaters:

Percentage. This is preferable, of course. Generally you get 35 percent of the door. Sometimes it might be 30 percent or 40 percent. In rare occurrences you might get 50 percent.

Four wall. This simply means renting the "four walls" of a theater (e.g., you rent the theater for a night or a week or more). Most independent theaters will do this and the terms can be negotiated (more discussion on this below). If you four wall, you won't have a paid ad or publicist commitment as outlined below.

Minimum guarantee (MG) against a percentage. You agree to pay the theater a minimum if the percentage gross does not equal a certain amount (often their four-wall rate). You may have to pay this money up front. Whatever you earn comes back to you until your MG is recouped. After that the percentage split resumes.

2. Additional Terms:

Paid ads: In New York and LA, you will probably be required to spend a certain amount of money (at least a couple thousand dollars in each city) on print ads. Often the theaters already have ad buys that they want you to participate in. The theaters will also have people who will place your ad and/or whom you can pay to create an ad from your key art. However, of course, it is usually more cost-effective for you to do this on your own.

Publicist requirement: In New York especially, theaters may contractually require you to hire a publicist from a list of people they feel comfortable with.

Materials: All theaters will request other promotional material such as posters, trailers, and postcards. In New York and L.A. they will require it. They should be able to handle the 25x37-inch size that is the cheapest for you to produce (slightly smaller than the normal size of a movie poster).

3. Payment

All of my theaters paid me, usually within 30 days. I found all the independent theater owners lovely to work with and incredibly honest and supportive. I had to hound only one a bit (I waited until after 30 days to do so), and ironically it was the theater that gave me the best deal.

On *Cleopatra's Second Husband*, the distributor who released the film had trouble getting paid by the larger chains (or at least that is what they told me).

A note on payment: You might offer up your film for free to theaters as a way to motivate them to book your film. That way, you can tell them, the risk is more equal and is balanced more in their favor. This is the B-Side approach. After all, your motive for doing conventional theatrical is generally not to make money.

4. Length of Run

Your runs will usually be standard weeklong runs from Friday to Thursday. However, in some cities, where either there is only one movie theater or the market is extremely crowded, you might be offered shorter runs. This might be for one or two nights. Or a theater might restrict how many weekend screenings you can have — for example, only the 8 p.m. and 10 p.m. slots on Friday and Saturday nights. It can be easier to get short-term bookings from theaters, so that is something you might offer them or be agreeable to. As you will see in the next chapter, I am a believer in short runs.

5. Some Thoughts on Four-Wall Bookings

For *Bomb It*, I made a great effort not to four-wall any theaters because we didn't have the money for it. But it did seem at one point that we might have to four-wall New York, which can cost $10,000 to $18,000 per week. Fortunately, by the time I booked New York, I already had 10 respected theaters lined up in the rest of the country. This helped convince the New York programmer that I was legit. This is an instance where starting in small markets can help.

In general, four-walling is prohibitively expensive for most filmmakers going the DIY route. However, if you can't get a percentage booking in a regular theater, it might be your last resort.

Interestingly, in Los Angeles I had to play a bit of chicken with the theater programmer. He had said that he would give me a week, and most likely would guarantee it. But certain weeks that I wanted were busy; additionally, he said that he might have to push my booking if someone offered to rent the theater. The implication was that if I wanted a locked date, I would need to four-wall the theater. Fortunately, I didn't have to. I was able to convince him to give me a hard date and our film turned out to be the top performer that week in all of their theaters in Los Angeles.

6. Another Way to Think of Four Wall

If you feel confident that you can sell out your screenings, it can be much more profitable to four-wall. Filmmaker Gary Hustwit was very successful booking one-night-event screenings for his film *Helvetica*, four-walling the theater, selling it out for tickets up to $20 a piece, and doing very well. He was able to do this because he had a built-in niche audience of graphic designers around the country and worked with local chapters of national graphic artist associations to make his screenings special events for their members. He is now repeating this process with his new film *Objectified*.

7. Execute

After you book your film, you have to be able to execute and deliver the screening(s). This point was brought up repeatedly in my conversations with filmmakers and bookers when interviewing them.

Delivery includes much of what we have already discussed so far, but I will reiterate it here because it is so important:

- Promotional material in advance: posters, postcards, press kit, stills, 35mm trailers.

- Print ad slicks/artwork.

- Getting the print of the film to the theater on time, in the format the theater can play.

- Press advance work.

- Marketing campaign for that city.

- Your availability for local press.

Programmers talk to each other, and if you burn one, it will be harder to get other bookings. If too many filmmakers burn programmers, you'll be screwing it up for the rest of the DIY community. Be respectful and make sure you can execute their requirements before you start.

8. Theaters Will Help You

Like festivals, theaters know their local markets and have established relationships in their community.

In many of the smaller markets for *Bomb It*, the theaters handled getting the film out to the local reviewers. They also had connections to local radio for promotions and interviews.

LOS ANGELES/NEW YORK OR MULTI-CITY

Some people argue that that the only cities that matter are New York and Los Angeles. I would say that it depends on the film and what you want from your release.

Large Market Launch

One way of booking films that has become standard recently is to start in New York and let the New York press and grosses help book your film in the rest of the country.

I understand the New York/Los Angeles logic if all you want from your release are reviews out of those two markets, which are important reviews.

Another argument is that starting in New York, provided you do well, will translate into multiple bookings throughout the U.S. Small-market theaters still look toward New York box office returns and reviews to see what they might want to book.

This can be a double-edged sword, because if you don't do well in New York (and it is difficult to do well there), it might hurt your chances of booking in other cities around the country.

If you are working with a tighter timeframe (such as the two-month window I described in Chapter 14), you don't have enough time to wait for New York success to influence other theaters.

Considering the crowded marketplace and your limited resources, it might be better to book your smaller markets in advance if you want to screen in multiple markets.

Small-Market Launch

Small-market launches were used by the independent film distribution pioneers. Starting in smaller markets would help build word of mouth, thereby helping the release nationally. However, this approach is very labor intensive, one of the reasons that independent film shifted to opening films in New York and L.A.

I believe filmmakers also became fearful that their small-market releases might not perform well enough for a distributor, and then they might never get their New York and/or L.A. premiere, which they needed/wanted for the New York/L.A. reviews.

Advantages of Starting in Small Markets

1. You are also creating multiple events across the country to promote around, thereby raising awareness for your film.

2. Your film might have strong audiences in a specific region of the country, so it will be easier to perform well and build word of mouth out of those areas.

3. It is less expensive to promote and easier to get coverage in smaller markets, especially if you can create an event around your screenings.

4. You are able to learn from your mistakes and grow your abilities as a distributor/promoter by the time you get to larger/tougher markets.

With *Bomb It*, I was hampered by not having enough prep time for my theatrical because I had to fire my distributor and pick up the pieces. My posters and trailers arrived late in my early cities, and these theaters were generally forgiving of my errors. I also did not have enough lead time for street promotion in the smaller markets.

Even though nearly all of the theaters were satisfied with our performance, the first month and a half of our release was my learning curve, and I don't think I really nailed it until our June 2 release in Los Angeles. This was partly the learning curve and partly that Los Angeles was the only city for which we really had a full two months to promote — I recommend that much lead time for all of your important markets.

I also think our L.A. turnout was successful because it was our home market, and we had not done any screenings up until this time.

Home markets, especially in smaller markets, make sense for opening dates. Most likely you have your greatest resources and fans in your home market. It is easier to promote in your home market just because of the fact that you live there.

Disadvantages of a Small-Market Launch

Starting with small markets implies doing a number of cities. This is a lot more work — you have to interact with more theaters and deliver to them. Some cities won't be much more work; the theater just wants the film and they will promote it. But other mi-size cities, can be more involved to book and promote.

You can also get stuck with a bad review from a small-market weekly that will live with you and be reprinted in every city where that weekly has an outlet. For instance, instead of the *Village Voice* assigning one of their own reporters to do an article in-house (like the one who loved *Bomb It* and was dying to write a review on it for the *Voice*), they used the bad review that ran in the *Seattle Weekly*. This also ran in the *L.A. Weekly.* Win some, lose some.

Chapter 16 Conclusion

In retrospect, one side of me feels that I should have just done New York and Los Angeles for *Bomb It* because of the amount of work involved in the smaller cities.

However, it was easier to get the smaller city bookings first, and these helped me obtain my New York and L.A. bookings. In fact, I don't think I would have had my New York booking without my other bookings around the country. So I had no choice, and you may not, either.

In addition, as time passes and the pain of the experience fades, I am glad that we have played in as many cities as we have. It made for a much more robust release, helped all of our ancillaries, and enabled many more people to see the film.

incorporating aspects of an event into your screenings is the future of independent live event/theatrical releases.

CREATING A LIVE EVENT EXPERIENCE

Because of the traditional weeklong-run structure of conventional theatrical, it has been harder for filmmakers to create a sense of an event around their films than it is for musicians to generate buzz when they're on tour.

I have found that the closer your film screening approximates an event, the more successful it will be. Even if you have a traditional weeklong run, it is best to treat at least the opening night of each city as an event.

An event will help you break through the crowded media landscape and give the press a reason to cover you.

An event creates a must see feel around the screening/release.

An event helps build buzz — instead of your screening being just another film playing at another theater.

It might be harder to get conventional film reviews in some markets with a short run; however, I feel that this is changing. Film review staffs are being cut everywhere, so even if you lose a traditional review, you might get more non-traditional press for your event than what a conventional screening would garner you.

★ **I believe that incorporating aspects of an event into your screenings is the future of independent live event/theatrical releases.**

EMBRACE THE SHORT RUN — IT CAN BE YOUR BEST FRIEND

At first I was upset that some of my theaters in smaller markets were offering me less than a week run, especially New Orleans. I pleaded and cajoled to no avail. However, in retrospect, it was one of the best things for the film. Weeklong runs are difficult to maintain. In my opinion they are becoming outdated for independent film. In most cases with my film, we made much more money when the film played one or two nights instead of a whole week, especially in New Orleans.

Having the film on one or two nights makes the screening much more of a must-see event. With a weeklong run there is a lot of "I don't need to see it now, I can see it on Monday." Then Monday comes, and "I can see it Thursday," and then Thursday comes and it's "I'll add it to my Netflix queue." Theater owners in small markets give you short runs by necessity; there are not that many screens for indie films, so they have to rotate films at a much higher rate.

However, the savvy filmmaker might ask for the one-night screening. This will also make it easier to book your film in a crowded marketplace. Many theaters will be happy to give you their Thursday night (or Monday, Tuesday, Wednesday).

> Whether or not you are screening for one day or a week, you should endeavor to create the sense of an event.

WAYS TO CREATE A SENSE OF AN EVENT:

1. Personal Appearance by the Filmmaker/Cast

This is the usual way that filmmakers create events around their screenings. This does help box office on the nights the filmmaker or, better yet, the stars are there. However, if they are available at every screening, is it an event? It depends a bit on how well known the filmmaker is and how many screenings they are attending.

One of the most successful special guest appearances that has built tremendous word of mouth has been when the band Anvil starts playing live during the end credits of *Anvil! The Story of Anvil*. They go on to give the film audience members a mini concert. Defying your audience's expectations is a great way to build word of mouth. Note that *Anvil! The Story of Anvil* plays regular weeklong runs but still maintains this sense of an event.

Ben Niles, whose film *Note by Note* is about the making of a Steinway grand piano, recounts how local Steinway dealers would bring a piano to screenings, usually booking a pianist to play. This was not to accompany the film, nor to replace the soundtrack, but to broaden the event aspect of the screening. While this happened on an ad hoc basis during the film's initial theatrical release, Ben will be taking his film on a second tour, with a piano concert at each theater.

2. Personal Appearance by a Celebrity

You can have celebrities who are not in the film come to a screening event. In their world-wide two night screening spectacular, *The Age of Stupid* had Kofi Annan, Moby, Radiohead's Thom Yorke, Heather Graham attend, speak and perform either in person or via satellite at the premiere which was then sat cast to 700 cinemas in 50 countries.

3. Parties

Opening-night parties are another way to create an event for one night of a weeklong run. The more creative your party, the more of an event feel it will have and the more it will aid your promotion.

Try to find venues or vendors/alcohol sponsors willing to comp your event. If you have to pay for the vendor, alcohol, and DJs, it can be more expensive than it's worth. I have found that there are plenty of venues and vendors that are willing to lend a hand. Because of the amount of work required to put these together, I would limit the number of parties you have, unless you have local partners putting them on and handling all of the logistics. It's better to become a part of an already existing and promoted party.

4. Partner with an Organization

Make your opening night a fundraising event for an interest group. That group will have extra motivation to promote your screening and get an audience out. You will also be able to build publicity around the organization for which the fundraising is taking place.

5. Sell Advance Tickets

Just by virtue of having tickets available for sale in advance gives your screening the sense of being an event. Even more so if some of your screenings sell out. This gives you some news to further promote. Some venues are set up for this. There are also online ticket vendors such as brownpapertickets.com that you can use for your non-conventional or four-walled screenings.

6. Live Audience Participation Part 1

There are two types of live audience participation. The old school form of audience participation is where the audience reacts to the narrative, but the narrative does not interact with them.

The Rocky Horror Picture Show is the classic example of this form of audience participation in which the audience talks back to or repeats the lines of the film. The modern equivalent of this is Tommy Wiseau's *The Room*, which was released in 2003 and continues to play at midnight screenings to this day, with much audience participation based on the film's "unique qualities". It has been referred to as one of the worst films ever made.[6] The audience reacts accordingly.

TRANSMEDIA ASPECTS TO SCREENINGS

In a transmedia event, the audience interacts with the film in a larger context that uses multiple media platforms, including the Internet, mobile phones, and gaming devices, to create an experience that extends the narrative beyond the projected image. Filmmakers are only beginning to explore the creative potential of this mode of content creation and dissemination.

1. Live Musical Remix

DJ Spooky has taken a couple of films on the road as events, such as his remix of *Birth of a Nation*. We were considering having a live DJ remix the *Bomb It* soundtrack on certain nights of our engagement; it ended up being too difficult to pull off with my short timeline. However, it is something I would consider for the future for a second run.

6   HTTP://WWW.INDEPENDENT.CO.UK/ARTS-ENTERTAINMENT/FILMS/FEATURES/THE-COUCH-SURFER-IT-MAY-BE-SUB-LIMELY-RUBBISH-BUT-THE-ROOM-MAKES-AUDIENCES-HAPPY-1752708.HTML

2. Live Film Mixing

Dena points out that Peter Greenaway has been live veejaying his current film, *the Tulse Luper Suitcases*, meaning he mixes the film live. Each audience thereby sees the film in a different way.

3. Add Live Storytelling Elements
to Your Screening

Swanberg is considering designing his next film to only play in theaters where the actors will travel with the film and perform parts of the story as the film plays.

With *Head Trauma*, Weiler took this one step further, interacting with his audience via text messages in addition to having a live performance component.

Creating a transmedia experience is one way to encourage audiences to see the film in a live event/theatrical context, because it is the only way that they will have a complete experience of the narrative.

ONE-NIGHT EVENTS

This is an emerging model used by *The Age of Stupid* and *I.O.U.S.A.* These types of events do require a bit of an infrastructure to pull off and would be difficult to DIY.

However, if you have an issue-oriented documentary and an organization concerned about that issue funding your release, and one of the primary goals is to raise awareness about that issue, a one-night national release might be the right approach.

By having many screenings across the country on one day, your film has the potential of becoming a press-worthy national event. *I.O.U.S.A.* sold 45,000 tickets and screened in 430 theaters on one night, which served as a kickoff to a 12-city conventional theatrical. *I.O.U.S.A.* also illustrates how you can have a national live event component after your screening: They had a town hall meeting broadcast from Omaha, Nebraska, featuring Warren Buffet. But you could have bands play, comedians, any kind of event you can think of.

Fathom organized *I.O.U.S.A.* Besides *I.O.U.S.A.*, Fathom is best known for doing one-night screenings of the Metropolitan Opera in movie theaters all over the country.

According to Broderick, these one-night events can be as expensive to organize as a large-scale national theatrical, costing anywhere from $115,000 to $125,000. They also take at least four months of prep time to coordinate properly.

In addition, companies that organize these events can require a 120-day window for DVDs, which is an incredibly long time and seems to defeat the purpose of a national one-night event.

As with everything, you need to see how a one-night event fits with your overall strategy. But having witnessed *The Age of Stupid* premiere, it can be very exciting!

THE FILM TOUR

A number of filmmakers are looking to their counterparts in the music scene to see how the tour model works. One of the reasons that I fell in love with the power of film was my own experience touring with Target Video back in the early '80s.

Target was a punk rock collective documenting primarily West Coast punk bands. It was back in 1981 while working at Target Video, that I first recognized that distribution was as integral to filmmaking as production. Sure, you could pull off production in a DIY manner, as Target had been doing since 1977. But unless you took back the means of distribution, your impact was limited.

When I arrived at Target, they had recently enjoyed a very successful run of screenings at the FNAC department store in Paris, which had its own theater. Later, a music festival in Bologna, Italy, led us to Rome, where we projected our documentary outdoors next to the Coliseum to a crowd of thousands. More than anything, the power of these screenings convinced me to abandon my pursuit of a Ph.D. in economics at Stanford for a rat-infested loft in San Francisco.

For the next two years I booked five tours of Europe and the United States of Target Video programs. We screened in community centers, bars, and theaters. We traversed Europe, from Stockholm to Naples via Berlin (when it was still behind the wall). We did so in a beat-up VW bus, in which we built a platform to sleep on when we couldn't get a room included with the booking. Under the platform was just enough room for an NTSC Barco video projector, a full-size Sony U-matic video deck, our video camera, and a portable U-matic recorder (the latter two were used to film bands while we were on tour for future programs).

RANGE LIFE

Sklar has reinvented this touring model for modern independent filmmakers. Since his first tour with his film *Box Elder*, he has gone out on the road again with a four-film package event. Each film is screened for one night only in each city. He is continuing this effort with a third tour and developing his company, Range Life Entertainment, into a marketing and distribution venture based on this model.

When Range Life arrives in a city, usually on a Friday, they spend the first few days promoting their event and working with their marketing partners. This on-site promotion builds to event-like screenings at an art-house theater close to a college campus.

Sklar was generous to share his approach, tips, and strategy with me. Some of it repeats what I have written, but this will help get the point across and also allows Todd's model to stand on its own. Most of what he says can apply to any film booking, not just to a touring model, so listen up.

1. Book the first screening where you have the most support.

Since *Box Elder* was made in Columbia, Missouri, and they had a lot of support in Columbia, they decided that Columbia would be the first booking. The film played for a month and set a box office record. Since he did not have a film festival cachet, this box office cachet is what helped him book subsequent cities.

2. Choose your theaters strategically.

Don't just book any theater. Book a theater where your target audience goes to see movies. He prefers art houses because of the press that they garner. For him it was also important to book near a college campus, since that is where his audience is. "Have a battle plan. You are building a story — like releasing a product."

3. Booking is based on relationships — the phone is important.

Theater programmers are more phone-oriented, since they are all about the relationships. Related to this:

4. Book for the future.

Developing a relationship with a theater programmer will help you book your films in the future. These relationships will be more important than the money you make. Theater bookers are not in the business for the money. They will be around for a long time and have long memories.

5. Film festivals are resources, not problem solvers.

They have an unparalleled ability to tap into a local audience. Connect with them. What can you provide them? Film festivals are connected to the local art houses. Often the theater/festival programmers are either one in the same or they have a strong relationship with one another.

6. Don't compete with people's weekend plans.

Sklar utilizes the weekend to get to a new city and begin marketing screenings, which he schedules Mondays through Thursdays. He doesn't want to compete with other events.

7. Plan meticulously.

If you arrive in a town and don't have every hour accounted for, drive to the next town.

8. Don't worry about terms.

Ultimately, 35 percent of the door versus 50 percent doesn't matter. Volume is more important. It is better to be seen in more places than to do financially well in less places. Volume of screenings helps build audience — which is the point of a theatrical release, anyway. Put another way:

9. Audience is value.

The release helps you build long-term value in your brand.

10. The reward is not monetary — it is connection to people.

Sklar refers to a kid he met in Sante Fe, New Mexico, who fell in love with the tour's films. The kid then went all the way to San Francisco to see the films again and help out the tour. Todd also met a couple outside a theater in San Francisco whom he talked into seeing the movie and let them go in for free. They came back later with their friends and bought a DVD. The relationship with your audience is what it is all about.

In Sklar's approach, filmgoers actually become a part of the community, and it is as exciting for him and his team as it is for the audience. I still remember the punks I met in Bologna on my first European tour with Target. We were there for a few days, hung out with them, filmed them, and as a result they became part of the next Target Video program. I kept in touch with them for many years.

Chapter 17 Conclusion

This new system also gives filmmakers the opportunity to enjoy city-to-city touring that bands have enjoyed for so long. One of the reasons I made *Bomb It* was because the production enabled me to travel the world and meet interesting people. Fortunately, the distribution has provided me with the same experience.

Using a new definition of theatrical, filmmakers will not only take back one of the most important means of communicating with their audiences, but they can have a blast doing it. Live events provide a direct experience with your audience, both during and after your screenings.

If you are doing any kind of conventional theatrical release you should combine as many alternative theatrical screenings into the mix

BOOKING NON-, SEMI-, AND ALTERNATIVE THEATRICAL — AN INTRODUCTION TO GRASSROOTS/COMMUNITY SCREENINGS

Alternative theatrical screenings are a huge growth area for independent films. It is essential that filmmakers look to these types of screenings to build awareness. If you are doing any kind of conventional theatrical release you should combine as many alternative theatrical screenings into the mix. In addition, alternative theatrical screenings provide a way for more filmmakers to experience a live events/theatrical release for less money than ever before.

DEFINITIONS

Here are the standard definitions of various unconventional theatrical screenings:

"Non-theatrical" is a free screening — anything where an admission is not charged (such as college screenings, a free screening at a church, etc).

"Semi-theatrical" is everything else that is not conventional theatrical (e.g., any screening where an admission is charged but the venue is not a conventional movie theater).

"Grassroots and community screenings" are defined by the environment of the screening, not the admission fee. According to Boyle: "Community and grassroots screenings take place in settings where films are not typically screened, among them farms, summer camps, churches, grocery stores, barns, and sports fields. They bring films out of the anonymity of the conventional movie house and into a communal and socially-oriented space." Organizers of grassroots or community screenings occasionally charge admission or pass the hat at the end of the night, but often do not. In either case, the label emphasizes that the screening is either initiated directly by the viewer (a member of a church or a nonprofit advocacy group, for example), or is part of a concerted issue- or advocacy-oriented screenings campaign coordinated by the filmmakers, sometimes with the support and co-sponsorship of an organization for whom the film's message is particularly resonant.

Old-school distribution contracts that are still in use employ *non-* and *semi-theatrical* as legal terms, so it is important that you recognize and understand them to be aware of what rights you are (or are not) allocating to whom.

For this section of the book I will henceforth refer to screenings not booked in conventional theaters as "alternative theatrical." This term has come to describe all of the above markets together.

There are quite a number of alternative theatrical venues. A very non-inclusive list would include:

- College auditoriums

- Museums

- Clubs and bars

- Churches

- Galleries

- Parking lots

- Rooftops

- Public parks

- Libraries

- Community centers

- Gymnasiums

- Bookstores

- Union halls

- Living rooms

Essentially it is any public place where a projector, screen, and sound system can be set up and a film can be screened to an audience.

ALTERNATIVE THEATRICAL BOOKERS AND CONSULTANTS

Just as you can hire a booker for conventional theatrical, you can do the same for alternative theatrical. You hire these people to either consult (less money and consisting of start-up advice, with some additional advice sprinkled here and there), or they can work with you throughout the release and actually do the work of researching/ booking your alternative theatrical venues (more money, but worth it if your film warrants a large alternative theatrical strategy).

For consulting, you will probably pay a base fee that will include viewing the film plus a few hours of consultation. Any time after that is billed hourly.

To hire a full-time alternative theatrical booker, you will either pay a monthly fee and/or a percentage of the revenue. Fees are always negotiable and depend on the interest the consultant/booker has in your film, how much work it involves, and what return they expect. Sometimes you can pay a smaller monthly fee and a higher percentage or, inversely, a higher monthly and smaller percentage.

TIMING OF ALTERNATIVE THEATRICAL

Because I believe that all public screenings hold the same value, I believe they should be scheduled to start concurrently and continue throughout the life of the film (for example, we are still booking both conventional theatrical and alternative theatrical for *Bomb It*). As a result, I feel that you should start setting up your alternative theatrical at the same time as your theatrical. The more screenings (combined conventional and alternative) you set up, the more it seems like your film is something to take notice of. You will reap both economies of scale on the simultaneous release, as well as a greater critical mass of buzz and publicity.

It might even make sense for your film (if you have a strong community-based film) to have its alternative theatrical before its conventional theatrical. If you are lucky and have a film that can hit the zeitgeist at just the right moment, the success you have in an alternative theatrical could spawn a larger theatrical release. This was the case with Robert Greenwald's *Uncovered* and *Outfoxed*. However, it is very difficult to pull this off, and usually it does not happen by intention. I would caution against the time involved in essentially two separate theatrical releases.

I believe that alternative theatrical screenings, because they don't have an established infrastructure around them, are probably one of the best forms of continuing a theatrical release after a film festival premiere as discussed in chapter 13. Chances are you have been communicating with your audience and organizational base throughout the production, so it might be an easier transition into these types of screenings from your festival premiere than to conventional theatrical screenings. You might then dovetail the alternative theatrical into a conventional theatrical. This might be a good solution for those wanting to retain the attention from the festival but unable to set up a theatrical release immediately after the festival.

If you are holding back DVD sales of your film for the theatrical as required by conventional theaters, you will be able to charge more for your alternative theatrical during this time period, because it is not available any other way. Even though most people who regularly program film into venues realize that they have to pay for screening the film, many non-pros don't know that a DVD does not convey public performance rights — and you need to inform them.

For many films, however, it makes more financial sense to sell DVDs during your grassroots/community screening campaign. Depending on your film and your audience, you can sell a lot of DVDs this way. This might be an argument have your grassroots/community screenings at the tail end of your theatrical or to just not tell your conventional theaters that you are selling DVDs at your grassroots events.

PHILOSOPHIES OF CHARGING FOR ALTERNATIVE THEATRICAL

There are three schools of thought about getting your film out to the alternative theatrical world:

1. Make your film free to screen to anyone who wants to.

The reasoning behind this is that any kind of film screening builds awareness for your film. That awareness is necessary for your film to have a commercial life. Charging for a screening only creates barriers to screening and hence recognition. I discussed this briefly in the chapter on DIY theatrical.

2. Make your film accessible, but charge a modest licensing fee to those groups who request to screen the film in a public setting.

Boyle encourages filmmakers to take this route. Because an alternative theatrical release requires expenditures for, at the very least, DVD production, shipping and postage, promotion, and implementation, charging a modest fee for public exhibition rights can help underwrite the campaign itself. In some cases, these fees also become a distribution revenue stream in and of themselves. The most successful alternative theatrical campaigns not only cover their own basic expenses, but also provide for the ongoing outreach and advocacy of the film, and generate modest income for the filmmaker.

Perhaps more important, according to Boyle, is the way in which the licensing transaction encourages interaction, cooperation, and engagement between the filmmaker and the screening partner. By supporting the film both economically and organizationally, even in the most modest of ways, an organization or exhibitor contributes directly to the film's financial viability and to its value as a tool of advocacy and education.

We made more money for less cost and less work on *Bomb It*'s alternative theatrical screenings than on our theatrical screenings, and we continue to make revenue from them.

3. Hybrid approach.

Have an initial window in which you charge for the alternative theatrical screenings. After the film has been in release for some time and is available in other markets (online or as a DVD), then open the film up for free screenings to further promote it.

Finally, if you did not have time to plan your DVD or digital release close to your theatrical, a secondary, free alternative screening window can help increase sales and awareness for these other formats. We are currently having free screenings of *Bomb It* throughout the world to promote the launch on babelgum.com. We are doing these screenings in conjunction with a global graffiti live painting event group *Meeting of Styles*.

SETTING UP ALTERNATIVE THEATRICAL

1. Determine What "Success" Is for Your Film

We discussed this before in the beginning of the book, but it is especially important to readdress it in terms of your alternative theatrical release because of the money/audience calculation you need to make outlined above.

1. Determine what your end goals are. Do you need to make money or are you more concerned about social change and conveying a message? Your emphasis will determine your release strategy.

2. Will success be evaluated by money raised, number of screenings, and the amount of people you connected to, or will it be about engaging in a letter-writing campaign and getting a screener to 100 congressmen because of the momentum of the film? The better you know, the better you can strategize and have reasonable expectations, whatever those may be, about your results when it's all said and done.

2. Picking Your Moment

Timing has already been discussed, but it's even more pertinent to grassroots/community screenings because of the number of special days, weeks, and months set up for causes to organize around: Earth Day, Earth Month, African American Awareness Week, etc.

Organizations and schools need programming for these times. Accommodate them and watch your sales grow.

3. Research

I will reiterate some key points here: Who is the audience for your film? How do you reach that audience? What organizations care about these issues and/or cater to your audience?

If you engage the organizations that are interested in your film from the beginning, they will be invested in the success of your film.

Boyle Tip: Use LISTSERVs to reach out to organized groups. LISTSERVs are old-school email lists. Caitlin finds these much more useful than email lists. To accomplish this: Join LISTSERVs. Submit news about the film on the LISTSERVs. Start this in prep. Presumably you have an interest in the subject, so write emails that will be of interest to the whole group. If you just seem like you are promoting or shilling for your film, you will get kicked off the list.

---

4. Modify Your Website

You should have a prominently displayed button on your website for anyone who wants to screen a film. This button should lead to a page that not only entices people to screen your film, but also contains a form that people can fill out (online and by download).

The button should be titled "Host a Screening" — something simple and direct. You can check out the *Bomb It* site, of course, but *Made In LA, Under Our Skin, Crawford, Note by Note, Pray the Devil Back to Hell,* and *The End of the Line* provide some other good examples.

Boyle suggests having the screening request process be as turnkey and as friendly as possible.

Such a page will make you seem more real and more official for many of the programmers from established organizations, such as colleges and schools. It should answer a lot of their questions so they have less hesitation about making the decision to program your film. And as always, the more you can convey an appearance of "having it together," the better off you will be.

However, Boyle feels that it is still important to have a personal connection with all the people screening your film. You could turn the
alternative theatrical booking process over to your fulfillment house
(e.g., people would buy the DVD to screen the film from your fulfillment company at a higher screening fee), but Boyle recommends
instead maintaining an open line of communication with anyone
who screens your film. Smithline concurs; she feels that much of
this process is about relationship-building.

★ **Your page should be composed of the following items (if you
are using Wordpress, this will be relatively easy to set up):**

1. A friendly invitation to screen. Your page should be warm, enticing, and upbeat.

2. Endorsements about your film such as film festival laurels,
   awards, important press quotes, and images that convey
   something compelling about your film. "Pitch" the film through
   your site.

3. A direct personal email address and a phone number that people can call. Some people still like to know there is a person at
   the other end.

4. Very clear instructions as to how people can arrange for
   a screening.

5. Have a two-tiered pricing structure to give potential screening
   facilities a choice. For example, you could charge $195 to or-
   ganizations that are not going to charge for the screening, and
   $295 for places that are.

   The pricing structure is another reason you want to interface
   with people screening your film. If you find that the organizer
   is planning to charge a relatively high admission price for your
   film (people have charged up to $30 per ticket and sold out
   venues for high-demand films), you will want to propose a split
   of the door against a guarantee.

6. An option to bring you to the screening as a guest. This is best
   done by request, since you will be asking for travel in addition
   to a speaking fee (in addition to the screening fee). Broderick
   suggests a 75/25 split/proportion for speaker fee/screening
   fee. For example, if the organization has $1,000 for you and
   the film, then you get $750 and the film gets $250. While this
   might seem overly generous to the filmmaker, when you fac-

tor in travel time (often at two full days), I have to agree with Broderick on this.

5. Personal Outreach

Boyle stresses that the most valuable part of a grassroots/community screenings campaign is the personal connection you can make with your audiences. She advocates that filmmakers offer the following when implemening their campaigns:

- **The human voice** A little human interaction is critical. Resist the temptation to promote your film solely through e-blasts and social media websites. Instead, cultivate a relationship.

- **Accessibility** Maintain a flexible schedule, and encourage viewers to call back with questions or concerns as they arise. Return calls and emails as quickly as you can.

- **Education** For many viewers, your film may be their first encounter with independent media. Guide them through the film distribution process, explain how the economics work, and make clear your goals and hopes.

- **Reciprocity** Find out how your campaign can help both your film and your audience. Offer opportunities to cross-promote and collaborate.

- **Feedback** When your campaign is over, provide participants with information about your successes and pitfalls. Solicit feedback and advice from them, too.

6. Authoring the DVD

In chapter 25 Educational Sales, we will look at the reasons for having different editions of your DVD for public and private home use. You may want to avoid having your community participants from screening your home-use DVD publicly and show everyone an FBI warning that disallows public performance!

You might also want to create a Blu-ray DVD for screenings so that the experience is better for the live audience.

7. Screening Primer

Since this might be the first time a person or organization has ever screened a film publicly, provide a one- to two-page "Guide to Hosting a Screening." This would include:

- What equipment they need to have (projector, DVD player, sound, etc.)

- Publicity and marketing tips (a how-to on reaching out to local press, sponsors, etc.)

- Suggesting that they have a sound-video check if it is a non-traditional screening space.

8. Capitalize on the Energy of the Screenings

People will be most energized right after they have seen your film. Capture that energy by:

- Selling DVDs and other merchandise.

- Collecting email addresses *at every* screening.

- Ask the presenter about other people who might want to screen the film (you can do this before the screening as well).

- Have your presenter post the experience on his or her LIST-SERVs. Everyone who screens your film is a resource: develop the relationships organically. This is another argument against an automated system.

- Request that the audience promote your film on their social networks (turn them into digital street-teamers).

THE B-SIDE MODEL

B-Side is a new breed of distributor, one that is using hybrid strategies within a distribution company structure that includes marketing, a DVD output deal, digital rights deals, and so on. Specifically, they have created a grassroots theatrical model to mobilize publicity around their films. Chris Hyams, the head of B-Side, feels that there is money to be made from distributing movies — the key is to not lose money the way other people do. In his opinion, the primary way that people lose money distributing movies is through their theatrical releases.

As a solution to this loss-leader scenario, B-Side's approach to theatrical is as follows:

- Each film is to be treated differently, with its own release strategy.

- Anyone can set up a screening of one of their films during the "theatrical release window" for that film without paying B-side for the right to do so.

By not charging a fee for screenings and opening it up to the community, you can motivate more people to screen the film, and it frees up resources for them to promote the screening, further increasing awareness. Plus, you are motivating those who screen the film to work that much harder to promote the film, since they keep all the profits.

Hyams applies this philosophy to conventional theatrical and alternative theatrical. If a conventional theater knows that they can keep 100 percent of the door, they are more likely to take a risk on a film and book it.

If statistically all theatrical releases lose money, why try to make money by spending money on the theatrical release? Wouldn't it be better to *not* charge for the screening and require the theaters or organizers to spend money on it? You do not reap theatrical benefits, but at the same time you are not at risk for the loss.

B-Side's biggest success story to date has been *Super High Me*, which is a stoner take on *Super Size Me*. The following is from a write-up by Chris Hyams about the *Super High Me* screenings (the whole write-up, including how B-Side got involved in this model, is available for download on our website):

> At the *Super High Me* SXSW premiere we announced that starting on 4/20 — the national stoner holiday — fans could "Roll Your Own" screening of *Super High Me*. We launched our community website, and had 150 sign-ups the first weekend. We found new partners this time in NORML (the National Organization for the Reform of Marijuana Laws), SSDP (Students for a Sensible Drug Policy), *High Times* magazine, and as it turned out, dozens of comedy clubs. Barely a month later, on 4/20, we had 1,076 screenings of *Super High Me* in 822 cities all over the U.S.... And with screening hosts paying just the shipping and handling for DVDs, the entire program cost only $8,000 — less than a 2-inch ad in the *New York Times*.... Throughout the weekend of 4/20, the term "super high me" remained in the top 100 Google "hot

trends" search list, which measures search terms with "sudden surges in popularity." It peaked on Sunday morning at number 29 on the list nationwide. Only one other feature film in release that weekend, *Forgetting Sarah Marshall*, even showed up on the list.... This free, crowdsourced alternative theatrical has the same goals of any other theatrical release. Namely, to promote the DVD release of the film. To date, *Super High Me* has sold 81,000 DVD units for $1.7 million in gross sales revenue, and has done an additional $1.6 million in rental revenue.

I think this is a great example of everything we have discussed in this chapter:

- Use alternative screening venues and empower your audience to set up screenings for you.

- Work with partner organizations to set up screenings and promote them.

- Utilize any kind of live event that screens your film to organize promotion around your film and create awareness.

- Create a coordinated campaign of screenings to create even greater awareness.

While they didn't organize the sale of DVDs at the initial screenings for *Super High Me*, B-Side does this for other films of theirs, which provides an alternative way to make money at free screenings. One note: Chris will readily tell you that their model works for niche-oriented documentaries, which is their specialty, although they are currently trying it out on a narrative called *Visioneers* and may continue to do so.

ONLINE GRASSROOTS NETWORKS

Brave New Theaters

Established by Robert Greenwald and Jim Gilliam as a public service to filmmakers wanting to connect directly with an audience, Brave New Theaters is a network focused on connecting films with those who want to screen them to their local communities directly, without a middleman.

The website bravenewtheaters.com allows any filmmaker to post information about their film free of charge and to solicit screenings from any potential screening host. Filmmakers can provide their film for free, for the cost of a DVD, or charge a screening fee — it is up to the filmmaker.

People in communities will host a screening either in their living rooms or in some other accessible public space. In general the people hosting screenings are interested in social-issue documentaries, but this model does not need to be limited to this genre.

Filmmakers can also try to work out an arrangement to sell DVDs at the screenings, but this can get more complicated. Do you charge up front for the DVDs or provide them on consignment?

With *Made in LA*, Robert Bahar pioneered a "pays for itself" screening package that he sells from his website, which includes DVDs for the promoters to sell at the screening, as well as posters and postcards. The promoter keeps the money from all that he sells to help pay for the screening.

Indiescreenings.net

The people who brought you *The Age of Stupid* have created a website to allow filmmakers to bring their films to their audiences similar to the way that Brave New Theaters does. Currently it is only for use in the U.K., but they have plans to expand to the United States and the rest of Europe.

The key difference between Brave New Theaters and Indie Screenings appears to be that Indie Screenings includes a path of monetization within their program, which calculates a fee based on venue, amount of audience, admission charged, etc. I eagerly await their arrival in the U.S.

NON-THEATRICAL/EDUCATIONAL DISTRIBUTORS

The non-theatrical screening territory has been largely the domain of educational distributors, and hence there is some crossover between alternative theatrical and educational distributors. I will address this in Chapter 25, which is about educational distribution, except for the following:

The College Circuit

There are some distributors who are specialized just to handle the college semi-theatrical (admission charged) market, the largest one being Swank. The unfortunate situation with Swank is that they are geared toward monetizing studio films on the college circuit. And while they have started up an indie division, unless you had a very large theatrical release with a lot of traditional press, chances are that Swank will consider your film too small and too hard to book. However, they are worth contacting if you've had a breakout success.

DIY College

You can contact student associate bookers yourself. It does take a fair amount of work, and part of your struggle will be finding the people to book with, but it is a possibility nonetheless. Keep in mind that the college market is especially tough to DIY because the people who book a lot of the events for colleges are college students themselves, and these people change every year, if not every semester.

However, this is an added benefit of high search-engine rankings. Provided you are near the top of searches that make sense for your film, some colleges may find you.

NACA

If you have a film very well suited to the college market, you might spend the time and money to attend a convention hosted by NACA, or the National Association of College Activities (naca.org). They hold conventions throughout the year that are attended by the people who book events for student organizations. You can actually register to go to one of these conventions (be warned that it isn't cheap) and talk to the student programmers directly. It can be lucrative. The producers of *Good Dick* pursued this strategy and they set up eight events for $5,000 each! This included personal appearance fees for the director and/or actors.

It does cost to join NACA as an associate or affiliate member. Depending on your membership level, you can attend the national convention held in February each year. More than 2,000 delegates from 450 schools attend NACA's national convention to network with close to 240 artists and agencies. In addition, NACA hosts six regional conferences in the fall and two regional events in the spring.

To pursue this strategy, you need to have a film that will appeal to college students not only on an entertainment level, but (hopefully) on an issue level as well.

Chapter 18 Conclusion

The alternative theatrical grassroots screening model has shown the way to democratize and return a shared film experience to the control of individuals and groups. With that newfound power, people will continue to find new ways to exhibit and congregate in order to watch films.

A budget for distribution is as important as one for production and should be included in the production budget.

CHAPTER 19

BUDGETING DISTRIBUTION AND MARKETING

A budget for distribution is as important as one for production and should be included in the production budget. I have compiled a variety of sample budgets, which includes most of what you would encounter for all aspects of a hybrid, split rights release, including theatrical. You should be able to use these budgets as guides and create an approximate budget using those expenses that relate to your specific release.

BUDGET CATEGORIES

Column A: Contains the budget category numbers. I started with 9000 because I feel that this budget should not be a separate budget, but a part of your overall film production budget.

Column B: is the general category of the expense.

Column C: is the specific line item description.

RANGE OF EXPENSES

Column D: is the range of the specific expense, from the least amount you can spend to the highest for each line item. Of course, you can choose to not spend anything, to not do it, or to do it yourself.

SAMPLE THEATRICAL BUDGETS

These budgets are not exact, but are intended to give you an idea of how the expenses might play out for different types of releases. How you choose to release your film will, of course, cause these figures to change.

Column E High 35mm Service is a for a $180,000 theatrical release on 35mm prints, using a distributor for hire in seven cities, including New York and Los Angeles. It assumes that all creative has already been done.

Column F Mid 35mm Service is for the same release as E, but with lower ad commitments — essentially a streamlined release. It assumes that all creative has already been done.

Column G Low 35mm Service is for the same release as E, but only for two cities: New York and Los Angeles. It assumes that all creative has already been done.

The above three budgets are for a more conventional theatrical release. They don't include any money for travel or grassroots/community outreach.

Column H Low Service/Grassroots is for a 12-city theatrical release, with additional non-theatrical bookings beyond the original 12 cities. It assumes all creative except a trailer has been done. Some bookings are in film, some are on video. Note that it has a fee for grassroots/community outreach included. This budget reflects movement toward a more hybrid approach.

BOMB IT ACTUALIZED EXPENSES

Column I Bomb It Actualized Theatrical Expenses (e.g., what I actually spent on the theatrical release). As you can see, I spent a bit more than the $13,000 I originally allocated (column K). In addition, I gave myself a small stipend for the six months of work ($5,000 total), which you may or may not do. Areas in which I felt I could have saved money are postcard production, street teams (although these were very helpful for the DVD), and travel. Overall, for a 17-city release I feel I did pretty well, considering a modest servicing deal for two to 10 cities starts at about $60,000.

Column J Bomb It Actualized Non Theatrical Expenses lists the actualized expenses that we have paid on the distribution and marketing of *Bomb It* to date that do not relate to the theatrical release.

Column K Bomb It Budget is my stripped-down, $13,000 DIY budget proposal to my investor. How I ever thought I could do the release for this much money, I have no idea.

Column L Mid Video Service is for a two-city release (New York and L.A.) projected on video with a distributor for hire and the theaters are four-walled. It assumes that all creative has already been done.

BUDGET CATEGORIES EXPLAINED

9100: Distribution Labor and Fees

This is for all distribution labor, from consultants to lawyers, as well as fees for services.

9110: Distribution Consultant This is for your overall strategist and consultant. The total can go higher as you use them for more and more time throughout your release. The very low end for a few hours of consultation is $500; it can go to $5,000 and above over the course of the release.

9120: Conventional Theatrical Booking Fee This is for the person booking your film into conventional theatrical theaters and at the higher end, organizing the distribution — essentially it's the distribution fee. I ended up taking $5,000 for the six months of full-time work I spent on the theatrical release of *Bomb It*. If I could have found a theatrical booker for the low end indicated here, I wish I would have gone that route and saved myself some grief. Depending on the financial arrangements, I do feel it is important for filmmakers to take some money for their labor on their release.

9130: Alternative Theatrical/Community Consultant The range depends on whether you use the consultant as just an initial consultation or if he or she is handling the entire release. In the low service deal budget, the $10,000 is all in for consulting and labor.

9140: Alternative Theatrical Researcher/Booker Again, the cost depends on whether you have someone doing all of the work in 9130 and how long your release is. You can also offer this person a percentage of the bookings.

9150: Distribution Assistant Can be the same as 9140 and, of course, depends on the length of your release. $150 to $250 a week for at least 16 weeks at the low end.

9160: Legal How much you spend on legal depends on how many deals you end up doing. Each deal will cost you additional. It also depends on how complicated the deals are.

9170: DVD Fulfillment Company Fulfillment companies usually charge a start-up fee and a monthly fee. Start-up is about $250.

9180: DVD Fulfillment Company Monthly Charges About $30 a month. I am not putting them in the budget, since this will be a cost off the top of your earnings.

9200: Materials — Creative

9210: Key Art Creative This is the cost of paying a graphic designer to create your key art. It is very difficult to get good key art for $1,000 — but you usually don't need to spend $20,000. $5,000 to $10,000 is a decent range. Note: In my budget, key art is $0, since it was paid for by the foreign sales company.

9220: Graphic Design Miscellaneous This is the cost of a designer to take your key art and create other elements for your print promotion — web banners, postcard backs, emails, etc. Over time, this can add up, even if you are only paying a small sum each time.

9230: Print Advertising Design This is the cost of creating your print ad slicks — the variety of ad sizes based on your key art that newspapers will need in order to place your ad.

9240: DVD Cover Design Your key art should be on the cover, but you need a back and you need to size it to the DVD duplicator's specifications.

9250: Trailer Creative This is the creative cost of your trailer, including copy creation, editing, sound editing, voice over, etc. You can do this for free if you have people. The high end reflects a traditional trailer house. Our editors cut our trailers for *Bomb It*.

9260: EPK Creative People to cut your electronic press kit. I would also include the people cutting your webisodes and other web promotion here. I would definitely use up-and-comers. A very talented intern cut the EPK for *Bomb It*.

9270: DVD Authoring NTSC The cost of authoring your DVD, which you or someone you know can do for free using DVD Studio Pro, or you can pay $800 for a very simple DVD, or more for more. I didn't pay for this because New Video paid for these expenses as part of our deal.

9273: DVD Authoring PAL I'm paying about $1,000 for the very complicated PAL version of *Bomb It*, which includes about $400 for encoding.

9275: Translations You can spend nothing, but I found it hard to spend absolutely nothing.

9300: Materials — Printing

9310: Posters, Full-Size You can either do a small amount of full-size posters one by one, essentially laser printed, for $75 to $100 each. Or you can spend $1200 and have 2,000 posters printed 25x37 inches. Or you can spend $3,000 for a large run of conventionally sized film posters.

9320: 11x17 Posters One of the best printing bargains around. You use these for stores, giveaways, and for sale on your website.

9330: Postcards, 5,000/each The amounts are for a total expenditure. Each 5,000 should cost around $100 to $120, plus about $30 to $60 in shipping.

9340: Stickers Individually cut stickers can get expensive. They are also not as useful for guerrilla promotion and are mainly used for giveaways by hand or making sticker packs to sell. People like stickers, but a decent sized run can cost $300 to $1,000.

9350: Roll Stickers These are cheaper to print and are easier to guerrilla. You can get 5,000 for $500. But guerrilla stickering is, of course, not for every film.

9360: Promotional T-Shirts T-shirts for giveaway, not for sale. This amount is $100 at $4 each — the very low end. You can spend more. I would include the T-shirt design as an expense in 9220: Graphic Design Misc. We spent about $6,500 on printing T-shirts. We've made back about $4,000. We'll probably break even when we sell them all.

9370: Miscellaneous Promotional Printing This is for printing buttons, condoms, sandwich wrappers — whatever you think will work for your film.

9400: Print and Master Materials

9410: 35mm Transfer from Video If you are doing a wider

conventional theatrical release, it is still easier if you have a 35mm print. This will continue to change over time. The transfer will cost on the low end $30,000 to $40,000. It can cost much more, depending on your digital intermediate (DI). These budgets all assume that you already have your DI and/or film negative if you originally shot on 35mm.

9420: Release Prints These are the "prints" of prints and advertising. For a 7- to 10-city release, you can usually get by with about five prints, because you normally won't be doing all 10 cities at the same time.

9430: 35mm Trailer Conform If you are cutting a 35mm trailer from a 35mm negative. This is the cost of conforming your trailer to your offline edit.

9440: Trailer Blowup This is the cost of creating a 35mm master of your digital or video trailer.

9450: Trailer Prints The actual 35mm trailers. They cost only $25 each — you should make a bunch. This is some of the best free advertising available to you. Get these out as early as possible.

9460: Video Copies Your video dubs for your theatrical, if you are doing a video release. These are also your DVD copies for preview and review copies.

9470: Landmark Digital Conversion If you screen at Landmark Theaters, they will require you to conform your video master to their digital screening format.

9480: DVD Replication NTSC This is for basic DVD-5 with a black plastic case and full-color insert cover. If you want to get fancier for special sales, it will cost more.

9483: DVD Replication PAL

9485: European Glass Master If you are going to replicate your PAL DVD in Europe, you will need to pay for a "glass master." Approximately $250.

9490: iTunes Encoding If you go with Distribbr to do your encoding, you should budget $1,300 plus $80 a year. New Video is our aggregator and handled this for us.

9500: Marketing and Publicity

9510: New York and National Publicist Note the range of $5,000 to $15,000. The New York publicist is one of the people doing your national publicity as well.

9511: Los Angeles and National Publicist Again, note the range. Frankly, on a budget you should have your national publicist cover Los Angeles. Whether or not you use a New York or L.A. focused national publicist depends on where you need the most connections.

9512: Regional Publicists You can hire people to do other major regional centers, such as San Francisco, Seattle, and Chicago. This can cost as low as $500 a city. But many theater programmers know these people and will handle this themselves.

9513: Affinity Publicist This is the publicist who handles your niche.

9520: Press Screenings For DIY, you are sending out screeners. For a few hundred dollars you can usually arrange to use the theater you are screening in for a press screening. The next step up is multiple screenings in New York and L.A.

9521: Press Kit You should be doing this yourself, but if you are spending money, a publicist can make the press kit better.

9522: Miscellaneous PR Expenses This includes copying, shipping, etc.

9530: Viral Marketing Team and Campaign This is for people pushing your content, trying to get you traffic and awareness on the web. You can do this for free if you are capable or already have someone on your team. But if you can find someone who knows what they are doing, this can also be some of the best money you spend.

9531: Social Network Promotion Normally this would be included in 9530, but I separated it because you can find up-and-comers who like to social network whom you can pay a small amount of money to do this specialized task.

9532: Email List Buy Depending on the situation, you can sometimes buy a very good list that targets a particular niche or community. If you have partnerships with organizations, however, you shouldn't be paying for this.

9533: *Website Design* Approximately $1,000 to $4,000, which should include basic search engine optimization.

9534: *Web Hosting* $130 a year for however many years you think you need.

9536: *Email Service/Blasts* Such as Constant Contact or other. There are many free services available these days as well.

9540: *Street Teams, N.Y./L.A.* These are traditional street teams. You can pay either monthly, starting at $250 a month, or per 1,000 postcards distributed (e.g., about $150). For the latter, those people should be very experienced and really targeting your niche. They commonly provide you with some photographic evidence of placement and/or recipients of the postcards. New York, of course, is the most expensive city for this — like everything else.

9541: Street Teams, Smaller Cities

9550: *L.A. Party/Events* The costs in my budget here are for DJs and a sound system. For L.A. this was important, since this was our L.A. premiere. It also gave us an additional event to promote around and served as our cast and crew party.

9551: *New York Party/Events* We had a party in NYC but didn't pay for it. A sponsor, *Bombin' Magazine*, threw our New York party, with swag provided by All City NRG.

9600: THEATER EXPENSES

9610: *Four-Wall NYC* If you need to rent your New York theater, this is what it can cost for a week's run. Hopefully you won't have to if you don't want to or can't afford it. If it is your plan to four-wall and to reap all the income, then go for it.

9620: *Four-Wall L.A.* Ditto on L.A.

9630: *Special Video Equipment* Some theaters will charge you for their video equipment (even though they own it!). If you are doing screenings in some non-conventional venues, you may need to rent equipment (or buy it) yourself.

9700: DIRECT MEDIA

Direct media are your advertising expenses.

9700: Print Media The $2,800 I spent was the barest of minimums for New York and L.A. It was only allowed because of the massive street promotion and parties I was doing. I think unless you are spending tens of thousands of dollars, anything less is a waste of money in New York and L.A., since you can't penetrate public consciousness with $5,000 of media buys in major markets. I also feel that, in general, almost all of the money spent here is better spent on web promotion.

9710: TV/Radio Buys If you are in the $200,000 and under range, chances are you can't afford this and shouldn't be spending money on TV and radio advertising.

9720: Web Advertising Google and Facebook ads. Try $50 to start and see how it works for you; then, if it works, slowly increase your expenditure if it makes sense.

9800: TRAVEL EXPENSES

You shouldn't forget this expense if you are traveling and promoting your film in person. You might also want to fly one or more actors to some of the screenings.

9810: Travel Expenses Alternative theatrical venues will often pay your way. The $2,700 I spent includes separate trips to San Francisco, Portland, Denver (they paid nearly all), New Orleans, and a combined trip to New York and Chicago.

9900: GENERAL EXPENSE

If you are paying a distribution fee, they should be covering all of these expenses except print shipping, which is the bulk of your shipping. If you are doing DIY or hybrid, you need to include these expenses, which can add up.

9910: Telephone and Fax I will call theaters from a land line since I find my cell unreliable for critical first calls and VOIP is usually funky. Remember, you usually only have one shot to pitch yourself.

9920: Postage and Shipping Print shipping can add up for a 35mm release, as reflected in the budgets. It is not nearly as expensive for a video release.

9930: Office Supplies

9940: *Messengers* No matter how hard you try to minimize this expense, there are always a few things that have to get there *today*. You will spend more on this if you are understaffed.

9950: *Accounting* Your distributor for hire should be handling this. For DIY, get Quicken and do it yourself.

9960: *Bank Fees* Operating on a tight budget, you're going to incur some overdraft charges and interest on credit cards.

9970: *Errors and Omissions (E&O) Insurance* Some contracts with companies (home video, television) will require that you spend this. $3,500 is the lowest I have found.

WHAT THIS BUDGET DOESN'T INCLUDE

This budget does not include standard delivery requirements that are commonly part of conventional budgets. These expenses include:

Print Masters

If you shot on 35mm, you will need an interpositive, internegative, and check prints.

Video Masters

NTSC and PAL HD Masters with Digibeta downconverts of your theatrical masters, television masters, 4:3 extractions if necessary, textless backgrounds. Usually you need your LTRT mix on channels 1 and 2 and your music and effects (M&E) on channels 3 and 4.

M&E Mix

Music and effects mix for foreign sales. This should be included in your sound mix package, and can cost approximately $4,000 on the low end.

Dialogue List

This is the time-coded spoken language in your film. You can have an intern do it or pay, at the low end, $1,000.

Closed Captioning

Some television deals require this. Approximately $2,000 from a good dialogue list at the low end.

SECTION 3 CONCLUSION

"Live theatrical" experiences are here to stay, and I believe they will become more powerful for independent filmmakers in the years to come. People need to be around people; they need to engage with them and have shared narrative experiences. It has been happening since our ancestors told stories in front of fires. The technology and setting for those "fires" has and will change, but we will always be compelled to get out of our homes and gather with other people to share a story.

Once filmmakers throw off the fetters of the conventional theatrical release as the only worthwhile means of public screenings for their films, they will discover a myriad of ways to interact with their audiences. I even feel that some filmmakers can make a profit doing this.

The online press and blogosphere have already embraced this new reality. They don't care if a screening is in a regular theater or an outdoor park. Little by little the conventional press has already begun to value alternative screenings and venues as much as conventional releases. The more they do so, the more it will help this process evolve.

I am hugely excited about the different ways that independent filmmakers will push the boundaries of this experience. Please let me know if you are up to something new and exciting!

A	B	C — Description	D — The Range (what you can spend)	E — High 35MM Service	F — Mid 35MM Service	G — Low 35MM Service	H — Low Service/ Grassroots
9100		**DISTRIBUTION LABOR AND FEES**					
9110		Distribution Consultant/Strategist	$500-$5,000+				
		Conventional Theatrical					
9120		Booking Fee	$0-$25,000	$25,000	$20,000	$15,000	$4,500
		Alternative Theatrical/Community					
9130		Consultant	$500-$10,000+				$10,000
9140		Researcher/Distribution Assistant	$1000-$6000+				
9150		Distribution Assistant	$2500-10,000				
9160		Legal	$1000-$10,000				
		DVD Sales					
9170		Fulfillment Company Startup Fees	$250				
9175		Webstore Conform	$500				
9180		Fulfillment Company Monthly Charges	Approx $30/mo.				
		Subtotal Distribution Labor and Fees	**$5500 - 66,000**	**$25,000**	**$20,000**	**$15,000**	**$14,500**
9200		**MATERIALS CREATIVE**					
		Graphic Design					
9210		Key Art Creative	$1000-$25,000	$15,000	$10,000	$5,000	
9220		Graphic Design Misc	$2000+				
9230		Print Advertising Design	$200-1000	$1,000	$1,000	$1,000	
9240		DVD Cover Design	$0-500				
		Editing					
9250		Trailer Creative	$1000-$25,000				$5,000
9260		EPK Creative	$1000-$5000				
		DVD Authoring					
9270		DVD Authoring NTSC	$0-$5000				
9273		DVD Authoring PAL	$0-$2000				
9275		Subtitles	$0-1000+				
		Subtotal Materials Creative	**$3200 - $66,000**	**$16,000**	**$11,000**	**$6,000**	**$5,000**
9300		**MATERIALS PRINTING**					
9310		Posters Full Size	$600-$4000	$1,200	$600	$600	$1,200
9320		11x17 Posters	$300	$300	$300		$300
9330		Postcards	$300-$2000	$1,500	$1,000	$500	$2,000
9340		Stickers Individual Cut	$1000 - 2000				
9350		Roll Stickers	$500-$1000				
9360		Promotional T Shirts	$400-$1000+				
9370		Miscellaneous Promotional Printing	$400+				
		Subtotal Materials Printing	**$3100 - $10,700**	**$3,000**	**$1,900**	**$1,100**	**$3,500**
9400		**PRINT AND MASTER MATERIALS**					
		35MM Film Print					
9410		35 MM Transfer from Video	$30,000-$40,000				
9420		Release Prints	$1500 Each	$7,500	$7,500	$3,000	$2,500
		Trailers					
9430		35MM Trailer Conform	$2,000	$1,800	$1,800	$1,800	
9440		Trailer Blow Up	$1,300				$1,900
9450		Trailer Prints	$200	$200	$200	$100	$300
		Video Screeners					
9460		Video Copies	$300-$1000	$100	$100	$50	$300
9470		Digital Screening Copy/Landmark	$5,000				

A	B	Description C	The Range (what you can spend) D	High 35MM Service E	Mid 35MM Service F	Low 35MM Service G	Low Service/ Grassroots H
9400		**PRINT AND MASTER MATERIALS CONT**					
	DVD Replication						
9480		DVD Replication NTSC	About $1.10- $1.30@				
9483		DVD Replication PAL	About $1.10- $1.30@				
9485		European Glass Master	$250				
9490		iTunes Encoding	$1,300				
		Subtotal Print and Master Materials	**$0 - $50,000+**	**$9,600**	**$9,600**	**$4,950**	**$5,000**
9500		**MARKETING AND PUBLICITY**					
	Publicists						
9510		NY and National Publicist	$5,000-$15,000	$12,000	$12,000	$6,000	$8,000
9511		Los Angeles and National Publicist Publicis	$5,000-$15,000	$12,000	$12,000	$6,000	$4,000
9512		Regional Publicists	$500-$5000	$5,000	$2,000	$0	
9513		Affinity Publicist	$500-$5000				
	Supplies/Purchases						
9520		Press Screenings	$200-$5000	$5,000	$2,500	$2,000	$2,000
9521		Press Kit	$0-$2000	$2,000			
9522		Misc PR Expenses	$400-$2500	$2,500	$1,500	$500	
	Web Marketing						
9530		Viral Marketing Team and Campaign	$0-$20,000	$20,000	$10,000	$5,000	
9531		Social Network Promotion	$0-$4000				
9532		Supplemental Email List Buy	$100-$750				
9533		Webdesign	$1000-$2000				
9534		Webhosting	$130 a year				
9536		Email Blasts	$0-$300+				
	Streat Teams						
9540		Street teams NY/LA	$0-$3000				$3,000
9541		Street Teams Small Cities	$0-$750				
	Events						
9550		LA Party/Events	$0-$5000+				
9551		NY Party	$0-$5000+				
		Subtotal Marketing and Publicity	**$0 - $78,050**	**$58,500**	**$40,000**	**$19,500**	**$17,000**
9600		**THEATRE EXPENSES**					
9610		Four Wall NYC	$0-$18,000				
9620		Four Wall LA	$0-$5000				
9630		Special Video Equipment	$0-$2000				
		Subtotal Theater Expenses	**$0 - $25,000**				
9700		**DIRECT MEDIA**					
9700		Print Media	$2500-$75,000	$75,000	$50,000	$40,000	$10,000
9710		TV/Radio Buys	$0				
9720		Web Advertising	$500				
		Subtotal Direct Media	**$0 - $78,000**	**$75,000**	**$50,000**	**$40,000**	**$10,000**
9800		**TRAVEL EXPENSES**					
9810		Travel Expenses	$0-$5000+				$5,000
		Subtotal Travel	**$0 - $5000+**	**$0**	**$0**	**$0**	**$5,000**
9800		**GENERAL EXPENSE**					
9910		Telephone & Fax	$0-$500			$1,000	
9920		Postage and Shipping	$400-$2500	$2,500	$2,500	$1,200	$1,500
9930		Office Supplies	$0-$500				
9940		Messengers	$0-$300				
9950		Accounting	$0-$2250				
9960		Bank Fees	$0-$300				
9970		E&O Insurance	$3500-$10,000				
		Subtotal General Expense	**$0 - $16,350**	**$2,500**	**$2,500**	**$2,200**	**$1,500**
		GRAND TOTAL:		$189,600	$135,000	$88,750	$61,500

A	B	Description (C)	The Range (what you can spend) (D)	Bomb It Theatrical Expenses (I)	Bomb It Expenses other than Theatrical (J)	Bomb It Budget (K)	Mid Video Service (L)
9100		**DISTRIBUTION LABOR AND FEES**					
	9110	Distribution Consultant/Strategist	$500-$5,000+	$0		$0	
		Conventional Theatrical					
	9120	Booking Fee	$0-$25,000	$5,000			$15,000
		Alternative Theatrical/Community					
	9130	Consultant	$500-$10,000+		$500		
	9140	Researcher/Distribution Assistant	$1000-$6000+	$700			
	9150	Distribution Assistant	$2500-10,000		$6,000		
	9160	Legal	$1000-$10,000		$5,000		
		DVD Sales					
	9170	Fulfillment Company Startup Fees	$250		$240		
	9175	Webstore Conform	$500				
	9180	Fulfillment Company Monthly Charges	Approx $30/mo.				
		Subtotal Distribution Labor and Fees	**$5500 - 66,000**	**$5,700**	**$11,740**	**$0**	**$15,000**
9200		**MATERIALS CREATIVE**					
		Graphic Design					
	9210	Key Art Creative	$1000-$25,000	$0		$0	$10,000
	9220	Graphic Design Misc	$2000+	$150	$2,000	$0	$0
	9230	Print Advertising Design	$200-1000	$150		$0	$500
	9240	DVD Cover Design	$0-500		$300		
		Editing					
	9250	Trailer Creative	$1000-$25,000	$250			
	9260	EPK Creative	$1000-$5000				
		DVD Authoring					
	9270	DVD Authoring NTSC	$0-$5000				
	9273	DVD Authoring PAL	$0-$2000		$1,000		
	9275	Subtitles	$0-1000+		$600		
		Subtotal Materials Creative	**$3200 - $66,000**	**$550**	**$3,300**	**$0**	**$10,500**
9300		**MATERIALS PRINTING**					
	9310	Posters Full Size	$600-$4000	$2,000	$0	$0	$240
	9320	11x17 Posters	$300	$325		$0	$0
	9330	Postcards	$300-$2000	$2,500		$1,000	$200
	9340	Stickers Individual Cut	$1000 - 2000	$800		$900	$0
	9350	Roll Stickers	$500-$1000		$500		
	9360	Promotional T Shirts	$400-$1000+		$6,000		
	9370	Miscellaneous Promotional Printing	$400+				
		Subtotal Materials Printing	**$3100 - $10,700**	**$5,625**	**$6,500**	**$1,900**	**$440**
9400		**PRINT AND MASTER MATERIALS**					
		35MM Film Print					
	9410	35 MM Transfer from Video	$30,000-$40,000				
	9420	Release Prints	$1500 Each				
		Trailers					
	9430	35MM Trailer Conform	$2,000				
	9440	Trailer Blow Up	$1,300	$1,340		$0	$2,500
	9450	Trailer Prints	$200	$250		$0	$160
		Video Screeners					
	9460	Video Copies	$300-$1000	$314		$0	$600
	9470	Digital Screening Copy/Landmark	$5,000				

A	B	Description (C)	The Range (what you can spend) (D)	Bomb It Theatrical Expenses (I)	Bomb It Expenses other than Theatrical (J)	Bomb It Budget (K)	Mid Video Service (L)
9400		PRINT AND MASTER MATERIALS CONT					
		DVD Replication					
9480		DVD Replication NTSC	About $1.10- $1.30@				
9483		DVD Replication PAL	About $1.10- $1.30@		$1,300		
9485		European Glass Master	$250		$250		
9490		iTunes Encoding	$1,300				
		Subtotal Print and Master Materials	**$0 - $50,000+**	**$1,904**	**$1,550**	**$0**	**$3,260**
9500		MARKETING AND PUBLICITY					
		Publicists					
9510		NY and National Publicist	$5,000-$15,000	$7,500		$7,500	$15,000
9511		Los Angeles and National Publicist Public	$5,000-$15,000				$15,000
9512		Regional Publicists	$500-$5000				
9513		Affinity Publicist	$500-$5000	$500			
		Supplies/Purchases					
9520		Press Screenings	$200-$5000	$0		$0	$1,600
9521		Press Kit	$0-$2000				
9522		Misc PR Expenses	$400-$2500	$100			
		Web Marketing					
9530		Viral Marketing Team and Campaign	$0-$20,000	$150		$0	$3,000
9531		Social Network Promotion	$0-$4000	$600		$0	$0
9532		Supplemental Email List Buy	$100-$750	$200		$0	$0
9533		Webdesign	$1000-$2000				
9534		Webhosting	$130 a year		$650		
9536		Email Blasts	$0-$300+				
		Streat Teams					
9540		Street teams NY/LA	$0-$3000	$2,700		$1,600	$0
9541		Street Teams Small Cities	$0-$750	$600		$0	$0
		Events					
9550		LA Party/Events	$0-$5000+	$1,000		$1,000	$0
9551		NY Party	$0-$5000+	$0		$500	$0
		Subtotal Marketing and Publicity	**$0 - $78,050**	**$13,350**	**$650**	**$10,600**	**$34,600**
9600		THEATRE EXPENSES					
9610		Four Wall NYC	$0-$18,000	$0		$0	$10,000
9620		Four Wall LA	$0-$5000	$0		$0	$6,000
9630		Special Video Equipment	$0-$2000	$0		$0	$2,000
		Subtotal Theater Expenses	**$0 - $25,000**	**$0**	**$0**	**$0**	**$18,000**
9700		DIRECT MEDIA					
9700		Print Media	$2500-$75,000	$2,800		$0	$15,000
9710		TV/Radio Buys	$0				
9720		Web Advertising	$500				
		Subtotal Direct Media	**$0 - $78,000**	**$2,800**	**$0**	**$0**	**$15,000**
9800		TRAVEL EXPENSES					
9810		Travel Expenses	$0-$5000+	$2,673		$0	$0
		Subtotal Travel	**$0 - $5000+**	**$2,673**	**$0**	**$0**	**$0**
9800		GENERAL EXPENSE					
9910		Telephone & Fax	$0-$500	$0	200	$150	$0
9920		Postage and Shipping	$400-$2500	$1,136	$1,200	$300	$600
9930		Office Supplies	$0-$500	$130	$300	$50	$0
9940		Messengers	$0-$300	$150		$0	$0
9950		Accounting	$0-$2250	$0		$0	$2,250
9960		Bank Fees	$0-$300	$300		$0	$0
9970		E&O Insurance	$3500-$10,000	$0	$3,500	$0	
		Subtotal General Expense	**$0 - $16,350**	**$1,716**	**$5,200**	**$500**	**$2,850**
		GRAND TOTAL:		**$34,318**	**$28,940**	**$13,000**	**$99,650**

Section 4
Marketing and Publicity

In earlier chapters we talked about the publicity and marketing work you should be doing before your film is finished and continuing through to the release. In this section, we will address the publicity and marketing you should be doing during your release, capitalizing on the foundation that you have laid down in prep, production, and post.

The goal is to have your publicity peak at the point in time when you will be able to monetize your rights most effectively (or otherwise reap the success of your film). This is not necessarily during the theatrical, as the theatrical is also part of your publicity building to the ancillary rights, such as DVD and digital sales, where you have the best chance of monetizing your content.

CHAPTER 20

CONVENTIONAL PUBLICITY

Conventional publicity still plays a large role in the independent film market, despite the rapid shrinkage of print media. Here's why:

1. Conventional publicity and reviews still raise awareness of your film.

2. Reviews will help further distribution of your film and help your career and future projects.

3. If you are booking into conventional theaters, many of them will require a certain amount of conventional publicity and marketing expenditures.

4. Conventional publicity can be cost-effective and can be done yourself.

5. Some conventional publicity can still be effective for sales.

The most effective time to do conventional publicity is when you have an event to rally around — for independent film, it is usually a screening event. The more unique you can make that event, the better.

TYPES OF PUBLICITY

Smithline makes an important distinction between three different kinds of publicity.

1. **Press About Your Film:** Traditional film press or press in a certain niche that relates to your film.

2. **Press About the Issue/Subject of Your Film:** "Off entertainment press." In regard to community- or grassroots-oriented films, this is press that builds issue awareness. People

want to see the film because they are concerned about the underlying issue. This is not limited to documentaries. It applies to narrative films based on interesting real-life people, historical incidents, the author of the book the film is based on, etc.

For *Better Living Through Circuitry*, we were lucky in that three films about rave culture and electronic music were released at the same time. Instead of each film detracting from the others' press, the issue about rave culture became the "off entertainment press" issue.

3. *Free Media:* This is related to No. 2 in that it has to do with your issue, but instead of you cultivating the issue, you are breaking into an existing news cycle.

For instance, say Daryl Hannah is camped out in a tree, about to be hauled off to jail. Even though she is not in your rainforest film, you could connect to the organization involved with the protest and try to post a clip of your film to their site. This might spark some coverage from the media looking for a new angle to the issue.

Taking this one step further, you should consider creating your own event to generate publicity around your issue or niche. Even if you don't have a star in your film, perhaps you can get a celebrity to be involved in the cause that the film concerns and build awareness around that.

Think about the timing of your release in terms of free media events that you can become a part of.

For narrative films, perhaps the author of the book on which your film is based has a new book coming out — that might be a good time to release your film. Or an anniversary of an event or birth date of an important real life character in or related to your film.

TARGETING PUBLICITY

Swartz: "The role of publicity is to pitch people who might be interested before you pitch them (you just need to know who those people might be)."

Part of a publicist's job is to target a receptive press audience. If you are doing your own publicity, you need to be aware of a reviewer or journalist's likes and dislikes and make sure you approach the right person. In other words, do your research.

TIMING PUBLICITY — OR, NOT ALL PUBLICITY IS GOOD PUBLICITY

Swartz and McInnis agree that not all publicity is good publicity, especially if that publicity comes at the wrong time. This usually arises in the case of festival publicity. The best-case scenario if you are not releasing your film day and date with a festival is that a lot of reviewers see your film at the festival, love it, and will hold those reviews for the theatrical release.

If, on the other hand, the paper runs a review or feature during the festival, usually they will *not* run it again during the theatrical release. A seasoned publicist who has relationships with the press will discuss this with the reviewers and request that they hold the review. For the same reason, don't do every interview at a festival, since the paper may not hold it, and then you would lose the feature story with that paper. If you don't have a publicist, try to work this out with the journalists on your own — but be sensitive to the fact that journalists *do not like being told what to do*. However, if they are a fan of your film, they will want to help you.

Knowing about positive reviews waiting for a theatrical release will definitely help you book your film. However, if you don't have a lot of these reviews, you should try to garner some good press to come out during your premiere festival to help you book your film, or garner other distribution. Trade reviews (*Variety, Hollywood Reporter*) can be very helpful in this regard if they are positive. This can give the film some credibility with theater owners (if the reviews pump up your theatrical potential) but does not take away from the press you need for the release.

Swartz advises against spending too much money on publicity on your premiere festival. (Not every actor needs you to pay them to go to Sundance. One can be enough.)

Furthermore, don't ask too much of your actors too soon. If you have them do a lot of press at a festival, they will be less inclined to do the press at your release. Always remember, you have one best opportunity for press exposure — use it wisely.

All of this is moot, of course, if you are intending your festival run to be your theatrical or planning to run them concurrently. Then you want to use that time to get as much press as possible.

AVENUES OF PRESS PUBLICITY

1. Long Lead This is press that is planned and prepared a long time before it is to run. In general these are the nationally released monthlies such as *Vanity Fair, Vogue, Rolling Stone* (which comes out twice monthly), etc. If you don't know your start date six to eight months in advance, it will hurt your chances of getting long lead press. However, in general, it is hard for indies to get this kind of press without big stars either in or in support of the film, or some other amazing hook. For instance, Mick Jagger doing the sound-track.

There is affinity/niche press that is long lead. For *Bomb It*, a few monthlies such as *Juxtapose, Complex*, and *VICE* made sense. McKinnis also points out that in-flight magazines get a lot of eye-balls, and this could be valuable if you are doing a release near a small airline's home base. They might even agree to do a sponsor-ship with you.

2. Short Lead This is generally local press that can be garnered in a few weeks to a month. Weekly and daily papers are in this cat-egory, as well as nearly all blogs.

3. Super-Long Lead This is for most blogs (and fan sites) in your niche that you want to be working with. You create a long-term awareness for your film in your target audience, which builds expec-tation for your film. You want to involve these people in production, perhaps even prep.

4. Radio While you probably can't afford radio ads, there is plenty of free publicity to get from radio. There are a wide variety of sta-tions and programs within stations, especially on public radio. You can do on-air interviews and special programs. You can also do on-air promotions with your merchandise and free ticket giveaways, and DVD giveaways when your DVD launches.

5. TV In general, getting TV coverage is tough for independents. If you or anyone on your film has a local angle (i.e., if the film was shot in a small town or the actors are from there) or you have a human interest story, it might be worth investigating.

TV publicity is more likely if you can break into a news cycle, or something regarding your film is developing heat of its own.

Onto the materials you will need to get the above publicity going.

Key art and
printmedia:
posters,
postcards,
stickers

Media buys,
including
print ads

Trailers

Parties

Promotions

CHAPTER 21

CREATING PUBLICITY MATERIALS & EVENTS

In this chapter we will examine the following:

- Key art and print media: posters, postcards, stickers
- Street teaming/"wild posting"
- Media buys, including print ads
- Trailers
- Parties
- Promotions
- Sponsorships
- Partnerships
- Guerrilla and stunt events (While this is not "conventional," I will address all non-web-based types of publicity in this chapter.)

KEY ART

Good key art can not be underestimated — it is the one visual that will sell your film (even more than your photos).

You will use this key art for all of your graphic design: your website design, your paid ads, your postcards, and, of course, your poster.

Good key art can be expensive ($10,000 on the low end for poster art), but there are some resources on the web to help you get around this.

Crowdsourcing Key Art

Crowdspring.com lets you create a posting explaining what you need and what you are willing to pay, then designers from all over the world will submit artwork to you. You pick your favorite one and pay the artist.

PRINT MEDIA: FULL-SIZE POSTERS

If you are on a budget, use slightly smaller 24.5x37 posters at $1,300 for 2,000 posters as opposed to $2500 for 2000, if you can live with them being slightly smaller. While this is not the standard poster size, most theaters are willing to work with it.

If you are going to make more than 10 posters, it doesn't make sense economically to print less than 2,000 posters. You can use leftovers for promotions at the theater and in selling the DVD.

Unfortunately, it is more expensive and difficult to put posters around town than it seems. This "wild posting" is controlled by a few companies in most cities. They lease the space from building owners and put up contracted posters themselves. If you put up your own posters on their sites (which are usually all the legal spots in town), they can and will track you down and at best have you fined.

If you are feeling adventurous, you could consider printing 18x24-inch posters to fit on electrical boxes à la street artists. I would recommend making a poster with a street-art feel and without anyone's name on it. As it is, the local law enforcement might track the poster back to you and fine you (this goes for stickers as well). Be cautious about this kind of guerrilla marketing.

PRINT MEDIA: 11x17 POSTERS

Print 11x17-inch mini posters for promotion and sale: $300 for 1,000. Stores can put these up much more readily than full-size posters. People like to buy them for their bedrooms as well, since they don't take up so much space. Since they are cheap, they make good giveaways, too.

PRINT MEDIA: POSTCARDS

Use online printers for your postcards — $130 for 5,000 is the approximate going rate. Make sure you pay attention to and include the shipping costs from the printer to you on all print media. You may pay a higher price using a printer that's closer to you, but that can be more than made up for in shipping costs.

While postcards are cheap and they are still great for festivals, they seem to be going out of style for basic street promotion. You need to make sure they are useful to your target market. Sklar (and many street marketers) do not give out a postcard before having a personal connection/conversation with the person receiving the card. Consequently, the postcard ends up serving as a reminder instead of an addition to the recycling bin.

If you have a film that relates to the club circuit, it might make sense to use old-school street teams. We actually spent a fair amount of money on street teams and, adding it all up, we could have afforded a decent social-network viral electronic street team that probably would have been more effective.

MEDIA BUYS AND PRINT ADS

Media buys are generally not affordable for independent filmmakers doing releases on their own. To make a difference in TV and radio, you usually have to spend millions of dollars. Unless you have a studio-level saturation campaign, it is unclear whether these buys have much of an effect. You would get much more bang for your buck by saturating the online space.

If you are doing a theatrical release in New York and Los Angeles and you have a conventional booking in a conventional theater, chances are that you will be required to buy some print ad space. It is usually best to have your low-cost graphic designer make a variety of different-size ads for you. The theaters can also make ads for you — but they will charge you.

In New York and L.A. there is usually a minimal print ad buy in your contract with the theater, starting at $2,000 and going up. Personally, I think tiny print ads are a waste of money, which in New York and L.A. is about all that $2,000 buys you — for one week.

However, in smaller markets you can get better rates and buy much larger ads for less money. Often theaters will have "co-op" ad rates, in which you share space with other films and take advantage of the theaters buying power. Thus, a few hundred dollars in San Francisco would get you a ¼ page . That might be worth it for the right film in the right paper. Larger ads do give you some awareness. More on co-op ads later, when we talk about partnerships.

TRAILERS

One of the benefits of a theatrical release is to have your trailer played in theaters repeatedly in the weeks leading up to your screening. Free advertising to a captive, potentially relevant audience. This trailer will need to be 35mm.

The least expensive way is to do a film transfer from a high-res digital output. If you shot on film, cutting and conforming a trailer from your negative will cost from $2000 to $5,000. This is probably out of your DIY budget. If you are on a budget, I recommend using a high-res copy of your digital trailer and having a lab print the 35mm copy, which costs approximately $1,200.

PROMOTIONS

Promotions involving some kind of merchandise are a great way to garner ticket sales or awareness. Here are some of the promotions we did for *Bomb It*:

- T-shirt and poster giveaways/contests on radio stations and websites. They talk about your film while giving away the product.

- DVD giveaways during PBS and NPR pledge drives. For the low cost of 10 to 20 DVDs, you get countless plugs. Often they will buy the DVDs wholesale if they want a lot of them.

- We had a limited number of silk-screened printed versions of our poster signed by artist Shepard Fairey. We raffled one off for each of the nighttime screenings on Friday and Saturday of our opening weekend at the Laemmle Theater in Los Angeles. We promoted this "raffle" on the web and at graffiti shops around town. Everyone who came to one of those screenings got a regular glossy full-size poster. This is the modern version of the dish giveaways that theaters started doing when television started taking away theatrical audiences in the 1950s.

PREMIERES & ADVANCE SCREENINGS

The primary purpose of an advance premiere screening is to get local press out to cover the event and the stars attending. This helps garner local television news and entertainment coverage. If you don't have big stars, a premiere is a waste of money since chances are the press will not show. Even Harris felt that the L.A. premiere for *Bottle Shock*, with an $8 million P&A, was a waste. However, they did one in Napa that was sponsored by a winery which helped raise awareness with their niche.

With a premiere, you are actually giving away potential ticket sales from your opening weekend. Premieres are also expensive to put on. Your limited resources are better spent elsewhere. If you do have one, have it on a Monday or Tuesday night so that the press has material to run before your opening on the weekend. It makes no sense to have a premiere on the Friday of your release, the press for which will then run on the following Tuesday.   The caveat to this is the festival premiere, which has many other benefits that a DIY premiere does not have in terms of promotion.   In addition the festival screening might be the only screening in that city.

Cast and Crew Screenings

I advise against cast and crew screenings if you are concerned about box office and expense. It will cost you to rent a theater and you will lose opening weekend ticket sales. Invite the cast and crew to buy a ticket, support the film and come celebrate one more time at opening night. It is usually good to then try to get a sponsored party afterwards as a bonus for the cast and crew. Also, if you have your DVD ready, this would be a good time to hand them out to your cast and crew. It saves you shipping and hassle and it feels like an even exchange if they buy a ticket to opening night. Also give everyone a poster. We did this for *Bomb It* and everyone loved being part of the sold-out event and seemed happy to get their DVD and poster.

Word-of-Mouth Screenings

These will most likely sap away your audience. They take a fair amount of coordination to set up with local colleges. Also, a free screening at a university can take away a paid college screening. The best of both worlds would be a paid college screening in advance of your theatrical.

⭐ Either way, you need to discuss your advance screening plans with your conventional theater. They may be more concerned about the lost ticket sales than you are and disallow it.

Press Screenings

The local theater will either provide one for free or at a reduced price. However, more and more journalists are watching films on DVD, obviating the need for a press screening.

PARTIES: PREMIERE AND OTHERWISE

Unless you are using them to create an event, parties can be expensive and can be of limited promotional value. I would only do one if your film appeals to people who would go to the party.

If you want to have one for your cast and crew, here are some ways to make it worth your while:

- Get the club to give you the space for free. Usually they will do this for a couple of hours (e.g., from 10 p.m. to 12 a.m.).

- Use a DJ from the local radio station for your party. He or she will sometimes promote your film and party on air. We were lucky enough to have Garth Trinidad and Jeremy Sole of KCRW deejay our L.A. premiere party.

- Find a liquor sponsor so you can offer free drinks.

- Try to get stars to attend. If your party has stars, you *might* get TV coverage.

ADVANCE EVENTS

Better than premiere or afterparties are advance events where you show trailers and do promotion for the film.

For *Bomb It*, we created a "party reel" that ran in the background at clubs and gallery openings or other existing non-film events in town. We then cobranded these events with the original promoter of the event. They were able to associate themselves with our film. We were able to get the word out about our film to our target demographic. We did five of these events before our L.A. screening. These are very effective.

For any social-issue film, consider a large fundraiser in the city on the Monday or Tuesday before a Friday-night opening. Try to get some stars concerned about the issue to attend to entice the press to cover it. Do this in conjunction with some of your organizational partners and have them handle the event organization and costs. You get an event to promote your film, the organization gets an event to raise money.

SPONSORSHIPS

Sponsorships are a great thing. The producer of *Better Living Through Circuitry*, Brian McNelis, raised over $25,000 for the P&A of that release through sponsorships.

Sponsorships take a long lead time. Sponsors generally are a corporation or other institution, and they determine their marketing budgets far in advance. For *Bomb It*, we established a number of sponsorship arrangements with All City NRG/Arizona Ice Tea, *URB* magazine and Fusicology — but I believe we could have had more with more time. McNelis has started talking to some of the sponsors in production. Note that the *URB* and Fusicology sponsorships were marketing partnerships — they emailed to their list and we posted banners for their site on our site.

There are sponsorship agents who can broker sponsorships for you. They sometimes work for a flat fee and sometimes on a percentage basis (up to 25 percent).

The Sponsorship Deck

To garner sponsorships, you will need a "deck". The sponsor deck is very similar to a business plan. In fact, you can readily modify your business plan into a sponsor deck. It should include:

- The film — short and long synopsis.

- The audience (demographic).

- What kind of sponsorship you are looking for — cash, goods and services, or both.

- Specifics of special events and promotions that the sponsor can be involved in and use for their brand awareness.

What you can provide the sponsor?

- Banner placement at the event.

- Product giveaways (swag bags and samples) — this gets their product into the hands of their target demo.

- Co-op ad opportunities — for instance, if you have a party, the sponsor might split an ad in a weekly paper with you, or they might pay for the ad to be associated with a movie that is relevant to their demographic.

- Logo placement on postcards that you distribute (a potential reason to print and distribute postcards).

- Pre-roll or post-roll ad space on your trailer or webisode.

- A piece of media that they can have exclusively for their website.

PARTNERS

Related to sponsors are partners. Whereas sponsors provide you with cash and services in exchange for promotion and placement, partners get more involved with the promotion in exchange for the brand awareness.   Here is an excellent hypothetical example provided by McInnis:

> You have a romantic comedy. You decide to have a speed-dating event in the lobby of the theater on the night of the premiere. You partner with a speed-dating service that hosts the event as a way to associate themselves with your film, thus heightening the awareness of their service in your demographic. They promote the event, thereby promoting your movie.

A sponsor, on the other hand, might buy 20 tickets to give away in exchange for awareness at the event. You have to put on the event, but the sponsor gives you cash.

The partner instead throws the event *and* promotes the event to your target demo. Much better than a little cash.

★ McInnis is big on getting value for value. If someone is offering the value of five extra tickets sold but the process is costing you 80 hours of work, that is not a proper exchange. Only create events and marketing relationships that will give you appropriate value for the time, effort, and money expended. You are in short supply of all of these things, so use them wisely.

A DIY APPROACH TO PUBLICITY AND MARKETING: THE RANGE LIFE TOUR

Sklar has based his approach to marketing on promotion for bands and musicians. Since it is so expensive and time-consuming to market a film, if you don't do it strategically, you won't get very far.

The Range Life marketing strategy has three primary elements:

1. A Strong Online Presence Utilize social networks and reach out to tastemaker blogs. In addition, get emails from your organizational partners whom you've set up in advance and send out a few thousand emails in each market. Range Life starts the local social network outreach two-and-a-half weeks before screening in a particular market.

2. Grassroots/Community Outreach On Site Range Life sends an advance team 10 days before arriving in a city to figure out how best to promote the tour in that city at that specific time. What events are going on that they can work with? The main team then arrives four days in advance and starts the person-to-person outreach. This involves going to local hot spots and continues through the end of the screenings. Three top outreach locales for Range Life:

- Coffee shops

- Sandwich shops: Make sandwich wrappers with your film's information and give them to the local shops to wrap the sandwiches in.

- Bars

Be creative in your giveaways — condoms are always good. Don't give away anything that can't fit in someone's pocket. If you have a gambling film, use poker chips. People always like stickers, but even those are getting old. Posters and postcards are overrated.

3. Utilizing Existing Campus Organizations and Structures for Marketing

- Contact student activities in advance.

- Go to relevant classes that relate to your niche.

- Work with what is already happening on campus. Events, fraternity parties, etc. Promote at those events, and give free tickets and/or merchandise away.

- Do workshops on campus — film schools are a natural — but be creative. Give a talk on narrative process to an English class.

Sklar's Marketing Tips

Tip 1: Market to someone who is going to like the film, but still let them feel like they are taking a risk and be excited about it.

Tip 2: Market to the most strategic people within your audience, the impassioned ones who will be word-of-mouth champions. It's not just about pure numbers.

Tip 3: Tailor everything to your audience. Examine what films are similar to yours and how they marketed to their audience.

Tip 4: Look at Trailers. What makes you want to see a movie? Do the same with film festival catalogs.

Tip 5: Don't have pre-screening parties. Afterparties are much better — they get people talking about the film, and give people an excuse to come.

Tip 6: Reach out and get marketing partners. Convey what could be in it for them.

Tip 7: Don't spend money on ads or too much time on conventional publicity.

Tip 8: Viral marketing is much more effective than reviews and conventional press, and takes much less time.

Tip 9: Use conventional press to reinvigorate your existing base. Get it to people so they care more about your film.

Tip 10: Link to reviews in your online promotion. This is more effective than putting up pull quotes.

Enough of all these tried-and-true conventional promotional tools. It's time to move on to the Wild West of web marketing.

CHAPTER 22

PUSHING CONTENT ON THE WEB

While the term *viral* is overused (and loathed by some web marketing people), it is still the term that best describes a piece of media taking off like wildfire on the Internet. Generally for something to go viral, it has to:

- Be something that people want to see and share with their friends.

- Get over a critical threshold.

THE ECONOMICS OF THE WEB

Di Minico observes that the web has become a combination of:

An exchange-based economy — you are trying to get something from the consumer; what are you providing them in return?

A self-promotion economy. Millions of people are putting themselves and their work and interests out into the world (which contributes to the clutter).

A referral economy (where sharing information is king).

How do you tap into these exchanges to promote your film?

Here are some of Di Minico's suggestions:

- Create content that is worth viewing recommending, tagging, etc..

- Look at your film's characters lives beyond the screen — the extra diegetic material I talked about in chapter 12 — what kind of original material can you create to extend their stories into the digital space?

- Integrate your media to create a convection effect - a creative loop that keeps your audience cycling through your various content.

- Control migration. Keep people reliant on your site to complete their experience. Embed as much material as possible; open a new page or pop up within your site instead of redirecting to another location. Invite your fans to contribute to your site/community in some way (uploads, comments, etc.).

- Don't lose your audience's trust.

- Have unique, downloadable content (aka digital swag) available to your audience, from mosaic posters to branded screensavers, etc.

- Build your audience using the most appropriate social tools. Being everywhere can often get you nowhere. Be smart and strategic.

CONTENT IS KING

Everyone I spoke to about Internet marketing emphasized that content is king. Content gives people a reason to follow you. And this content does not necessarily mean your film; it usually means the short clips that you create to promote your film, whether it's your trailer or other short content. These are more digestible than longer content. As Sklar points out, you should remember the behavioral aspects of the online audience. They will stay on your site for two to three minutes, tops (usually 30 seconds). If you can't give them everything in that time, you've lost them.

HOW TO PUSH YOUR CONTENT

What follows are some suggestions from Kate Christensen and Hung Nguyen for how to help push your content out to web. Both Christensen (one of *Bomb It*'s producers) and Nguyen work in the web marketing world and helped with the web campaign for *Bomb It*'s theatrical and DVD release.

1. Events matter.

It is hard to create an online event. Online is about the flow of information. If you have a live event-like a screening, it will give you something to organize your online campaign around. See chapter 17.

2. Momentum builds momentum.

On the Internet, success is the event. This is why the "viral" video or publicity is so important. When something gets a lot of hits, it feeds its own success, creating an event in and of itself.

3. Relationships matter.

Big media players parlay online media buys into coverage from the online world, just as been the case in offline publicity for years. PR firms have relationships with bloggers and favors are exchanged (the exchange economy). You can either hire a PR person so that you can use their relationships, or provide bloggers with something that will motivate them. Offer them a great piece of content (perhaps exclusive) to play. If it works out, you have provided an opportunity for that person to be a hero in the online world or in his company. Continue to cultivate and maintain that relationship. If they run your piece, email them and thank them. Send them a gift, a T-shirt.

4. Don't sell the movie — sell a piece of content.

In turn, the content will sell the film. The piece of content needs to be independent enough to be able to go viral, but close enough to the film to sell it.

5. Your email address and subject line are critical when pitching.

The only thing the recipients of your emails can see in their inbox is your email address and subject line. And they get hundreds or thousands of emails a day. Some pointers for making sure your email gets read:

- Don't email from a gmail address — it feels like spam and is amateurish. Invest in a good domain name that sells.

- The subject line should be creative and speak to the recipient's blog or something in the zeitgeist.

6. Use links to YouTube.

YouTube is a standard that everyone knows and has social options for sharing. Christensen and Nguyen recommend against embedding the trailer in an email into your email as file sizes can be too big. Don't annoy your audience with long load times or you'll lose them.

7. Be creative in pitching content.

Be a creative copywriter when writing your pitch. Short and creative. Something that will entice a click on the link.

8. The title of your clip is important.

Some guidelines:

- The title of the clip should *not* be the title of your film. Remember, it needs to stand alone from the film.

- The title should be funny, sexy, or intriguing.

- Don't be afraid to give away the content of the clip in the title — it might be what gets people to watch.

9. Expand your vertical.

Film blogs provide you access to only one audience, so broaden the targets you market to. For instance, with *Bomb It*, we targeted graffiti blogs, music blogs, urban gear blogs, art blogs, design blogs, etc.

10. Try to find the trendsetting blogs in your niche.

These blogs are the key influencers. If you have local events, invite local trendsetting bloggers and give them free stuff. Use web tools such as *Technorati* or *Alexa* to determine the relative popularity of a particular blog - and the size of its readership.

11. Energize your base and get them involved.

Ask questions. Make people feel that this is their movie. Motivate them to evangelize online for you.

12. When shooting your film, keep an eye out for web-worthy content.

Take note if a cast member has a funny bit or does something outrageous or inspiring.

13. Don't be precious with your footage.

Just get people to look at it.

14. Email people who have commented or blogged about your video.

Invite them to your premiere or offer a discount coupon/promotion for your DVD (e.g., DVD/poster combo).

15. Make people feel special.

The Internet is alienating. If you can target and connect with the right person, then you are helping your cause.

DIGITAL STREET TEAMS

Fancorps.com and fanrising.com are digital street teams that function similarly to conventional street teams, except that they work in the online arena as opposed to nightclubs. Neoflix is also setting up a digital street team for filmmakers.

With a digital street team, you can convert some of your more excited fans into digital street team members. They can earn points by how much work they do for you and your film. These points earn them swag and access to higher and higher levels of exclusive content. You can reward them with items listed in chapter 10, such as a chance to have a drink with you when your film comes to town, seats to the premiere, etc.

GOING PROFESSIONAL: HIRING WEB MARKETERS

Of course, you can hire people to do much of what we have just discussed. Because there is some proprietary technology that enables effective viral marketers to do their job, it can be worth hiring these people as part of your team. They also have relationships with bloggers, which they can use to your advantage.

Instead of paying a lot of money for web marketing, you can sometimes work out a creative solution, as we did for *Bomb It*. Christensen worked a deal with a group of web marketers who agreed to promote our clips as long as we put a post-roll ad for them on the clips. We timed this for the three weeks leading up to the DVD release. They then promoted the trailers to the relevant video bloggers around the Net. This campaign ran at the beginning of our DVD release, and we subsequently saw a definite spike in web activity and sales.

TIMING IS EVERYTHING

Finally, be measured about what you put on the web until you have a product to deliver. You don't want to peak too soon, or have the experience end in the online space. That's why we released the viral clips for *Bomb It* three weeks before the DVD release (not for the theatrical), since we wanted to support the sales of the DVDs, not the theatrical loss leader.

Snakes on a Plane is the primary industry example of a film's web buzz peaking too soon. They had an incredible online presence in the months leading up to the release and thought the film would be a huge hit. Unfortunately, the online experience didn't translate into a theatergoing experience. People had gotten all the experience they needed in the online world.

CHAPTER 23

DIRECT WEB MARKETING BASICS

You can push people to your site to act. But you must give them ways to act, otherwise you are wasting your marketing efforts.

ALTERING YOUR WEBSITE FOR SALES

Your website should already feature "calls to action" that enable people to sign up for your email list, become your Facebook friend, follow you on Twitter, "support" your film by making a donation, etc. When your film is ready to go to market, you need to set up other calls to action, such as the "Set Up a Screening" button that we previously discussed. Now is the time to set up "Buy the DVD" and "Download the Film." Marc Rosenbush, a filmmaker and guru on Internet marketing for filmmakers, states that the two main purposes of your website are:

1. To get people to buy your film or content.

2. To get them to give you their email address.

Rosenbush actually recommends placing a click-to-buy button on your website three times, in three different ways, on your home page. Take a look at the front page of his site for *Zen Noir*. Rosenbush suggests designing all of your web pages to convert visitors to buyers, and that your website as a whole should be primarily geared to this purpose (if this is your main intention).

How much you can apply the hard sell, though, depends on the type of film you have, the type of audience you have, and whether the purpose of your website/blog is strictly sales or if it's also for creating relationships with other organizations. Depending on your profile and purpose, you may want to take a softer approach.

However, take heed on his main point. That is, to make the website clear and simple for the viewer to take the action you want them to.

EMAIL MARKETING

Remember those emails you have been collecting? It is time to put them into action.

For live screenings, you want to remind people of the film and where the screenings are. This is why it's important to collect ZIP codes, so that you only email the people in areas where screenings are taking place. You don't want to bombard every member with every screening. In fact, you want to be cautious about overblasting your list in general. People will start deleting your messages and removing themselves from your list. Once a month seems to be a good frequency to send a blast, and you can step it up when things are really happening; just pull back when they are not.

Provide a way for people to buy advance tickets for screenings as discussed in chapter 17.

For the DVD, email fans with incentives to buy your film, such as coupons, special packages, autographed copies, etc. After our sales started slowing down in the nine months after the release, we created special packages of our products and promoted them to our email lists. Our sales surged dramatically. Check out the *Bomb It* store for current specials!

Rosenbush has a lot of great marketing suggestions to make both your email campaigns and landing pages more effective. If you want to know how his program works, just sign up for his mailing list and you will see how hard he works to get you to buy — it's very instructive.

ADVERTISING

There are a number of ways that you can buy advertising on the web. However, you need to be cautious about how you spend this money, because it can add up quickly. You will be paying a rate based on CPM (cost per thousand impressions). And remember, impressions don't guarantee clicks, and clicks don't guarantee sales. But if you are going to advertise, you can do so utilizing a variety of means:

★ Static Banner Ads

If you have spent any time at all on the Internet, you know what a banner ad is. You create a set of banner ads for your film in standard sizes, with eye-catching graphics and motivational copy so people click through. In addition to placing banners on websites, you can place banner ads in your emails. Here is a website that shows standard banner ad sizes: webpencil.com/bannersizes.php.

★ Flash Banners

The same as a static banners, but they have flash animation to make them more eye-catching (or annoying). Some people turn off flash advertising in their browsers, so these people won't be able to see your ad.

★ Text Ad

These are ads that employ only text. They are commonly used in emails or for search engine advertising programs.

★ Google AdWords

Google is the king of online advertising. Because Google is the most used search engine, your ads have the greatest potential audience in the open Internet. Google AdWords is very simple. You tell Google what keyword searches your ad should appear next to. In this way, you are only targeting people whom you think might be interested in your product. In addition, you pay Google only when someone clicks on your ad. Facebook has a similar program.

★ Conversion/Conversion Rate

To "convert" is to get a viewer to take a specific action, and how often your viewers take action is tracked as a conversion rate. For example, the number of people who click on your Google ad and then buy something from your store is measured as a conversion rate. The conversion rate is expressed as a percentage. Generally a conversion rate of 2 percent is considered very good. So for every 1,000 visitors to your site, 2 percent might click through to your store. Of those clicks, perhaps 2 percent might buy something. So, to get two buyers, you would need 10,000 visitors to your site. 10,000 visitors translates to 200 clicks to the store, and that results in two sales. As Rosenbush points out, this is a business of volume. You need to get massive amounts of people to your site or landing page. This also shows why you want to reduce the number of clicks that someone needs to make in order to buy your product. Each time you make someone click, it reduces the chance that they will follow through.

PICTURE 4 - *BOMB IT* LANDING PAGE

LANDING PAGES

A landing page is an intermediary page where you can send people after they click on any text link or ad. Landing pages are very helpful because you can create a more sales-oriented presentation for potential buyers than the one that might be on your website. From a sales perspective, the purpose of a landing page is to close the sale and to give the customer only one available action — to buy (or whatever else you want them to do). Even the most targeted film websites give people several options of actions on their homepages: join the email list, set up a screening, find out about the film. The potential buyer might get distracted. On your landing page, potential customers only get as distracted as you want.

You are hoping that many of the people who click through from ads or affiliate marketing are not aware of your film. Landing pages give these people just enough information about your film to convert them into customers. See Picture 4 for the *Bomb It* landing page — it has some quotes and, most importantly, the embedded trailer. I have also included the top portion of Rosenbush's *Zen Noir* landing page (Picture 5) as an alternative; it shows off a lot of his marketing ideas. You may even want to consider not having an embedded trailer on the landing page to avoid the time lag that comes with loading the trailer, since time is money on the Internet.

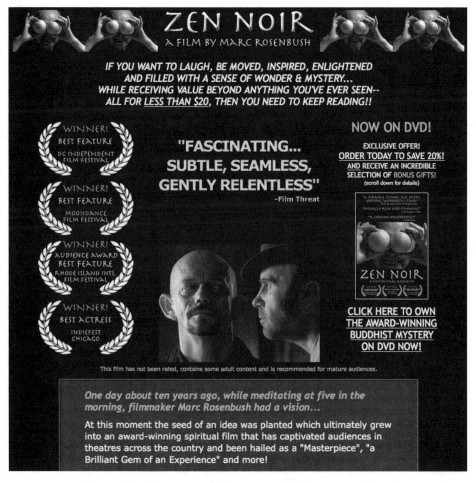

PICTURE 5 - ROSENBUSH'S *ZEN NOIR* LANDING PAGE

AFFILIATE MARKETING

Affiliate marketing is when you engage other people or organizations to promote your film (your affiliates) and they receive payment based on what people do in specific relation to your promotion. You can pay affiliates for impressions, clicks, or purchases. Most likely you will be giving an affiliate a percentage of any sale. It is a way to reward people to promote your film, whether by email blasts or links/ads on their website. The more attractive you make the program to the affiliates, the more they will push your film. I pay affiliates 20 percent of the any sale originating with them. There are many affiliate marketing programs on the web. Neoflix has their own affiliate marketing program called Indieclix, which is integrated into any web store you have with them. Here's how it works:

1. <u>Sign Up as a Merchant</u> As part of this process, you deposit money into your account so the affiliates can get paid.

2. <u>Program Creation</u> A "program" consists of the parameters by which you pay for web activities generated by your affiliates. You can offer the same program to many affiliates. For example, one program would give affiliates 20 percent of any sale from your web store.

3. <u>Upload Your Banner and/or Text Ads</u> You should create a variety of banner sizes so that your affiliates have a choice (most affiliates will only have certain sizes available on their sites). Indieclix will embed these banners/text links with the code needed for any activity to be credited to the affiliates.

4. <u>Invite Affiliates to Join</u> The affiliates must sign up on Indieclix, where they can get the codes to embed on their sites. These codes will have the banners automatically embedded in them and will track any activity from their promotion.

5. <u>Tracking Activity on Your Website</u> One way for you to check the effectiveness of your web marketing (from your website or blog) is to set yourself up as an affiliate. You set up this program to pay you pennies for clicks, sales, and impressions for the banners on your site. (Obviously you don't need to be paying yourself 20 percent for the sales you yourself generate.) You then sign up as an affiliate for this program and use that program's text links and banner ads on your site, and it will track the results.

Affiliate marketing is an important way to build relationships through-out the web and with supporting organizations. It is also a way to further advance the relationships that you have already created. To be honest, it doesn't result in a ton of sales, but it does allow for a way to reward partnerships and gives people incentive to raise awareness of your film. I offer our affiliate program to every blog or web magazine that writes a piece about us.

Some Web Marketing Definitions

Impression When a viewer comes into contact with your site or ad. They don't need to look at it (you can't *yet* monitor eye lines of web denizens). The ad just needs to appear on a page that the viewer has on his/her screen.

CPM Cost per thousand impressions. The amount you pay a website for 1,000 impressions of your ad placed on their site.

Click or Click-Through When someone clicks on an ad, taking them to either the sales portal or a landing page.

Click-Through Rate The average number of click-throughs per hundred ad impressions, expressed as a percentage.

Conversion/Conversion Rate To "convert" is to get a visitor to your site to do something specific — usually to click or buy. The conversion rate is expressed as a percentage.

Landing Page Sometimes known as a lead capture page, it is the page that appears when a potential customer clicks on an advertisement or a search-engine result link. The landing page gives more detail about the product offered with a controlled path to action/purchase.

Sale is what you want: a potential customer actually buying your DVD or other merchandise.

we should approach it from the point of view of making provoca- tive, mov- ing, cre- atively challenging work that also promotes the work itself.

CHAPTER 24

TRANSMEDIA, PART 2

I was torn about where to put the second chapter on transmedia.

I don't really love that it exists in the marketing and publicity section, since I feel that viewing transmedia as an just an avenue for marketing is limiting and contributes to the banality of many of the uses of the techniques.

But since most transmedia experiences to date have been used for promotion, I felt that this was acceptable for this edition of the book.

I feel that it is up to filmmakers to make transmedia as creative as possible. In the spirit of moving beyond the dualism of art and commerce, we should approach it from the point of view of making provocative, moving, creatively challenging work that also promotes the work itself.

When I teach the new models of distribution and marketing to my graduate students at CalArts, I hear a common complaint that many of the techniques work best for documentary filmmakers. They are constantly asking, "How do my narrative films fit into this model?" I think transmedia has tremendous potential for how narrative filmmakers can find new audiences and engage with them. Again, this is not just about marketing, it is about finding and engaging the audience for your film and your oeuvre.

TYPES OF MEDIA

Anything can be a storytelling device. Dena outlines some of the various media that can be used to engage your audience:

- Email

- Messages, either text or multimedia

- Live events

- Websites

- Social networks

- Google maps

- Mobisodes — episodes that you download onto your phone

- Games

- Pay phones

- Cakes

- T-shirts (Nine Inch Nails used tour T-shirts for their alternate reality game)

- Stickers

- Stencils

- Graphic novels

- Fictional characters in blogs

- Fictional newspapers and website

- Skywriting

- Billboards

- Flash media drives

- XML code

FRACTURED MARKETPLACE

Dena and Weiler both reference a fractured marketplace for media. Audiences don't consume media as they once did. They have their own preferences, whether it is a movie theater, DVR, their iPhone, Xbox console, etc. Audiences have media and art form preferences. You can't bend them, you must accommodate them.

Weiler feels that transmedia has the potential to create a virtual water cooler, because it allows people to be social around film. The interaction between viewers doesn't always have to be about the story — story is the point of engagement — but the audience might leave that at any moment and engage with each other in a personal way outside of the narrative.

PARTICIPATORY CULTURE

Weiler feels that social media tools can be used to extend the cinematic experience. Audiences want to participate with culture. By allowing them to participate, filmmakers open themselves up to a deeper relationship with their audiences.

He feels that obviously not all of your audience is going to engage in this way, but that there will be a devoted core who will. It is this core that you can turn to as advocates of your work, who by participating in the expanded experience you provide for them will actually become your distributors.

But more than that, these techniques also provide a way to engage with your audience throughout the creation of your piece. It can be a way to workshop your projects and make them stronger.

By allowing this participation to occur, it creates a longer life for the film or content. Part of the death of DVDs has been due to people realizing that they didn't need to watch a film more than once. Transmedia creates a life beyond the one viewing of a film.

SIMPLE FORMS OF PARTICIPATION

Transmedia does not have to be a lot of work. Weiler suggests that filmmakers not be so proprietary with their media. Give people assets — footage, sounds, environments. Let them re-edit your scenes. It doesn't take much to get started.

LANCE WEILER'S HOPE IS MISSING MIG

What follows is the article that Lance Weiler wrote for *Filmmaker* magazine about his Media Integrated Gameplay experience that he created to promote the VOD release of his film *Head Trauma*. I think it is such an excellent introduction to transmedia for independent filmmakers that I am reprinting it in its entirety with Lance's blessing:

"<u>The Evolution:</u> Over the last six months, I've been experimenting with a collision of gaming, movies, music and technology known as a MIG (media-integrated game play). The MIG is a way in which the audience can experience a story across multiple platforms and devices. Characters from a film interact directly with an audience via live encounters, phone calls, text messages and e-mails. These interactions lead to clues consisting of hidden media, sites, blogs and social networking pages, all of which extend the film's storyline and provide life for its characters beyond the screen.

The driving force behind my experimentation is my constant quest to reach audiences in new ways. The advent of DVRs (digital video recorders), portable media players and an increase in connectivity has enabled a new exchange of media that is social and places the power smack in the palm of the viewer. A rapidly expanding on-demand culture offers independent filmmakers new distribution outlets, modes of interaction, promotion and revenue streams.

<u>Beyond The Console</u> Often the term *gaming* conjures up the image of first-person shooters like *Halo*, or old-school console games like *Donkey Kong*. But the conventions of play are changing thanks in part to an emerging independent gaming movement.

From the ITVS-funded political ARG (alternate-reality game) *World Without Oil* to the controversial RPG (role-playing game) *Super Columbine Massacre*, games are tackling important social issues.

In other cases, ARGs and MMOGs (massively multiplayer online games) have become hot new promotional and advertising platforms for Madison Avenue and Hollywood. TV shows like *Lost* and *Heroes* have employed ARGs to expand the reach of their series beyond the set, and upcoming releases by J.J. Abrams (*Cloverfield*) and Christopher Nolan (*The Dark Knight*) are using ARGs to promote the films far in advance of the theatrical release.

When it comes to massive multiplayer online games, James Cameron and Steven Spielberg are creating whole worlds around their films complete with virtual currencies.

But the above are all studio-funded ventures. What can independent filmmakers gain from this convergence?

The Value *Hope is Missing* is a MIG that my company, Seize the Media, constructed to assist with the promotion of Warner Brothers' VOD (video-on-demand) release of my independent film, *Head Trauma*. At the heart of the MIG is the story of a young journalism student named Hope who returns home to find her mother exhibiting strange nocturnal behaviors. As she digs deeper she uncovers what is causing these behaviors, but before she can notify the authorities, she is abducted.

The narrative and game play are lead by Hope's fiancé, who is desperately searching for her. This storyline then begins to blend in elements of *Head Trauma* until the two become directly intertwined.

The *Hope is Missing* MIG consists of the following components:

MOBILE DRIVE-IN (mobmov.org screenings): Characters lead audience members to secret screening locations with phone calls and text messages. During screenings audience members can use their phones to interact with the film.

WEB SERIES: A four-part Web series is released weekly. In each episode a number of clues — "rabbit holes" — lead players to hidden media and sites across the Web.

REMIX: Through a collaboration with eyespot.com we built a special promotion that allows players to become contributors. As players remix media they unlock a series of hidden clues.

LIVE GAME BOARD: A map mash-up tracks elements of the game play and also holds a number of hidden clues.

MOBILE COMMUNICATION: Characters call and text audience members.

The *Hope is Missing MIG* was developed for less than $1,000. It started by crafting the game play and pitch. We built a pitch deck to convey our concept and then targeted outlets that could assist us with reaching a wider audience. To view a version of the *Hope is Missing* pitch deck visit workbookproject.com/mig.

In the end we assembled an impressive number of outlets and promotional partners: MySpace, Stage 6, Xbox, Eyespot, Twitter and Opera Mobile. This not only increased our reach but also created an effective national promotion for *Head Trauma*.

VOD releases tend to be fragmented due to the number of varying outlets. A unified promotional push can be difficult and costly. The MIG concept will allow us to reach an audience of more than 30 million people, and our promotional partners provided over $400,000 in placements across their networks and sites.

Once we had the commitment from the promotional partners we were able to leverage additional deals for the film and better placement within VOD catalogs. Over the coming months we will have a better understanding of the exact conversion rates of players to VOD purchases but we are seeing value from our efforts already.

New Streams Of Revenue The other element of a MIG that is exciting for independent filmmakers is that you can creatively build a game around your film, building and testing new storylines and properties in the process. For instance the *Hope is Missing* MIG has led to a number of high-level discussions about turning the concept into a fully funded, ongoing Web series.

After the *Head Trauma* cinema game experiments my whole focus around story has changed. I am now considering creating a world around each of my works — worlds that can cross devices, platforms and audiences. In fact, I have been writing game bibles (which overviews games and their rules) at the same time that I am scripting."

SECTION 4 CONCLUSION

While many independent filmmakers can readily tackle distribution, as in the delivery of their films to various outlets (much of this work is very similar to the daily grind of production), it is marketing that perhaps feels farther afield for most filmmakers.

My intention with this chapter was to somewhat demystify the process and to indicate a number of strategies available to you.

Again, each film is unique, and each will have its own marketing path, even more so than having a unique distribution path. You must find the most effective and cost-effective way to engage your audience.

Furthermore, we have only begun to see the potential of the web for marketing films. As new techniques evolve, I will post them on the website. If you are involved in a particularly exciting new form of marketing for films, please share that information with the rest of the film community, either on your own or via our website.

We will now proceed to one of the main ways in which filmmakers can apply the marketing techniques discussed in this section: *merchandise.*

Section 5

Merchandise

This section concerns the sale of hard-good consumer products: items that people can touch, hold in their hands, put on their wall, wear. As Dentler observes, people like to put things on their walls, shelves, and bodies that represent their lifestyle.

The most important merchandise for filmmakers to sell are their DVDs. We will address selling your DVDs through a distributor, selling DVDs on your own, and selling DVDs to the educational market.

Finally, we will spend some time with other forms of merchandise — posters, boxed sets, T-shirts, and soundtracks, to name a few.

CHAPTER 25

WORKING WITH A DVD DISTRIBUTOR

While sales of DVDs released by all content providers, studios included, are dropping at the moment, home video is still one of the most lucrative stages of a film's distribution.

People still respond to packaging, and the DVD is currently the only sales mechanism for films that includes packaging in the product. Hyams feels that you will sell a lot more DVDs through a distributor than off your website. They sold 80,000 units of *Super High Me* off of retail shelves. Only 600 were sold from their online store. I have had a similar experience with *Bomb It*, in which we have sold 9,000 units through Docurama but only 800 from our website. I do feel that we would have sold more DVDs through our website ws not handling the online sales and sales to brick-and-mortar stores, but I don't think we would have sold 10,000 units on our own.

Here are some reasons why distributors can be more effective than you in selling merchandise.

- Distributors have relationships with retailers and can push product to them. A good distributor will be talking up a product with a retailer for months. These are established relationships that individual filmmakers don't have.

- Distributors can also pay for placement on store shelves. Yes, this actually happens. With so much product and limited shelf space, much of that space goes to companies that pay.

- Similarly, a distributor has access to more online retailers than most filmmakers. Most filmmakers can get on Amazon and perhaps Barnes & Noble. But there are still many other web stores that people buy products from. It is helpful to get into those other retailers, because people buy from where they are used to buying.

- Even in the online world, you can pay retailers for where your product is placed for various search results. Does it come up on the top of a search for "graffiti" or on the second page?

Here are some reasons why brick and mortar stores are still effective at selling merchandise:

- People go to stores to purchase things. If they are in the store already, they are inclined to buy something. On the web they might be buying or not. The web provides many more opportunities for distraction than the store.

- Having an item on a store shelf allows the packaging to sell the product to them — this does not happen in the online space (or as effectively).

- People buy things where they are used to buying things either online or in brick and mortar. It takes extra effort for people to buy items from a new vendor, like your store.

Fortunately for filmmakers, there are still many DVD-only distributors who will take your DVD rights without taking any other rights. Before entering into an agreement with one, it is up to you to research whether or not these companies are reliable, trustworthy, and financially solvent. Ask people who have used them and ask your consultant and/or lawyer.

For *Bomb It*, we were lucky to garner a DVD-rights-only deal from Docurama/New Video. We had heard good things about Docurama's support of filmmakers — that they push their films and pay on time — so we proceeded with them.

CREATING A HYBRID RELATIONSHIP WITH A DISTRIBUTOR

When I partnered with Docurama/New Video, it did not mean I handed over my video master, sat back, and waited for the check. Any filmmaker who does that might be unpleasantly surprised when that check does arrive.

What I did was create a hybrid relationship with Docurama/New Video that allowed me to sell the DVD on my own from my website and to create the infrastructure and materials needed for me to sell my DVD worldwide myself.

I also coordinated all of my marketing with the DVD distributor and tailored my theatrical release to coincide with the DVD street date.

In order to proceed with such a strategy yourself, you need to integrate DVD sales into your overall release plan.

WORKING WITH A DVD DISTRIBUTION COMPANY

If you decide that you will benefit from a more traditional DVD distributor and a trustworthy one is interested in your film without demanding all other rights, here is what to negotiate for. None of these are unreasonable, so distributors should agree to these requests.

1. Advance vs. Better Terms

While the old way of thinking was to take any advance you could get, these days, advances are generally too low to make it worth your while to accept lesser terms. Put another way, it is more important to get better terms than to take a tiny advance. New Video offered us a $10,000 advance against a standard 50/50 profit split after all expenses. They agreed to cap expenses under this deal.

The other option was to take no advance, but take all the revenue after expenses, which would include a 25 percent distribution fee of gross sales for New Video. However, there would be no cap on expenses. New Video gave us spreadsheets indicating the monetary ramifications of each. Essentially, if we thought we would sell more than 10,000 DVDs, this second deal was better. We took it and have had no regrets.

2. The Right to Sell Your DVD From Your Own Web Store

This is a basic right. In general, the company will require you to buy the DVDs from them, but I have heard of the rare case in which they will let you sell your own version from your website. (This is very rare. Companies usually don't want competing products in the same market.)

3. Retain The Right to Sell DVDs at Your Public Appearances

Public appearances are one of the best places to sell since your audience is excited. They will want to share the film with their friends. Some theaters may have an issue with the DVD being available, but other theaters really won't care. If you are doing this, ask every venue where you are going to appear to supply someone to sell the DVDs for you at a little desk in the lobby. This allows you to focus on your Q&A and not worry about whether you were able to sell to the people leaving during your Q&A.

4. Negotiate a Reasonable Fee for Buying the DVD From Your Distributor

This should be no more than $5 and preferably less. And if you can, get them to kick in the "profit" from these sales into the general revenue pot. After all, you are selling the DVDs, and they only cost the distributor (at their bulk rates) $1 or less. (Currently, chances of getting the distributor to agree to this are slim, but as filmmakers, we should be pushing DVD companies to supply us with our DVDs at cost!)

5. Retain Access to DVD Authoring Materials

This depends on your deal. A distributor is more likely to allow this if you have a "costs off the top" deal because, in essence, you are already paying for the materials. Actually, any way you slice it, you are usually paying these expenses, so you should ask for it and receive it. This is important when you create your own international, multi-language, region-free NTSC DVD — it will save you time and money.

6. Encourage Your DVD Company to Create a Region-Free DVD

This will facilitate your ability to sell their version of your DVD in foreign territories and might obviate the need for you to re-author your film for the international market. If you don't have a large volume of foreign sales, making your domestic DVD foreign-compatible might be the most cost- and time-efficient method of creating DVDs for the foreign market.

The old way of looking at this is: The foreign sales company and the territories they sell to will be upset if the U.S. product is region-free. However, technology is making this issue moot. DVD players that can play region-encoded DVDs are becoming much more prevalent, and as a result, region coding is becoming obsolete. You can restrict sales to certain territories through your fulfillment company and through your distribution agreements. (There will always be some market bleed, in any case.) Explain to your home video distributor that region encoding doesn't benefit them; it only benefits the foreign territories.

7. Be Cautious as to What Digital Rights You Give to Your DVD Distributor

Some DVD companies like Docurama act as aggregators of content for iTunes and the like. Others do not, but want the rights anyway. Do some research and find out if the company really is an aggregator or not. If they are not an active aggregator, don't let them have your digital rights. If you let them have some digital rights, here are some tips:

Even rights within download-to-own should be carved out. For example, if your distributor aggregates to iTunes but no one else, only let them have the iTunes download to own rights. Try as hard as possible to only license non-exclusive rights. Non-exclusive is the name of the game at the moment, for digital rights anyway. Few entities can afford to or want to pay for exclusive digital rights, although I believe that this will start to change.

Argue for a different percentage of the digital rights than DVD revenues. DVD sales are a tough business and warrant a company taking 25 to 50 percent, depending on the deal. But when they aggregate digital rights, all they do is sell off the rights (plus a bit of encoding). Argue that digital rights are a 15 percent deal, or 25 percent max.

Retain the right to sell download-to-own and streams off your own website. Someone's going to offer it for free on YouTube or BitTorrent soon enough, so you might as well try to make a little money for it and offer a better-quality image.

GETTING PAID

Be prepared to wait for your money from DVD sales through a distributor, for a variety of reasons:

- First, when the current sales quarter closes, you usually wait up to 60 days for an accounting. And then you are only paid for the previous quarter 90 days after the close of the quarter.

- Second, there is a difference between "sales" and money collected. The distributor will only pay based on what is collected, and it can take them several quarters to collect from some retailers.

- Third, the distributor keeps a certain percentage of money for returns, or "holdback." Stores are allowed to return unsold merchandise within a set period of time. It is important to negotiate a low percentage rate of holdbacks, as well as the maximum length of time money can be held back.

I had a fit the first time I saw a statement from New Video. But I talked it through with my investor, who had been through this before, and he explained the process that I am now explaining to you. Since then we have started to be paid for the DVDs and we are getting happy.

NETFLIX

Netflix is a huge presence on the independent DVD scene. Filmmakers often try to get their friends to add their film to their queue to try to game the Netflix ordering system. The theory is that Netflix bases their orders partly on how many people have added the film in their queue.

Both Dentler and Hyams speak of the Netflix "halo effect": When a film is popular on Netflix's Watch Now program, it becomes more popular on DVD. The Watch Now program is subscription streaming, which is not and does not generally interfere with free streaming rights. Netflix members can watch certain films on their TVs via a set top box or on their computers. The idea is that people see it streaming and then want to buy it, or they tell their friends to buy it.

Dentler and Hyams point out that the Netflix rating system has real value for filmmakers. Higher-rated films translates into more views, rentals, and DVDs sold.

However, I have heard some complaints from filmmakers who have found their films on Netflix's queue without Netflix ever having bought DVDs from them. Hence you are in Netflix's system, people think they are participating in promoting your film by adding it to their queue, but Netflix has not and often will not purchase the film. In the meantime, the potential customer moves on to other films. Netflix adds films when they are added to the Internet Movie Database (IMDb), not when they purchase the films. One hopes that in the future, Netflix will only add films to their system that they intend to buy, or at least take films off their system when they have made a decision not to buy them.

Whether or not you work with a distributor, I presume you will be selling DVDS from your website. The next chapter should help you get started.

CHAPTER 26

DVD DIY

Whether you have a DVD company that you are working with or not, this chapter is designed to help you set up and maximize the DVDs that you sell on your own.

SELLING YOUR DVDS AS EARLY AS POSSIBLE

I recommend that you start selling your DVDs as soon as possible, as early as your festival run.

I understand why some people are still uncomfortable with this. The fear of selling your DVDs in advance of any potential sale is obvious: Video companies see that the film is in release and won't distribute it. I believe that is a false fear. First, any DVD company who is worried about your own personal sales is not worth making a deal with. Secondly, you can always fudge the truth and say the film is not in official release, and in a sense, that's true. Your distribution is not wide enough to be deemed a release in a distributor's eyes, so don't cop to it. You're just selling a few copies to ardent fans. Chances are that your efforts in home video marketing will, if anything, only boost the company's future sales.

Both of the documentaries *King Corn* and *Note by Note* had healthy DIY DVD sales before being picked up by Docurama. Docurama didn't care. They just required the filmmakers to stop selling it when the Docurama DVD (with extra features) came out.

The Bigger Issue Is This: Don't Wait for Distributors, Because They May or May Not Come

Selling Your DVDs During Your Festival Run

Live appearances are some of the best places to sell your DVD. If people love your film, they will want to buy one to show to their friends. As we have discussed, film festivals are the location of not just your first audiences, but of some of the most enthusiastic. Just as it might make sense to have your film available on VOD during its festival run, it makes as much sense to have your DVD available for sale during your festival run.

This DVD in no way needs to be the final DVD version of your film — this version can be a festival version, with no extra features.

Selling your DVDs day and date with your festival run will help you in a number of ways. First, you will make money at festivals and screenings right away. Some festivals will not let you do this; others will. But festivals can't stop you from selling DVDs at your parties or anywhere else. And as festivals start to realize that there is a new paradigm for an independent film's release, I believe they will realize their new place in the day-and-date window of DVD release.

During your festival run, you should consider setting up a store on your website and have the DVD for sale there as well. Because of the promotion of your film at the festival, people will be going to your website, and how great would it be to have something to sell them? However you might have an issue with your premiere festival, so be cautious about this. I would certainly be careful about having your DVD for sale in advance of your premiere festival. When in doubt you might ask your top festivals or at least suss it out.

One caveat to selling your DVDs from your website as soon as possible: You need to decide how to protect your educational sales, if those are an issue for you. We will address this in the next chapter.

SETTING UP YOUR FULFILLMENT COMPANY

When you are selling DVDs from your website, rarely are you actually selling them from "your" website. Nor are you shipping them out of your garage, with Gramps putting the stamps on and walking them to the post office. You're doing enough already releasing your own film without having to then deal with customer service and returns.

The sane alternative is to find a fulfillment company to do this work for you. A fulfillment company takes a percentage, but it is worth it. If you look on the web, you will find a number of types of fulfillment houses. Most of them are set up for big-volume customers. These larger houses don't set up your sales website (you still need to hire someone to do that). They often don't have customer service or credit card billing integrated (you will need to find that as well, or if they have it, you pay extra for that). These large houses will usually have a monthly minimum and don't make financial sense unless you plan to move tens of thousands of units (in which case, you are probably doing porn and don't really need this book).

There are, however, other filmmaker-friendly options that provide off-the-shelf web stores, where you can customize the look and feel of your store and plug in your merchandise. They handle customer service, billing, and fulfillment, and provide an accounting and check every month — all for the modest sum of 10 to 15 percent. A couple of top fulfillment companies are neoflix.com and breakthroughdistribution.com (they have an new arrangement with a fulfillment company). Another option would be to use a shopping cart such as E-junkie and link it with a fulfillment house that doesn't handle the shopping cart, such as youreeeka.com (mentioned in Chapter 34).

Fulfillment Company Comparison Check List

Here are some of the items that you should make sure your fulfillment company offers:

- A low percentage per transaction, with no hidden costs (e.g., "per pick").

- Low monthly fee.

- Low start-up fee.

- Low storage costs. Fulfillment companies charge you to store your merchandise — make sure this is as low as possible.

- Credit card billing included at no additional fee.

- Customer service included. You need to keep your customers happy. Speaking of those customers, a fulfillment company should provide you with your customer lists so that you are able to build your fan base. It is essential that your fulfillment company or e-commerce site provide this.

- Off-the-shelf web store templates that are easy for you to set up, match the look and feel of to your site, and modify so that you don't have to pay someone $1,000 to $2,000 or more to set this up for you. However, no matter what the off-the-shelf template looks like, you will still want to customize it and integrate it with your website. This can cost $500.

- The ability to have multiple products and separate them by category. For instance, if you don't have a distributor, you will want to have a variety of multipack DVD packages to sell wholesale in quantities of 10, 25, 50, and 100 preset on your store. You will also want to be able to sell t-shirts, books etc.

- Low shipping and handling fees. This is often a barrier to sales from your site, and when people can get free shipping from Amazon, it is an issue.

- The ability to use Amazon's checkout system. This allows customers to buy a product on your site, but enables them to use their already exiting Amazon account to pay for it. Often people would rather buy your product from Amazon not just because it can be cheaper, but, more importantly, because they don't have to give another online service all of their credit card and delivery information. By allowing people to use their Amazon account, you are removing this barrier to sales.

- The ability to sell your product on Amazon (let your fulfillment house deal with them), provided you don't have a DVD distributor who has an exclusive on Amazon.

- Timely sales reports, payment, and inventory, and a record of paying their clients. Do your research: Find out which other filmmakers are using the fulfillment company and contact those filmmakers before you commit.

- The ability and willingness to send merchandise for you without a sale. You can employ them to send DVDs and posters to theaters, festivals. They do charge for this.

- The ability to sell digital downloads of your film or stream your film.

- Marketing programs, such as an affiliate program, coupons, etc.

- An ability to grow with you and handle your specific needs. Since shipping is different for every international wholesale customer, this needs to be done manually for each order, not calculated automatically through the store.

AUTHORING YOUR DVD

If you don't have a DVD company that requires you to let them author your DVD, you will need to either do it yourself or have a professional house do it. Here are some things you need to keep in mind:

- Get quotes for the authoring. There are a number of reliable houses. Your fulfillment service might be able to provide you with someone.

- DIY. I found commercial authoring quotes pretty high. I then realized that two of my previous DVDs had been authored by former students and they turned out great *(Better Living Through Circuitry* and *SRL: 10 Years of Robotic Mayhem)*. Get an up-and-comer who knows DVD Studio Pro to do your authoring. If you have your HD master on hard drive, he or she can encode straight from that. However, the more complicated your DVD gets, the more time you may need. Our DIY PAL version of *Bomb It*, translated into seven languages with a stills photo gallery in addition to all the other extra features, has been quite a task.

- A caveat about DIY authoring: Encoding is becoming an art — how to keep your film looking its best while keeping the file size down. Smart encoders will bump the resolution of certain scenes to keep the look consistent. Get an experienced encoder, even if you DIY the authoring.

- Create your DVDs region-free. This will facilitate the sale of your own DVDs internationally.

- A note on multiple versions: Broderick recommends creating multiple versions, including a festival/theatrical version, a preview edition of the consumer DVD with no extras, a retail version of the consumer DVD with extras, and an educational version of the DVD with additional materials of curricular value not on the consumer DVD. However, you need to weigh this recommendation against your own ability to keep revisiting and working on your film. Certainly a "festival film only" version makes sense. Work out an agreement in advance with your authoring house so that you make one overall deal that allows you to come back to do more versions. They should cut you a break since you are not reinventing the wheel each time.

Handling Foreign Languages:

You may want to save subtitles for a later release on DVD, but if you are able, you may want to consider subtitling your film in its early DVD release so as to reduce the number of versions you need to create. Here are some tips:

* Dialogue and Subtitling Lists: Provide foreign film festivals with not just a dialogue list but an English subtitle list. Hence festivals will be translating for you line by line with the time code you will need for the subtitling document that you will later provide to your authoring house.

* The difference between a dialogue list and subtitle list is specificity. The latter has the time code for every time the image or line changes. The former is much more general and is hence less helpful. Doing this requires more work on the front end, but will save you time and money on the back end.

* Require as part of any foreign film festival deal that they provide you with not only the translation of the subtitle list, but also any files that they generate for the subtitling. You are looking specifically for .stl files or .son files. If these are not offered, try to get Final Cut Pro files, which you can later convert to .stl files with a piece of software. We obtained *Bomb It*'s Russian and Portuguese translations just by asking. We obtained our Spanish subtitles as part of a prearranged deal with a specific festival.

* As indicated in the chapter on delivery requirements, if you have subtitles in your film, you will probably want to create an intermediary, second textless version of the film: one that has all of the onscreen titles that you can live with *not* being translated into a foreign language but excluding any language subtitles. This will allow you to create a multi-language DVD without having to re-insert specialty titles and animations (don't forget to include all on-screen text in your subtitle lists).

Replication

As stated, there are two ways of manufacturing your DVDs: totally DIY (i.e., invest in a DVD duplicator and label printer), or hiring a professional house to replicate your DVDS. I recommend the latter. If you are going to sell DVDs at your festivals and screenings, you might consider having all of your early DVDs replicated.

Replicated DVDs as opposed to those *duplicated* on your computer will look nicer and be less likely to fail. And even if you have an intern or the people capacity to burn and label the hundreds of DVDs that you will need for festivals and press, at some point it will get to be a bit much and you will want to duplicate them professionally. DVD-to-DVD duplication can cost from $1.50 and up (not including case and cover). DVD replication *including* case and cover from a mastering house ranges from $1.25 to $1.50. In the end, you get more for your buck.

If you are going to do a lot of sales in Europe, you will need DVDs that are playable on their PAL standard. A few companies can actually produce your PAL DVDs in Europe and fulfill them from there, thereby making the shipping for your customers substantially cheaper.

DUPLICATION ON DEMAND

If you don't feel that you will use 1,000 DVDs — for instance, the film is an older title in your library — an alternative to replication is to set up duplication on demand. The most popular version of this is Amazon's CreateSpace, where filmmakers, writers, and musicians can have their DVDs, CDs, and books produced as orders come in. Lulu.com has a similar service as well.

Createspace

The advantage of CreateSpace is that you have the opportunity to be immediately listed on Amazon. As a print-on-demand company, CreateSpace manufactures and ships physical products when your customers order, eliminating the need for preexisting inventory.

When a sale of your title is made on amazon.com or your CreateSpace eStore page, CreateSpace will print a copy of your DVD and send it out. Here are some additional advantages:

- Printed with full-color, full-bleed, customizable disc and cover artwork

- Free UPC is assigned if you do not already own one

- Amazon.com orders may be eligible for Super Saver Shipping, One-Day Shipping, 1-Click® ordering, and Amazon Prime®. However, if your fulfillment house can sell through Amazon, your film will have the same advantages as these.

What You Pay

It's free to set up. You send them one authored DVD via FedEx and the artwork via email. Their share is calculated by taking a percentage of the list price plus a fixed charge. The fixed charge is $4.95 per unit, plus $2.50 per additional DVD in the same case (a case can hold up to four discs). The percentage of the list price varies depending on where each sale occurs. For your CreateSpace eStore, they take 15 percent, for amazon.com they take 45 percent.

For example, if you sold a DVD with a list price of $25 through a CreateSpace eStore, you would earn a royalty of $16.30. The calculation is as follows:

- List Price: $25.00

- Less Fixed Charge: $4.95 (one DVD-R in Amaray-style case)

- Percentage Share for eStore: $3.75 (15 percent of $25)

- Your Royalty: $16.30 (list price minus their share)

That is not a bad royalty for the sales that come from CreateSpace. However, if the sale is made on Amazon, the royalty is much less.

- List Price: $25.00

- Less Fixed Charge: $4.95 (one DVD-R in Amaray-style case)

- Percentage Share for eStore: $11.25 (45 percent of $25)

- Your Royalty: $ 8.80 (list price minus their share)

That is not such a good royalty. And in reality, the bulk of your sales will come from Amazon.

In addition, if you want DVDs for review or promotional copies, they will cost you $4.95 instead of approximately $1.25, which can add up if you are giving away a lot of copies.

As you can see, if you are doing small quantities, CreateSpace makes sense. If you are doing large quantities, it makes much more sense to invest in your own replication.

In sum, it is relatively easy to set up your own web store to handle your DVD sales through a fulfillment house. It's something every independent filmmaker should consider for their film, whether they have a distributor or not.

CHAPTER 27

EDUCATIONAL SALES

There is an established network of educational distributors as well as an emerging path of DIY educational sales. For most educational sales, you either need a documentary (one that deals with a specific educational subject area) or you need a narrative film that deals with said subject area in a manner that would provoke in-class discussion.

WHAT ARE EDUCATIONAL RIGHTS?

Educational rights traditionally include two types of rights: non-theatrical performance rights and purchases of the films/DVDs.

According to John Hoskyns-Abrahall from Bullfrog Films, one of the most highly regarded educational distributors in the country, 95 percent of educational sales comes from merchandise — the sale of a tape or DVD. It is typically sold as a license for the life of the piece of media. When the piece of media fails, the license ceases and another must be purchased.

The other 5 percent of their revenue comes from selling digital rights to educational institutions giving them the non-exclusive right to put a film on their server for on-demand streaming, plus rentals to colleges, public libraries, hospitals, prisons, and religious organizations where admission is not charged. Hoskyns-Abrahall notes that colleges and universities are by far the biggest sources of their revenue.

When a library or school purchases a life-of-copy license to use a tape or DVD, you can determine whether the film can be circulated out of the library, shared with other schools, and whether they can be screened for non-classroom, free public screenings.

Non-classroom screenings on college campuses, where admission is charged, becomes the domain of whoever controls the semi-theatrical rights.

WHAT CAN YOU CHARGE FOR EDUCATIONAL RIGHTS?

While prices vary, it is common to charge $85 to $295 or more for a one-screening rental.

Purchase of the DVD for classroom purposes and library usage can run from $50 for public libraries to $85/$95 for high schools to $295 for colleges and universities. If you are curious, visit the websites of some educational distributors.

Why are these prices so high? Alice Elliot from the New Day Films cooperative explains that libraries and educational institutions understand that paying this amount allows filmmakers who create niche content suited to the educational market to make a living and continue to produce these types of films. They understand that if they didn't pay this premium, these films would not be created. What a novel thought.

EDUCATIONAL DISTRIBUTORS

Some of the top names in the business are Bullfrog, Icarus, California Newsreel, and Cinema Guild.

These educational distributors tend to take 70 percent of sales. When I was first told this, I was shocked. But when you factor in how labor-intensive the educational market is, you begin to understand why they take 70 percent. Third World Newsreel, however, only takes 50 percent.

I have encountered a number of educational distributors who, in addition to wanting your educational rights and nontheatrical rights, also want your home video rights so that they can benefit from and control these rights.

The educational market is also beginning to go digital. Instructors desire access to titles on their school's online library in order to instantly screen films in class. These educational digital rights will need to be split off from the rest of your digital rights, if and when you make a deal with either a digital aggregator, digital distributor, or online site.

You should fight for the right to set up screenings through your website, and while you may not retain the right to non-theatrical college screenings, you should be able to request semi-theatrical college screenings as well as grassroots/community screenings.

I believe that many educational distributors are aware of the blurring of the alternative-theatrical rights market and will work with their filmmakers in parsing out these rights.

WHY IS AN EDUCATIONAL WINDOW IMPORTANT?

There is an exception in the copyright law that permits any legally bought DVD to be used for face-to-face instruction in the classroom. In other words, if your film is available for $24.95, it will be more difficult to get educational institutions to pay the higher price for the educational version.

However, home video DVDs may not be used by substitute teachers to fill up class time and cannot be used for assemblies. They are also not allowed to be circulated by the educational library. Many institutions do not want to police the usage of media on their campus and will buy an educational copy.

Most educational distributors will start off wanting a three-year educational window. A six-month educational window is considered very short. Many if not most educational distributors will not take your film if it has already been released on home video. I had this problem with *Bomb It*. We were approached by a couple of educational distributors, but they lost interest when they discovered that we had already released the film on home video.

I agree with Broderick that the three year window is very excessive for any title that has a potential popular home video market. He argues that home video only cuts down educational sales 30 to 40 percent. While this is a sizable chunk, it still leaves 60 to 70 percent, which is a substantial potential.

How long of a window you allow for educational rights depends on your film, how much value you feel it has in home video, and how much clout you have with an educational distributor who wants your rights. Some films have a lot of value on home video, and creating a very long educational window will hurt those sales.

However, Hoskyns-Abrahall points out that many films that are suited to the educational market do not have as much potential in the home video market. He feels that *all* filmmakers believe that their film will do well on home video, even if this is not the case. With the slumping home video market, it might make a lot of sense for you to allow for a longer educational window if your film warrants it.

PROTECTING EDUCATIONAL SALES WITH A SIMULTANEOUS HOME VIDEO RELEASE

Here are some other ways to reduce the bleed of your home-use-only DVD into the educational market:

- Create an enhanced honor system. Declare on your web store and on the DVD packaging that the DVD is licensed for home use only. Offer educational versions and/or educational licenses on your website. (See bombitstore.com for an example.)

- Prevent the DVD from being played from the beginning without a warning stating that the version is for home use only and no public or educational screenings are permitted. I got this tip from Robert Bahar, who did it for his film *Made in LA* (madein-la.com). He did a simultaneous home video and educational release with California Newsreel.

- Offer a special educational instructional disc when schools or institutions buy the film from you. Although this will not convince educational distributors to take you on after your home video release, it may convince some to buy it from you instead of from Amazon.

SPECIAL FEATURES FOR AN EDUCATIONAL DVD

Here are some features that can add value to your film in the educational market (however, Hoskyns-Abrahall emphasizes that it is the quality of the film itself that is the ultimate determinant of success in the educational market):

- Closed Captioning Departments of Education in several states include the hearing impaired as a group requiring equal access and as a result require closed captioning. This might be something to leave off your home video and put on your educational

DVD; however, it can cost approximately $600-$2000.

- <u>Chapterization</u> You might consider putting chapter markers at intervals not much longer than 5 minutes apart. This helps teachers use specific sections from your film in the course of instruction.

- <u>Study Guide</u> This consists of suggested discussion topics and/or questions. It can be a pamphlet or PDF in the extra features of the DVD. Hoskyns-Abrahall suggests not spending a lot of time or money on this unless you have secured a budget for it. I have also heard that colleges and universities tend not to use study guides, but that they are used by high school teachers. Hence, how much time you spend on the study guide may be related to what age group your film is most suited for.

- <u>Special Sections</u> In addition to chapterization, you may want to have some sections of the film separated in the extra features to tie into the study guide/discussion topics. Better still would be to provide extended sections where additional material is included with the section from the film. These are often called thematic modules.

APPROACHING AN EDUCATIONAL DISTRIBUTOR

Here is Hoskyns-Abrahall's advice to filmmakers on how to approach an educational distributor:

- The best films for the educational market are documentaries and for K-12 schools, animation.

- You should know what you are talking about and have your act together before contacting them. This means being able to specify which disciplines your film is relevant in the educational market.

- Know what types of thematic modules and teacher's guides might be suitable for your film.

- Use a clip of the film and still photos to sell your film, not just a trailer. Even the first three minutes of the film can work.

- Send an email, don't call — although this depends on how hot your film is.

NEW DAY FILMS AND EDUCATIONAL COOPERATIVES

New Day Films is a high-functioning cooperative that is composed of filmmakers each selling their own films to the educational market. I applied to New Day Films myself for *Bomb It*, and they would have taken me in had I not already released my film on home video. They felt this prior release would cause me to be disappointed with my educational sales.

Alice Elliot was the representative from New Day Films who interviewed me regarding my participation in the cooperative. She can be reached via email at director@welcomechange.org.

The benefit of an educational cooperative is that you share the workload of distributing your film with other filmmakers, yet keep nearly all of the revenue of your film. The revenue you keep can range from 70 to 95 percent of your gross sales, as opposed to 30 percent with a traditional educational distributor.

I am going to spend a little extra time describing how New Day Films works because, as I have said, I think distribution cooperatives have a lot of potential for independent film. New Day Films is actually creating a kit on how to form and run a cooperative, to sell to other potential cooperatives. This might be a great way to start your own distribution cooperative with some friends.

How New Day Films Works

New Day Films has 60 active members and holds two semi-annual meetings that members are required to attend and prepare for.

Each participating filmmaker needs to choose one area in which they will contribute labor to the organization. These fields include website maintenance, email supervision, acquisitions, and recruiting, and usually consists of a total of one week's worth of work a year. However, you don't do any work for the first six months after joining the cooperative, since New Day wants you to have time to launch your film and start making money.

Besides contributing work, you also contribute a portion of your earnings in the form of shares (which are also excused for the first six months). These shares are pro-rated by your gross sales relative to the cooperative gross.

You must apply to New Day Films. Alice first vets your film and personality. Regarding your film, they want to make sure that it has educational content, preferably related to social action, and that it will support the collection (e.g., provide something that is lacking or complementary to other films). Regarding the filmmaker, they want to make sure that you are someone whom they want to work with (e.g., that you have your shit together and are not overly needy, for instance calling repeatedly with endless questions whose answers can easily be researched). Even if you have a collection of films, they will only look at and take on one film at a time. Your application is voted on by the membership.

After acceptance, you get a "Topic Buddy/Launch Coach" who helps you start the educational distribution of your film. You have this coach for the first six months. You also get a sales list of proven buyers of similar films in the cooperative. The cooperative has an email czar to make sure that the group is not sending out too many emails to the same customers.

Filmmakers within the cooperative who share subject areas will share lists and often create master subject area lists.

With your lists, you approach potential buyers with an email and postcard campaign. Based on the cooperative's experience, buyers like to be approached in multiple ways. Phone calls are actually not as productive as email, postcards, and brochures. As for brochures, the cooperative feels that they are expensive and not necessary, unless you have many films to include in the brochure that would appeal to the same group of buyers. Eventually I might do a brochure for *Bomb It* and my Survival Research Laboratories films, since they would both appeal to art departments.

They encourage films in which their target niche has an annual conference, to go to these conferences in order to network and make presentations.

They also attend the American Library Association meetings every summer as well as the NACA conventions mentioned earlier in Chapter 18.

New Day Films works with their own fulfillment house, which ships the DVDs and keeps track of sales, sending a check and report every month to each individual filmmaker.

DIY EDUCATIONAL

You may decide to handle the educational sales yourself, if you feel that you can do as good a job on your own and don't want to relinquish the 70 percent to a distributor, or if you have not been approached by a distributor, or if you have not been accepted into a cooperative.

You should know that doing educational DIY can be very time-consuming, since you are doing all of the work outlined above, but by yourself, without a coach or *proven* email lists.

Here are some ways to contact departments and individuals who may be interested in buying your film:

- Utilize the help of a relevant interest group to reach out to their educational members. This hopefully is an organization that you have been in touch with since prep or production.

- Buy a list of relevant mail and email addresses of departments and educators from a company that sells them. Alice suggests Market Data Retrieval (MDR) at schooldata.com. The problem with buying lists is that you don't know if the people listed have a record of buying educational DVDs, or how up-to-date the information is. In addition, the lists are rather expensive. But these lists might be your only source of information, besides painstakingly going through department listings of universities around the country.

- Use an email and postcard campaign to sell your film.

- Use the similar outreach techniques described previously for grassroots and community screening campaigns. Many of these techniques apply, such as utilizing ListSERVs.

ALICE ELLIOT'S SUGGESTIONS FOR A DIY EDUCTIONAL RELEASE

In addition to many of the other items we have discussed in this book, such as having good key art, reaching out to affinity groups, and getting email addresses at every screening and event, Alice suggests the following tips specifically for the educational market:

★ Alice Elliot's Do's:

- On your promotional material, have quotes from the right people in the field who like your film. Be strategic if your topic is controversial.

- Get reviewed in educational journals, both in print and online. Ask your organizational partners what they read.

- Screen at conferences and conventions. Try for plenary sessions, kickoff speaker, or lunchtime slots.

- If you are going to a conference, ask if you can have one of your postcards placed in each of the conference packets.

- Do a newsletter about topics in the field: pending legislation, outstanding achievements, and other films or media. Be a trusted resource.

- Craft good sales emails with carefully constructed topic lines. Read about direct mail techniques.

- Share information with fellow filmmakers.

- Let people know your mission.

- Let your customers know where to find you. Stay with your film.

★ Alice Elliot's Don'ts:

- Don't be afraid to charge money for your film.

- Don't be embarrassed to ask about details with a distributor.

- Don't undervalue your work and time.

- Don't give up.

- Don't think you can't do this or that it will take too much time away from your filmmaking.

> A final thought from Alice: "Educational distribution can be the most satisfying and financially rewarding part of your filmmaking experience."

Remember, that merchandise can be points of entry for films or narrative extensions - so they can be important to a transmedia strategy.

CHAPTER 28

MERCHANDISING

There is a whole range of products that visual media content creators can produce to sell on their websites and in stores.

Filmmakers can look to musicians to see how they have expanded the types of products they market to support their careers and brand, from T-shirts to boxed sets. To get a sense of what is possible for filmmakers, check out the Rooster Teeth store. These are the people behind *Red vs. Blue*, the Halo Machina film. On their site, they not only have their upcoming DVD, but also a boxed set of *Red vs. Blue*, plus T-shirts, hoodies, posters, books, and music. You can also, of course, take a look at bombitstore.com to see our collection of T-shirts, DVDs, stickers, posters, and books.

I also recommend going to the Nine Inch Nails site because it shows what the future might be for popular filmmakers and filmmaker brands. They offer a plethora of ways for their fans to engage with them, both live and on the web. They have their own social network, updates from their tours, a place for fans to remix NIN music, and tons of merchandise. You may think, "Well, this is unrealistic. NIN is a hugely popular group and no way can this translate to independent filmmakers." I say you are just limiting your thinking. Look at the millions of hits and fans some media content creators already have on YouTube — why can't they do a portion of what NIN is doing to monetize their brand? If you have ardent fans, you are doing them and yourself a disservice by not providing them product.

Remember, that merchandise can be points of entry for films or narrative extensions – so they can be important to a transmedia strategy.

DVDS

We've discussed different content editions of your DVDs already, but now I would like to address packaging. Most filmmakers produce their DVDs in the cheapest way possible, in a black plastic case with a full-color insert. For filmmakers with a growing fan base, it might make a lot of sense to create collectors' editions of your films, something akin to the Criterion Collection. Nine Inch Nails has been a pioneer in this model, creating different pricing structures for different versions of their CDs. They seem to have realized that, in order for consumers to buy a media product, you cannot just sell the digital content. You have to create an interesting package that fans really want to engage with as a physical product.

The best example of NIN multiplexed product can be found at ghosts.nin.com/main/order_options. You will see the following options:

- A free download of nine tracks in a DRM free format, plus a downloadable PDF.

- A $5 download of all 36 tracks in a variety of digital formats, including a 40-page PDF.

- A $10, two-CD set in a six-panel Digipak with a 16-page booklet (That's a lot of product for only $10, and includes digital downloads as well.).

- A $75 Deluxe Edition Package: A hardcover fabric slipcase containing two audio CDs, one data DVD with all 36 tracks in multitrack format, and a Blu-ray disc with *Ghosts I-IV* in high-definition 96/24 stereo and a second book of photographs.

- A $300 Ultra-Deluxe Limited Edition Package (only 2500 produced and numbered), which includes everything in the Deluxe Edition pack, plus two additional books, one containing 48 pages of photos inspired by the music, and the other containing two selected photos as art prints.

Eventually there will be a six-DVD boxed set of *Bomb It* — with a full-color booklet to go with it! I have to start thinking about a deluxe collectors' edition, with one book of the six DVDs and another book of photos to go with it. Perhaps I'll do it when I retire!

PACKAGES

One of the advantages of producing your own merchandise is that you can offer it together with your DVD as exclusive packages. This provides motivation for people to go the extra mile (or few minutes that might feel like a mile to them) to buy the DVD from you instead of from Amazon. I would suggest offering the DVD on your site at the same price as Amazon's or less (but including a poster, or T-shirt, or something else) and talking to your fulfillment company about a special shipping-and-handling combined rate for this product. This serves several functions:

- It motivates people to buy the DVD as opposed to download-ing it for free somewhere else.

- Assuming they are going to buy it instead of download it, your profit margin is higher from your site.

- You get customer information from your fulfillment company so that you can promote other specials and future films to them. Amazon and other merchants will not give you this informa-tion.

SIGNED MERCHANDISE

Some of your ardent fans and supporters will want signed merchan-dise. Posters and DVDs work best for this. DVDs take a little plan-ning. Ask your DVD replicator to give you a stack of cover inserts before final packaging. You then sign them and give them back to the replicator; they then insert those signed covers into packaging and seal them. This saves you the hassle of opening up each DVD, signing them and then having someone re-shrink-wrap them. Don't sign the DVD itself; the ink has the potential to eat through the label and then interfere with the media.

SOUNDTRACKS

Soundtracks can actually be a bit of a hassle because of the sound-track royalty clause in your music clearances. Most music clearanc-es have a soundtrack clause that provides for a pro rata share of a small percentage of the retail price of the soundtrack. However, the market for soundtracks is relatively slim, and this combined share of royalties can actually add up. I was told by a small distributor that it can actually be a fair sum and ultimately cost more than you make from the sale of the actual CDs. Further, you still have to pay the royalty, even if you give the CD away for "free" in your DVD or on your website. This small distributor recommended using a flat buy-out clause instead of a royalty for the soundtrack rights. However, even if you pay $50 a "side," in actuality that is $100 for each track (each source cue requires two contracts — master and sync). For 16 tracks, that's $1,600. Not a lot, but considering the sales, per-haps not something you are going to recoup. Depending on your relationship with your musicians, of course, you can offer less. But if you are already begging for free music, it can be a stretch to ask for a $10 soundtrack buyout as well. It never hurts to ask. An alternative is to leave the soundtrack clause out of the licensing agreement initially and put in a clause that a buyout will be negotiated in good faith at a later date. Consult your lawyer. Consider what works best for your particular film.

If your music is composed, or even if half of your soundtrack is composed, and if you used a work-for-hire composer agreement, normally you will have the soundtrack rights included in those contracts for no extra money.

Digital Downloads

Instead of offering hard CD soundtracks, offer the music as a digital download from your site. You still have to pay royalties, however.

Extra Benefits of Music

Those caveats aside, there are some extra benefits of releasing music. Primarily, it gives you another way to promote your film. If your music and your audience align, then it can make a lot of sense to promote the music separately on your website and to potentially publish it in some form. Studios will usually release the soundtracks of movies in advance of the theatrical release as a way of building word of mouth and an audience. With enough planning and strategy, this might make sense for youth-oriented films.

GAMES

If sold as a piece of physical merchandise, games count here as well. While most independent filmmakers would think that games are out of their reach, Weiler is very involved in making game creation accessible to all. It is as much a part of his DIY Days as film. Again, you are only limited by your creativity.

GRAPHIC NOVELS & BOOKS

You can self publish these, just as you can self publish DVDs. Create Space and Lulu can print these on demand so the start up cost does not need to be very high. The book you are reading is self published – of course. If you think film royalties are bad, you should take a look at the publishing world.

TOYS

Are also not outside the realm for independents. Just on the verge of accessibility are 3D printers that will actually print objects on demand.

POSTERS

If you have a lot of posters leftover from your theatrical, sell them, of course. But you can also use them for promotions and giveaways, since they were cheap to produce. You can also sign them — signatures traditionally go on the bottom edge for the collectors' market.

If you have a particularly special piece of key art, as was the case with *Bomb It* (Shepard Fairey, who is in the movie, did the design), you might want to consider printing some of your posters on linen stock. The linen stock will produce a much nicer product that you can then sell at a higher price. We created signed (by me) and un-signed versions in a limited edition and added them to the store. We promoted these posters to the Shepard Fairey collector sites and sold quite a few. You can also produce a silk-screened version of the poster in even smaller quantities. We have 50 of these numbered and signed by Shepard and myself waiting to be sold.

T-SHIRTS

You should have a small quantity of T-shirts produced at least for use as web and radio promotion giveaways, as well as for thank-you gifts. Unless you have a large fan base, I don't recommend doing more than one T-shirt. They can take a lot of extra money and hassle, especially if you go for nicer shirts and printing methods, like we did.

The simplest route for printing them yourself is to use a local printer who prints with oil-based ink and has nice shirt blanks in stock to choose from. You can get T-shirts for about $5 each in this manner

— including printing and shirt. These are the ones you want to be using for your promotions. You can print some extra ones and have them available on your website.

You will need your graphic designer to modify your key art or create a new design, usually in a color-separated Adobe Illustrator file so that the printer can create color-separated films. Note that each additional color you print in will cost extra. Printers charge extra for the additional screen (about $50 flat) and per-shirt printing.

I suggest using a local printer if possible, because:

- T-shirts are heavy and the shipping can get expensive. Since you probably don't live close to your fulfillment warehouse, you need to decide if most of the shirts will be housed and shipped to there or at your office.

- If you are doing anything beyond the basics, you might want to discuss colors and printing methods with the printer.

Beyond T-shirt Basics

Beyond a simple design on a simple shirt using oil-based ink, you can get into various extras to make a better T-shirt product:

Use higher-quality T-shirt blanks. Many printers now stock American Apparel. I also recommend Alternative Apparel. You will pay up to two times more per shirt, but you might be able to charge more for these shirts than the basic shirts. You might also want to consider organic cotton, if you think it is something your audience would want.

Use water-based ink instead of oil-based ink. This will give you that faded-shirt look with a much softer feel. It is also more expensive. The screens are more expensive, up to two times more. And the printing is more expensive as well, per ink.

OTHER FABRIC PRINTING

Your T-shirt printer can also silk-screen any type of fabric, including hoodies, sweatpants, hats, messenger bags, etc. You can also find a separate company to stitch your hats instead of silk-screening them, which looks much nicer.

ON DEMAND PRINTING AND MANUFACTURE

The easiest way to produce T-shirts is to have them printed on demand through one of the many online T-shirt printing and fulfillment houses. The most popular one is Café Press, where you can upload your design and have it applied to any merchandise of your choosing, including shirts. You direct people to their site to buy your merchandise and then you receive a royalty check. Just as with DVDs, though, when someone else handles the vertical integration of manufacture through fulfillment, they take a bigger piece of the pie. As a result, your per-item profit is less than it would be if you did it on your own.

Regarding how much effort you put into a product in order to reap the highest return: The difference between DVDs and other merchandise is that DVDs are your core business; the other merchandise is not. You might not want to get distracted with the production of merchandise. In addition, just like DVDs, if you do not think that you are going to sell a large quantity of this other merchandise, it might be better for you to have it manufactured on demand and available for people to buy than to not have it available at all.

MISCELLANEOUS OBJECTS

Besides DVDs, T-shirts, and posters, there are a plethora of other products that you can create, from mousepads to laptop skins to mugs to buttons. Think of something that specifically relates to your film and produce that item. It makes the most sense to create these products through Café Press or a similar site, unless your brand has exploded. A note on iPod skins and laptop skins: These are very cool and a great way to promote your film. However, the sizes change rapidly and there are so many different computers and iPods out there that it might be hard to keep up economically.

WHAT DOES YOUR AUDIENCE BUY?

Before scrambling out to make a bunch of consumer products for your audience, you should consider what your audience purchases. Perhaps they don't wear hoodies and prefer trucker hats to baseball caps. Try to be in tune with your consumers and provide them with what they want, or what you can make them feel they need.

Section 6
Digital Rights

CHAPTER 29

REDEFINING DIGITAL RIGHTS

Two simultaneous events got me thinking about the nature of television and digital rights.

The first: I read about the next generation of televisions that are on the horizon (LG already offers one), which allow you to plug the Internet directly into a TV without an Apple TV, Roku box, or similar interface. By 2010, many more TVs will have this capability. I am already able to view my Netflix Watch Now queue on my TV via my son's Xbox.

The second: While negotiating one of my digital rights contracts, I was put into a situation of juggling my television rights in various territories for the digital rights acquisition.

I came to the following conclusions:

TELEVISION AND CABLE ARE DIGITAL RIGHTS.

DIGITAL RIGHTS ARE SLOWLY INVADING THE REALM OF CONVENTIONAL TELEVISION AND CABLE.

Put another way:

The television is just one viewing platform for digital rights. Cable is just one delivery system for digital rights. Many free streaming channels are building themselves as television channels for the future.

What is television? According to Shwarzstein, it's "a device that sits in your house that plays images in a rectangular frame."

In other words, it is a way to view content.

What is cable? Cable is a piece of wire that is used to deliver content.

Weiler puts digital rights into a different perspective. Digital-rights content can either be viewed via a:

- Computer with content commonly delivered through the Internet.
- A freestanding box in your house; usually, a television. This box receives signals through over-the-air broadcast, cable, or the Internet (via various devices like Xbox, PlayStation, Roku, Apple TV, etc.).

It's muddy territory. Filmmakers have to be very careful about how they handle their digital rights.

THE DIGITAL RIGHTS MINEFIELD

Filmmakers are given conflicting advice on their digital rights. Some people advise that giving your film away for free on the Internet creates awareness and leads to other sales.

Other people recommend that filmmakers hold onto every single digital right for fear of lost opportunity. It depends on the film, filmmaker, market, and audience for that film.

There are two certainties.

1. Companies buying your rights, whether digital, cable, home video, domestic or foreign, will try to get as many of your rights as they can, whether or not they have the ability to exploit those rights.

2. Little by little, television/cable/digital rights are competing for one another's business.

Filmmaker, be warned.

The television/cable/VOD/digital rights are all specified separately in contracts. Not only will this continue, but it will become even more specifically defined.

It is important that filmmakers see how the ways of monetizing their films might come into conflict with one another; or more optimistically, might work in collaboration with one another.

★ The Minefield

Digital rights need to be considered in conjunction with the following other rights (because distributors and channels will try to obtain these rights simultaneously): home video, television/cable, digital, and foreign.

It is a minefield because one ever so slight misstep can blow up in your face: deals cancelled, people pissed, money down the drain. I speak of what I know. It's not fun. But you can survive and even come out with more than you thought you could get (perhaps you'll lose a finger or hand but you'll make it through alive).

Jon Sloss, one of the premiere lawyers working in the independent film world for many years as well as the founder of independent film sales powerhouse Cinetic, believes that companies are omnivorous by nature — they ask for as many rights as possible.

I feel that it is worth looking at the probable reasons why companies want as many of your rights as possible:

- They are accustomed to obtaining these rights through tradition. Some foreign TV stations have no avenue to exploit digital rights and have no concern about competition. They just want the rights because that is part of their package on all their contracts. In other words, habit.

- They don't want to miss out on a potential revenue stream, even though they have nothing in place now to exploit it. In other words, fear.

- They are concerned about direct competition in their platforms from digital rights. This is a growing concern among cable operators. More fear.

- In the case of foreign sales agents, they want digital rights in their contracts because they feel that they need them to sell foreign television (or don't want to be bothered to ask). In other words, covering their ass (CYA).

- In the rare case, companies asking for digital rights actually have distribution channels with which to monetize these rights. For instance, a number of home video companies are now digital content aggregators.

The latter reason, in my opinion, is the only reason that is valid and that you can work with. For the other reasons, you need to fight to retain your rights. Fortunately, Sloss and Broderick and a few others have already been fighting for your rights. They have been able to establish a lot of precedent.

It is up to filmmakers to continue this fight.

An argument might be made that cable/television/digital platforms have a right to be concerned about competition from other platforms. I have two responses to this:

1. People are creatures of habit. As Dentler notes, they tend to get information and entertainment from trusted sources. Only the most technically minded consumers scour all available platforms on the Internet looking for media. Most consumers continue to buy from the sources they know.

Orly Ravid has worked in various areas of the film industry for 10 years, from festival programming to development to acquisitions and distribution, and is now the co-president of the marketing and distribution company New American Vision. Ravid argues that the Internet world is similar to the retail world. Just as many different retail stores can carry the same product, many different platforms can carry the same film.

2. If a company wants to control any of your rights exclusively, it should pay for that right. Continuing Ravid's analogy, certain brick-and-mortar stores do pay a premium for the exclusive rights for certain brands. If someone wants your rights exclusively, they should pay a similar premium for that privilege.

In dealing with a platform wanting a larger share of your digital rights (television/cable or Internet), you need to determine:

- What is the real desire of the entity requesting the rights?

- What is their real capability of monetizing those rights?

- What they are offering you to take those rights off the table (in order to mitigate their fear of competition or lost opportunity)?

If a company does not have the ability to sell your rights and is not willing to offer you something for those rights, you should push hard not to give up the rights.

The *Good Dick* team recounted a story in which a cable company wanted some of their digital rights. When push came to shove, it turned out that the cable company was not even going to have the capability to affect the rights they were requesting until well after the expiration of the term of the contract. The filmmakers then successfully carved those rights out of the contract.

★ Bomb Squads

Bomb squads are consultants and/or lawyers who are *very* well versed in the digital rights landscape. If you have a lawyer whom you like who does not have a lot of experience in this area, you might need to educate him or her. Oftentimes, it's like asking a general practitioner to do brain surgery. I'll repeat: Unless you are super savvy, and even if you are, get someone who knows this arena well to look over your agreements, to make sure you are protecting yourself and the revenue stream of your film. This might not be a lawyer; it might be a knowledgeable consultant who works in tandem with a lawyer.

This does not abrogate your responsibilities to look at the contracts. Two heads are always better than one, and you should read the contracts to try to understand what is happening within them. If you don't understand, ask questions.

I consider myself relatively savvy and pretty good at reading contracts and doing basic negotiations on my own. That said, I have still made mistakes in the digital arena. Seller, be warned.

★ A Map

I have mentioned this before, but because I naturally enjoy pushing metaphors, I will do so here. Create a map of the minefield so you can navigate it. Make a spreadsheet of all of your available rights and deals so that you can track whether and when they might come into conflict with one another.

as cable networks have matured, they have turned to series to bring back repeat viewers. Even indie stalwarts IFC and Sundance are buying fewer films

CHAPTER 30

TELEVISION/ CABLE

In our examination of digital rights, we'll address television and cable first. These rights were previously known to film-makers as a growing source of revenue, and have been recently known to independent filmmakers as a declining source of revenue.

I was puzzled about this precipitous drop in revenue, so I asked Shwarzstein about it. Here is his very interesting explanation:

Television's core business is repeat viewers.

It is difficult for television to command repeat viewers with indi-vidual films. When there was a plethora of fledgling channels such as HBO, Starz, Showtime, AMC, etc., they needed to buy movies to fill their schedules. But as those networks have matured, they have turned to series to bring back repeat viewers. Even indie stalwarts IFC and Sundance are buying fewer films in favor of series program-ming.

When television and cable entities buy movies, they do so for:

- Ratings — but the film needs to be very well known for the network to garner ratings from a feature film.

- A Loss Leader — A network might buy a huge film to provide a lead-in to a new show.

- Promotion — a film that will help brand a network and/or garner them press. Usually this is from a news-oriented or issue-ori-ented film. The network is hoping for as much publicity about the subject as the publicity accorded to the filmmaking.

That being said, there is still a consensus among people whom I spoke with that television/cable is one of the main ways to monetize independent films, even though the revenues have declined.

TELEVISION SALES AGENTS

Television is a market that is hard to monetize if you DIY. You should get yourself a TV sales agent if you can. These agents/reps deal with television buyers all the time; they also go to specific television sales markets throughout the world. You might consider getting a TV sales rep to handle all of your worldwide television, and let them handle North America as well.

Television sales reps typically take 25 percent of the sale as a fee, less expenses. Make sure you limit the rep's expenses in your agreement. At most, you should be paying a percentage of their market expenses. At best, you should not be required to reimburse them for market expenses, since they attend these markets with a large slate of films.

I would strongly recommend not giving the TV sales agent the ability to sell your digital rights. It is becoming more common for agents not to require digital rights, or they are okay with a contractual provision to deal with them on a case-by-case basis. In negotiating the deal points with your TV sales agent, you should look at my suggestions regarding foreign sales agents in Section 7.

If you have separate representatives handling your television rights and your digital rights, you need to coordinate their activities. This is one advantage to new specialty sales agents who can handle and/or coordinate both your digital rights and television rights. Provide all your representatives with full disclosure on all of your deals. Scan the deals and maintain them in a folder. Every time you get a new representative, give them the folder.

DIY TELEVISION

If you are going to try to contact networks directly, you should research each network and what it programs before making contact. Furthermore, just because a network has a certain reputation or has a certain kind of programming at a certain point in time, it does not mean they are looking to purchase the same programming in the future.

PUBLIC TELEVISION

Fortunately for independent filmmakers (especially documentary), there are still some slots on public television. POV and

Independent Lens are two series on public television that purchase independent film.

While it does help to have a sales agent to talk directly to the programmers, they take open submissions. They also pay attention to films on the festival circuit.

Besides these "strands," there are a couple of other ways to get your film on PBS and make some money. PBS consists of a network of local stations. You can either approach national PBS or the local stations individually for two options:

Sale of Underwriting

In this option, you offer the film for free but obtain the right to sell the underwriting time that PBS allocates at the beginning and end of the film. This time used to be worth several hundred thousand dollars. However, the money has dried up in the last couple of years as corporations and endowments are hurting for money, like everyone else. But if you can do it, it is a win-win situation for you and the station. The station gets free programming and you get a way to monetize your content. This depends, of course, on PBS wanting your film and it fitting in with the local station's or national network's brand.

There are people who actually work for a fee to sell this underwriting time. And you should know that it can take six months to a year to sell the time.

These sales agents commonly work for a guarantee against a percentage. The low end would be a three-month guarantee at about $2,000 a month, plus 15 percent of the underwriting obtained.

Niles obtained this type of PBS opportunity for *Note by Note*. His greatest regret from his entire release was that he tried to sell the underwriting himself. He didn't know about the existence of the special underwriting sales agents; no one bothered to tell him. He *strongly* warns against trying to do it yourself.

Alternatively, if you happen to be working with a well-endowed nonprofit that needs national visibility, they could pay for the underwriting and brand the broadcast.

Note: It would be relatively time-consuming to sell sponsorship time station to station across the country. It's better to sell national sponsorship time.

Sales of DVDs

A second alternative is to offer the film for the various pledge drives across the country in conjunction with your DVD company. The movie is shown for either a small fee or for free, but you wholesale the DVDs and/or boxed sets to the PBS station for resale as part of the pledge drive. So, they buy a DVD from you for $8 and then use it to raise $75 for a membership pledge.

VIDEO ON DEMAND (VOD)

VOD is emerging as a large source of potential revenue for filmmakers. Video on demand is delivered via cable television and is similar to a download-to-rent in the digital realm. A viewer pays from $1.99 to $8.99 or more to watch a film, which is made available for a specified period of time. Pay-per-view is essentially VOD, but for a onetime viewing, usually of live events.

Video on demand generally has its own window, usually after theatrical and before DVD. In order to take advantage of the publicity from a theatrical release, a VOD release allows consumers to see the film while it is in theaters, or soon after. Since the film is not available anywhere else (e.g., DVD, Internet), viewers are willing to pay a premium to see the film in this way.

Several companies are developing a business model based on a day and date theatrical/VOD release: IFC, Emerging Pictures, and Magnolia. Magnolia has an Ultra VOD program where they release the film on VOD three weeks before the film is available in theaters. This is an interesting way to build word of mouth for the theatrical.

Sloss feels that VOD is one of the greatest impulse-friendly technologies that can be monetized.

Deutchman from Emerging has a very interesting observation: In the retail world, the pricing of many products is based on evaluating the relative merits of:

- Convenience
- Selection
- Quality

He observes that the theatrical release, in general, does not provide the best available option. He feels that VOD is more convenient, has greater selection, and by virtue of the greater selection has the opportunity for greater quality (especially with the advances of home theater systems).

Deutchman feels that because of these advantages, VOD should be more, not less expensive than theatrical. For instance, a group of four friends can watch a film on VOD for $8 at any time on any night, with their popcorn machine in the next room — $2 a person, plus a few bucks for Cokes and popcorn. If they were to go out, the same experience would cost them $10 a person, plus another $30 in drinks and popcorn — $70 versus $10. The one kink in his argument is that it doesn't account for the value of the live theatrical experience. If you want a night out, you're not going to get that at home with your TV. When I mentioned this to Deutchman, he didn't disagree, but stated, "The question is whether, in most consumers' minds, all the negatives outweigh that one positive."

Swanberg, however, feels that there are a few kinks in the current VOD system:

- The VOD interface is confusing, making films hard to find. He remembers visiting a city and being unable find his film *Alexander the Last* on the IFC VOD page, though he found it in the title listings.

- For independents, sometimes there is not enough information for a consumer to make an informed choice. For instance, some systems have trailers available to help consumers decide on a film. Other systems only have a line or two of description for a film. The latter will result in more sales of blockbuster films with more stars, as opposed to independents.

- There still is some consumer reticence to VOD, although he feels that if someone tries it once or twice, they will get into the habit of using it more often.

- Most VOD platforms will remove a film after a month or three. This is similar to a theatrical release in the sense that if you don't see it in time, it will be gone.

I believe there is room for a variety of branded VOD services where consumers can go and expect to see a certain kind of content. For example, Cinetic has just launched a VOD service titled Film Buff, which will feature 15 films at a time with a 50 percent refresh every month. It is this kind of content selection and curating that will become a valuable commodity in the future, as consumers look for reliable sources of content that appeals specifically to them.

The digital rights landscape is changing constantly, with new companies and technologies emerging every day/week/month.

CHAPTER 31

AN INTRODUCTION TO DIGITAL RIGHTS

Internet rights are one of the most potentially lucrative sources of film revenue. The fact that a secure and profitable business model has not yet arisen to support films in the digital realm is a contributing factor in the contraction of conventional film production and distribution.

The digital rights landscape is changing constantly, with new companies and technologies emerging every day/week/month.

TYPES OF DIGITAL RIGHTS

The definitions of digital rights are becoming more well-defined as territories are being staked out by various vendors. However, as Broderick points out, the state of the industry is in such flux that different terms mean the same thing to different people and the same terms mean different things to different people. Again, be careful.

Free Streaming You watch content as it plays over the Internet, for free. YouTube videos are streamed. Hulu is an ad-supported free streaming service. Babelgum, an Internet platform, defines free streaming as Internet free on demand, or IFOD.

Subscription Streaming A customer pays a monthly fee for the ability to watch a catalog of content. Netflix's Watch Now is subscription streaming. I believe that more and more companies will start a monthly fee-based subscription service. There is a perception that creating the subscription-based model was one of HBO's strokes of genius for the early cable industry and that it can be replicated on the Internet. Netflix's Watch Now service might prove this to be true.

Pay Streaming You pay to watch content over the Internet as it streams.

<u>Download to Own</u> A customer can download a digital file to their computer or other storage device and owns the film in that form. iTunes' download to own is the most popular example.

<u>Download to Rent</u> Similar to download to own, but the customer does not own the film or file in perpetuity; they only rent it for a specific period of time.

<u>Mobile</u> The delivery of content to mobile phones. Some Internet companies are already asking for these rights to be included in their contracts, since mobile phones are able to access streaming content on the Internet. But it is not just mobile phones; there is a growing number of mobile devices, such as the PSP and iPod Touch, that can connect to the Internet and play content.

<u>Video on Demand</u> As discussed in the previous chapter, VOD is normally considered a cable right, since it is delivered via cable. However, it is increasingly being split off as a separate right, and the distinction between it and the digital rights listed above is lessening. If the film does not download to your cable device, it is most similar to pay streaming. If it downloads to your cable device, it is most similar to download to rent. Further confusing the issue is that some internet platforms such as Amazon call their download to rent service "VOD".

WAYS TO MONETIZE YOUR DIGITAL RIGHTS

There are currently a variety of means by which to monetize your digital rights.

<u>Fees Charged Per Download, Rental, or Viewing</u> The customer pays an up-front fee for the right to download or view the content. iTunes, Amazon Unbox, and Time Warner VOD are examples.

<u>Ad Revenue Share</u> A website charges companies to advertise while your content is playing. They share this revenue with you. YouTube and Hulu utilize these models.

<u>Subscription Fee</u> Instead of paying a fee per piece of content, users pay a subscription to either you individually, or to a service that has paid you for this right. Examples of this are David Lynch's website monthly membership fee and Netflix's Watch Now.

Merchandise Sales The site that hosts your film provides a link to a site that sells your merchandise. Examples of this are Snag Films' and YouTube's "Click to Buy" links.

General Promotion/Theatrical Launch Harder to track, but some sites will promote your film (maybe for your theatrical release) in exchange for running it exclusively on their site. This was the case for the launch of *End of the Line* on the streaming site Babelgum.

Ad Sales/Banner Ad Sales This is similar to ad revenue share, but on your own site. If you build up your audience enough, companies will pay you to place ads on your site. You need to be very popular for this to make an impact. On a smaller level, it might make sense to do banner exchanges with like-minded partners to help build awareness.

Branded Entertainment/Product Placement This is becoming prominent in television and on the web. Notice all the Coca-Cola branding on *American Idol*. Ileana Douglas has a web series on the IKEA website that revolves around her life as an out-of-work actress working in an IKEA store.

Sponsorship Companies will pay a fee to have a presence on your site.

Pay What You Want/Online Tip Jar This allows people to pay for your film or for your site for any reason. This is the model that Radiohead used for their last album release, which garnered a lot of attention. They dropped their label and ran with the idea that they could make more money and have more creative freedom by cutting out the middleman between themselves and their customers. They allowed anyone to download the album and pay what they wanted. The average "donation" has been reported to be $5, although the total sales figures have been disputed.

The theory behind this approach is that people *do* want to pay for content and *do* want to support artists when given an easy way to do so.

There are a number of services you can use for such a payment method. We decided on PayPal for its seeming simplicity. This allows people who have seen the film for free to contribute to the film.

GIVING AWAY YOUR FILM FOR FREE, PART 2

There are two basic schools of thought on giving your material away for free on the Internet. This argument is similar to the one discussed in Chapter 18, as to whether or not you should give out your film to be screened for free.

According to the first point of view, giving away your film for free can be beneficial because any publicity is good publicity. There are a number of extensions or justifications of this argument:

- By giving away something for free, you are consequently broadening the audience. This is important if you don't have an audience to begin with or any other way to gain an audience.

- An extension of this argument is to not worry about piracy, because when you are pirated, at least it means that people are interested in your work.

- In addition, you can't stop piracy anyway, so why not try to monetize piracy instead of fighting it?

- By building an audience for the film through making it free or allowing it to be pirated, you can monetize other revenue streams for the film, such as DVD.

- People only watch films for 15 minutes on the Internet, so free streaming is a great way to get people interested in the film. Then they will go buy it in some format that is more convenient for them.

- There is no other way to monetize streaming, so you might as well give it away for free and either ask for donations or hope it helps drive other sales.

- Having the film on one platform does not hurt it being available on other platforms — there is no cannibalization of one market to the next. In fact, the argument goes, all the different platforms by which the film can be obtained will help publicize one another and the film itself.

However, as I have already argued, each film is different and requires a different distribution and marketing approach. It is impossible that the arguments above could apply to all films and filmmakers.

The second point of view is that you have to look at your film and determine what Internet strategy makes the most sense. You need to plan how you are going to get your film out into the world, the Internet being only one method, and figure out how these different avenues are going to fit together to make your film a success.

Here are my responses to the above arguments:

1. By Itself, Free Only Equals Free

There is an argument I have heard on panels lately: Most filmmakers have a greater problem with anonymity than with piracy. I think this is a false argument. You still need to market your film to get people to see it. Is giving your film away for free the best way to market the film? Perhaps the problem is not whether or not to give the film away for free, but how to market the film in the first place.

Just because you have made a film doesn't mean that people are going to want to watch it. If a film is bad, nothing you do on the Internet will get an audience to continue watching after a few minutes, even if it is free. In addition, not all good films will generate an audience online — again, even if the film is free.

If you are going to give your film away for free through the Internet, you should integrate this free giveaway into an overall strategy.

2. Consider Creating an Internet Event

If you are going to have give something for free on the Internet, you might want to limit the free window to a day or weekend and try to turn it into an event and market it as such. Pollack points out that YouTube released Luc Besson's environmental documentary *Home* on World Environment Day to create a worldwide event around the film. They garnered 1.8 million views while also opening simultaneously in cinemas and on TV.

3. If a Site Wants Your Film for Free, How Will They Market It?

There are many Internet sites working on a catalog/library model, trying to add as many films to their arsenal as possible, either to have a bigger footprint on the Internet or perhaps for eventual sale. By giving your film to them for free, you are giving them value. What value are you receiving in return? Are they promising some form of enhanced placement or promotion?

4. Streaming Leads to Revenue from Ads and Merchandise Sales for Some Filmmakers But Not All

A number of filmmakers/visual content creators have made careers for themselves through their massively popular shorts on the Internet. Examples include Fred, JibJab, and Rooster Teeth/Red vs. Blue. Due to the large audience, these filmmakers can make money via ad revenue or merchandise sales.

While this model has worked for creators of short-form content that can readily become viral on the web and generate a large fan base, the jury is still out as to whether this holds true for feature films or material that doesn't lend itself to becoming viral, such as specific niche content.

Unless you have the kind of viewer numbers that you can convert into ad revenue or into merchandise sales, you should consider holding back your material until you can get value for it.

5. People Watch Whole Films Streaming, and This Will Increase Over Time

As more and more Internet streaming platforms become available on television sets, people will begin to watch content all the way through, or at least use this unlimited television access to certain films as their primary way of viewing those films. If a film is always available for free effectively on demand, what is the motivation for a consumer to buy a DVD or pay for a download?

I think streaming deals need to begin to incorporate some form of cycling or time-limited access, unless there is a large advance that makes sense for the film to always be available for free. For example, not all episodes of all HBO series are always available "On Demand" on cable. HBO chooses which episodes will be available during certain periods of time. If season four of *Entourage* is not available for free via cable, and I *have* to watch it, I'll look elsewhere and perhaps buy it on DVD or pay to download from iTunes.

6. Companies Are Beginning to Pay for Internet Exclusivity

I believe that as more and more Internet sites seek to differentiate themselves and the content they offer on their site, they will start to pay some kind of advance for this content. Babelgum has already started to do this. We are in a situation that is similar to when cable first began and there was a need for programming for start-up channels. The difference is not the need for content, since there is so much content available for free, but the need for curated content. As consumers look for better content on the web that's available in a way that is easier for them to obtain, and as sites try to promote themselves as quality destinations, there should be an opportunity for filmmakers to make some sales to streaming sites.

THE CASE OF PIRACY

Weiler has allowed me to quote liberally from an article that he originally wrote for *Filmmaker* magazine. In it he makes a convincing case for how and why filmmakers need to find ways to monetize peer-to-peer file sharing on the Internet (usually called piracy). What follows is an excerpt from that article:

> 'In a recent report by bandwidth-management firm Sandvine, 44 percent of all bandwidth consumed in North America is peer-to-peer traffic. And last fall the Pirate Bay, one of the largest torrent tracking sites, passed the 25 million peers mark while single-handedly accounting for over 50 percent of all public torrents....
>
> As the music industry abandons its fruitless war on piracy, many independent record labels and artists are turning to BitTorrent to ease distribution costs and, more importantly, to take the work to where the audience is — in other words, to mirror the audience's behavior....
>
> The film industry is running out of physical formats, and soon all media will be digital. A series of 1s and 0s that by its very nature is intended to be copied. Piracy is inevitable. DRM (digital rights management) has only frustrated consumers, often making it difficult for them to enjoy the media they have purchased on the device of their choosing, and in some cases leaving piracy as the only viable option. BitTorrent is the method of choice when it comes to file sharing. It scales effectively and, when files are seeded properly, can provide decent download speeds. But can the networks that fuel piracy also provide legitimate business models to filmmakers? Some British filmmakers seem to think so.
>
> When the time came for Jamie King and the Noble League of Peers to release their film entitled *Steal This Film*, a documentary

about copyright and intellectual property, they took it directly to where their audience lives. Through a promotional deal with a number of the top torrent tracker sites, King and company were able to secure various placements such as logo swaps and banners encouraging people to download the film for free. At the conclusion to the film there was a simple call to action that encouraged viewers to make a donation to help support the filmmakers' next project. To date, *Steal This Film* has received more than $30,000 in donations and, in the process, has been downloaded over six million times.

King believes that in the future it could be possible to have 0.5 percent of viewers donating if the filmmaker adds the right incentives. In fact, he believes this so strongly, he's decided to create a legitimate business model around it. This spring King is launching a new service entitled VODO (volunteer donation) that provides an easy way to assign and track donations made to a film's torrent file. The other side of the model is DISCO (distribution coalition), which will place participating films in front of upwards of 50 million people monthly. Current partners in DISCO are an impressive list of the largest torrent trackers in the world: the Pirate Bay, Mininova, isoHunt, and others.

When asked how his model will fare due to the fact that numerous tracker sites are under legal attack (the Pirate Bay was tried in Sweden and is awaiting a verdict in their case and Mininova goes to trial in May), King is quick to point out that as soon as one torrent site disappears, another rises from its ashes. But for King, it is not about any one outlet or file sharing protocol — his real goal is to create a legitimate model that is piracy-agnostic while providing opportunities for those seeking to monetize their films. At its core, the model is really quite simple, in the sense that it is centered on aggregating audiences and content. There are many sites and blogs that have large audiences, and under King's model, all of them could use elements of VODO and/or join DISCO.

Of course, donations are only one revenue model for a filmmaker, and some may argue against its efficacy. But King believes that audiences want to have a connection with those who make the work and are willing to support the things they are passionate about. VODO and DISCO are the first step in what King hopes will become a sustaining model for those who create content."

An aggrega-
tor is a com-
pany that
has relation-
ships with
the major
buyers in the
digital distri-
bution field
and acts as a
gatekeepeer

CHAPTER 32

SELLING YOUR DIGITAL RIGHTS

There are three basic ways to handle digital rights that are not mutually exclusive (this scenario is similar to your DVD rights):

1. Have someone else sell the content for you (an aggregator or distributor)

2. DIY

3. Hybrid (using elements from both)

AGGREGATORS

An aggregator is a company that has relationships with the major buyers in the digital distribution field and acts as a gatekeeper for content. A number of them are distributors in some fashion (most commonly DVD distributors) because they were already set up as gatekeepers in the film distribution world and had an existing acquisitions apparatus.

Back in the Wild West of digital rights a few years ago, iTunes welcomed all filmmakers to submit their films for inclusion. They were quickly overwhelmed. Now, iTunes only obtains content from aggregators. Hulu also obtains most of their material from studios and aggregators. Even with companies that do take material from individual filmmakers, you will have a leg up if you go through an aggregator. Aggregators will take anywhere from 15 to 30 percent of the money earned from the online service.

Most aggregators have relationships with certain digital rights entities, but not all. It is most important that they have a relationship with iTunes, since iTunes is the site that currently generates the most income for filmmakers.

★ New Video

New Video is a well-known aggregator for independent films. They aggregate for iTunes (for whom they represent *Bomb It*), Hulu, You-Tube (Premium Content Channels), Snag, Sony PlayStation, Netflix, Cinema Now, and Microsoft Xbox/Zune. Soon they will be offering content to VOD platforms globally. Their standard deal is 15 percent. They have a long-standing relationship with filmmakers and have a very good reputation with the indie community.

★ Wolfe Releasing

Wolfe Releasing has a deal with Warner Bros. for all its LGBT (lesbian/gay/bisexual/transgender) content. It also aggregates LGBT content for iTunes, Xbox, Sony PlayStation, Hulu, and Netflix's Watch Now program, and many other platforms as well. It has an output deal through Warner Bros. digital distribution services that feed over 80 million homes with satellite and cable VOD.

DISTRIBUTORS

In general, aggregators solely choose content, present it to the online services, and then prepare the material for delivery. There are a few emerging distributors of digital content who do much more. They function more like a traditional distributor because, in addition to selling your content, they will create a strategy for your digital rights and coordinate your digital rights with your other existing rights obligations. They will also position and market your content so as to increase its value. They have many more places to sell your content than the typical aggregator: Many aggregators only have two to three outlets for content, while a good distributor should have relationships and outlets all over the world.

These distributors will want all of your digital rights. Consequently, you should make sure that they are able to distribute your digital rights everywhere, to every platform; and if not, exclude from the contract the territories and rights they cannot help you with.

One benefit to having all of your rights deals under one roof is that you avoid confusion about who owns what, what the holdbacks are, and what the territories and terms are. The distributor should keep deals from interfering with each other — better yet, they should coordinate them.

Another benefit to a distributor is that they have already hammered out deal points with many of the digital rights companies that are more favorable than what you could have gotten on your own. Some of the hardest contracts I have ever had to read concern digital rights deals.

★ Cinetic Rights Management

Cinetic Rights Management (CRM) is one such distribution company. It was started by Sloss and, in his words, is intended to be a direct conduit between filmmakers and their audience.

Because of the expanded service they provide, they charge more than typical aggregators, around 25 to 50 percent, depending on the film. Dentler says that they are developing online release patterns similar to what has been commonplace in the theatrical realm.

CRM has a two-pronged approach. One is to work with filmmakers to release new films and content. The other is to work with so-called library titles (older films that have already had an initial release). Dentler uses the example of *Hoop Dreams*, the incredible groundbreaking basketball documentary directed by Steve James that was released in 1994. CRM is working to get *Hoop Dreams* in front of millions of new young basketball fans who were not previously aware of it.

Dentler feels that the titles that have the best potential for release on the Internet are those that:

- Are niche driven.

- Are cast driven.

- Have good word of mouth.

CRM has a marketing staff that pushes their content to niche communities online. CRM also has their own in-house counsel included in the fee. Not only is the counsel extremely versed in the complicated field of digital rights, they are already battling for filmmakers' rights with digital content providers in their standard deals. You get the benefit of their terms without the cost of paying a lawyer to get you partway there. Because the digital world is changing so rapidly, Sloss stresses that they want to keep the process as transparent as possible; he wants the filmmakers to learn as they are learning.

Dentler feels that once you have had some event screenings and played some festivals, you should make your film as widely available as possible. You also don't have to spend a lot of money. If you have a digibeta, you are good to go.

DIY

In this scenario, you sell your own digital rights from your website or through a third party connected to your website. You need to find a company to deliver and collect revenue from the sale of your digital content. The company, in turn, gives you all of the revenue from the sales, minus a fee or service charge. In essence, these are digital fulfillment companies similar to the DVD fulfillment companies. I will address this method in chapter 33.

HYBRID APPROACH

In this scenario, you would have an aggregator or distributor selling your content to larger entities, but you would continue to sell your content from your website in those rights and territories that remain unsold.

INDIEFLIX

IndieFlix is another new model of hybrid distributor. They operate non-exclusively with their filmmakers, with their primary businesses being digital rights and DVD. They will do the occasional theatrical for a cause-oriented film, and they have started doing some TV sales.

Their motto is "connecting people through movies," which indicates a social networking, Web 2.0 approach to film distribution. They want to provide a "forum for filmmakers and their audiences to interact, and to [build] a community that translates artistic vision into commercial success."

By being non-exclusive, they are set up as a hybrid solution for filmmakers who want to pursue a DIY model but also want to have a distributor working with them. Filmmakers keep all rights. IndieFlix pays quarterly with a 70/30 split (70 to the filmmaker) net. All costs are listed on their site. The average DVD cost to deliver is $4.75 and includes all artwork.

IndieFlix delivers PPV and DVDs directly. They aggregate to all the major digital platforms and also sell DVDs to brick-and-mortar stores.

They market films collectively and individually, promoting the film-makers via their weekly podcast and soon-to-be launched IndieFlix Internet radio program, "Listen to the Movies." They also organize special event screenings, educational tours, email blasts, offline marketing, festivals, and reviews.

NEGOTIATING A DEAL WITH AGGREGATORS AND DISTRIBUTORS

You should do this with a lawyer who can protect your rights, but you might need to educate your lawyer (and yourself) on some of the points you want. Here are some of those points:

1. DIY Rights The ability to sell digital rights from your website, either download to own, download to rent, or streaming. This is similar to your request for your home video deals. You need the right to not only sell the film from your website, but also deliver through a chosen service provider who links from your website.

2. Approval The ability to have approval (best) or meaningful con-sultation (okay) on individual deals organized by the aggregator. Some aggregators and distributors have output deals with certain services and may be reticent to provide you with the details of those deals.

3. Information Some knowledge of when the film will become avail-able on any digital platform. Sometimes the aggregator/distributor is not privy to this information, but you should still ask. You want this information so that you can promote the addition of the digital services to your fan base and keep track of the progress.

4. Encoding expenses covered Note that all aggregators and dis-tributors should also handle encoding your content for the licensed digital platforms. This is included in their percentage.

5. Territory Only give up the territories where they have relation-ships with online sites.

6. Rights Only give the company rights they have the abilitiy to sell. Some aggregators only aggregate for VOD. Other aggregators only do iTunes and Netflix.

7. Term Try to limit the term to one year. The field is changing so rapidly, who knows if they will even be in business in a year?

8. Accounting They should account for your film separately within any overall output deal.

9. Performance or escape clause You should try to get a performance clause. If the aggregator/distributor doesn't earn a certain dollar amount, you can get out of the agreement. However, since earnings are so low currently, you are unlikely to get this clause. More likely is a clause that lets you escape if the company is no longer in business or is not actively selling your film.

10. Assignment No assignment to third parties. You do not want to give the aggregator the right to sell you as part of a library to another distributor. Your deal is with them as aggregator/distributor alone.

11. No editing They should not have the right to edit your content without your permission, nor to pass this on to third parties.

12. A cap on expenses

13. Link A requirement that all deals must link back to your website. You can try for this, but it's unlikely that they will agree to this in all deals since they may not be able to enforce it. More likely you will get a clause that requests they try to affect this in third-party deals.

ORLY RAVID'S DIGITAL DISTRIBUTION TIPS FOR FILMMAKERS

Check Orly's Digital Distribution Guide at thefilmcollaborative.org. for up-to-date information about digital rights and platforms. Some of these repeat what I have already written - but they are worth repeating.

1. Take care Choosing the best platform/portal for your film must be done with care and must also take into account the type of film it is and its overall release plan. Some aggregators and distributors are better than others for your film, and in overall. Since Delivery costs money and time, prioritize the most appropriate and lucrative platforms.

2. Beware of exclusivity By way of comparison, such a request from a brick-and-mortar video store such as Blockbuster would be occasional at best, and then they would pay a lot for that right and it would only be for a short window of time, such as six months. A good thing to find out is the extent to which any given platform or distributor licensing to platforms has marketing tools and/or commitments in place. Will doing a deal with them be like having your film in the basement of a crap DVD store in a strip mall in Iowa (no offense to Iowans), or will it be like having the film on shelves facing out in a big chain with some advertising? Or will it be somewhere in between? Even getting onto iTunes presents options, and not all can give you marketing presence on the home page. One must analyze one's investment of time and costs in doing delivery before committing to any distribution option.

3. Think before you put all your eggs in one basket. Rights licensing nowadays is very tricky. Broadcasters and home video distributors sometimes want competing rights, and sometimes distributors want all rights and yet won't exploit them all. It's prudent to analyze options and the possibility of breaking up rights and windows so that you can explore available options with people who have experience in this area and can really help you.

4. Consult with someone who is up-to-date with industry standards, guidelines, and rights definitions, but most of all, someone who is experienced with revenue models and windows and all possibilities in negotiations.

5. Flexibility It's critical that one's contract contain language that covers a wide range of contingencies and possibilities in a rapidly changing and unpredictable landscape. Plan for changing revenue models, companies going out of business, and rights classes/categories to shift, and have your contract drafted accordingly. There is nothing you cannot protect yourself from in a contract, as long as you are reasonable, and no honest distributor will expect you not to cover yourself.

6. Balance All too often, filmmakers get screwed because of bad deals. It's also common for filmmakers to lose good offers because they want too much. Know your film, know your market, know your potential, and decide how much work you are willing to commit yourself to in order to maximize the distribution of your film, instead of solely relying on third parties.

7. Ask questions and ask for references There are a few aggregators and lots of distributors out there, so before committing yourself, weigh your options. Talk to other filmmakers who have worked with the company. Are they happy?

8. Mitigate the middlemen Ask for revenue potentials and examine how many layers of middlemen there are between the distributor/aggregator and the platforms that you most want to be on, assuming you cannot go direct (which is often the case). Make sure distributors are not going through too many middlemen, selling to themselves and double dipping, or simply offering to do something on your behalf that you could do yourself.

9. Recoup your expenses Get clear about expenses being recouped and marketing efforts that either you or your distributor (or both) need to undertake to have your film perform in the marketplace.

10. Think ahead It's hard to be certain which revenue streams and revenue models will win out, if any do. Assume all may be important down the line and be careful to advantageously participate in all, as directly as possible. Do so based on the revenue model (i.e. subscription, ad-supported, transactional) not on technology or way distributors categories. The fact that Netflix has deals with Sony Playstation and Xbox, that several studios just announced that they are are doing deals with a new download-to-own store from DivX, and the fact that the mobile device distribution space is just opening up, and that YouTube may start to charge for viewing films all suggest that the future cannot be predicted as far as which platforms or companies will ultimately have the widest reach down the line. Prepare for the future. Think ahead.

NEGOTIATING DEALS WITH ONLINE SITES

The second type of deal you will need to negotiate (other than with aggregators or distributors) has to do with relationships with online sites. A lot of these points are the same as those outlined above; I list them here for completeness but will not repeat their description:

1. Territory For some sites it is worldwide (mostly streaming sites). Download to own and rent usually go by territory.

2. Rights Limit the scope of rights. For example, if it is a streaming site, keep it to streaming. Keep this as narrow as possible.

3. Exclusivity This will often be linked to term. If there is exclusivity, then it should be limited to a shorter amount of time. Remember, don't give up exclusivity unless they pay you for it in a way that makes sense for you.

4. Term Limit it.

5. Limit the holdback The site might ask for a holdback, requiring you not to have your material shown in a competitive way for a period of time. You want to reduce the amount scope and time allowed for holdbacks in your deals.

6. Escape clause You can even put in a clause that if you get a better deal in the future, you are able pull out from their site (depending on what they are paying you, if anything).

7. Assignment No assignment to third parties. You are making the deal with them, not with some company that buys them or to whom they want to pawn you off.

8. No re-editing

9. Accounting If there is money being earned by your film, some schedule of accounting and payment should be provided.

10. Link A click-to-buy link or at least a link back to your site or landing page when your film appears.

11. Marketing and publicity What kind of promotion are they guaranteeing (if any)? What kind of placement? How often and for how long will you be on the homepage? This promotion can be as valuable or more valuable than an advance, and *might* be worth parting with some rights for.

You Still Need Someone Versed in the Digital Rights Field to Negotiate Your Deals

This could be a lawyer or a consultant. These days it is very likely that your consultant will negotiate the deal and you will have a lawyer finesse the language.

Even though streaming is currently the most difficult right to monetize, it is still the most popular way to consume film and video online.

CHAPTER 33

DIGITAL RIGHTS OUTLETS

There are a plethora of online sites selling or providing digital content, with more launching every day.

These sites can usually be categorized by the manner in which the content is delivered — either streaming or a form of download. I'm only going to address a number of the more established companies. For up-to-date listings, go to newamericanvision.com or to this book's website.

STREAMING

Even though streaming is the currently the most difficult right to monetize, it is still the most popular way to consume film and video online.

YouTube

YouTube is a global channel owned by Google and is the number-one site for online video. It accounts for:

- 31.3 percent of all online video being watched as of 2009.

- 73 percent of the visits to online video sites in the U.S. (according to Hitwise in April 2008)

- 1 million unique downloads and over 150,000 video uploads per day (according to YouTube).[7]

They have set up an online "Screening Room" to spotlight and help build audience awareness of feature films and shorts.

Monetization is threefold. It includes:

- Ad revenue share, which varies on the popularity of your page.

To do this, you need to become part of the their film partner program (youtube.com/partner)

- Click to Buy (DVDs or merchandise)

- Driving traffic to another site that you monetize.

There are quite a few success stories from YouTube — not just the
people who create short content, but for feature filmmakers as well.
Hunter Weeks, who made *10 MPH*, had success with the platform,
as did Arin Crumley with *Four Eyed Monsters*. For television, You-
Tube claims they helped reinvent Monty Python for a whole new
generation. Playing clips of Monty Python episodes lead to tens of
thousands of click-to-buy purchases.

YouTube has also launched the Screening Room, which highlights
selected feature films and promotes them in a special section of
the site.

YouTube is the ultimate democratic site. Nearly anyone can post
nearly anything, as long as they are the content creator. Moreover, a
very good aggregator/distributor can negotiate your ad revenue as
well as your market position within YouTube. It is also the industry
standard location for "viral videos." YouTube tracks your views and
posts them for everyone to see.

Here are Pollack's tips for best utilizing YouTube:

1. Post your content If it's a film, you should use the YouTube movie
section. If you are a hit, you'll be positioned on the homepage or
favorites page.

2. Push your content It goes back to marketing. For YouTube, you
should:

- Use social networks — when you post a video, automatically share it on MySpace, Facebook, etc. Get your friends to
share it.

- Use the "embed" feature to post the video in as many places
as possible: emails, different sites, your site, etc.

- Respond to each comment you receive. Create an email list
from these comments.

- Reach out to bloggers and ask them to post your content.

- Personalize your homepage.

- Watch other YouTube videos, see how they promote their content.

- Post your video as comments on other people's videos — especially popular ones. That way you'll branch out to new audiences.

- Tag your clips. The more metadata, the better. Look at metadata on popular videos. See how they do it and how it relates to you.

<u>3. Think about what content is more suited for online viewing</u> (although this will change over time). Thirty-second spots that have a beginning, middle, and an end are best. Bonus: If you can do this well, you can potentially parlay this into directing commercials.

<u>4. Create content in popular online genres</u> Certain content works better for the web (see Sara's recommendations in Chapter 7).

<u>5. Tap into online fan culture</u> Related to No. 4, but more targeted. Sara used the example of *The Hunt For Gollum*, which has over a million views (4,000 comments) and was able to tap into the large online *Lord of The Rings* community.

<u>6. Post frequently</u>

Hulu

Set up in 2007 by NBC Universal and News Corp as a response to YouTube, Hulu is an online video service that offers hit TV shows, movies, and clips for free in the United States. It generates income from advertising revenue.

Hulu videos are also available on AOL, Comcast, MSN, MySpace, and Yahoo! in the U.S., as well as on a growing network of personal blogs, fan sites, and other websites where users choose to embed the Hulu video player. They are reportedly the second highest revenue generator in the digital distribution space (iTunes is No. 1), and companies such as B-Side, CRM, and many others distribute to them.

Babelgum

Babelgum is a new model of streaming site, one that focuses on curating content for specific audiences instead of trying to supply the mass audience. I see this as the wave of the future for online sites, in which they create a brand for themselves — as cable channels have done. People looking for specific kinds of content will then be attracted to those sites. In addition, the sites can market themselves to specific audiences.

Laurence Billiet, who runs Babelgum's Metropolis channel, explains that over the last few years the excitement about video on the Internet came from the fact that it could be watched. But as the medium matures, people will be looking for great content. Babelgum intends to have a clear editorial position in order to curate select content.

While anyone can submit to Babelgum, they are not interested in traditional user-generated video of cats in Kleenex boxes; they want professionally made content. As long as the submitted content is of a high enough quality, they will consider it. However, it must fit within their five channels and complement the indie/edgy feel of the site. Once you submit and are "published" (passing their rigorous quality control), then you are on the platform.

However, for people to see your content, it must be programmed, and Babelgum admits that they tend to favor the content they have curated. Still, one of their most popular clips, "Crevasse," was user-generated and submitted.

Within the Babelgum umbrella are five main channels: Film, Music, Comedy, Our Earth, Metropolis. All are self-explanatory, except perhaps Metropolis, which is urban. Metropolis is the home of the *Bomb It* branded channel and "super landing page." Within each channel are other branded channels like *Bomb It*'s: within comedy is Funny Or Die; within film are IndieFlix and FilmBuff. They also create exclusive series, such as *Radar* by the Workbook Project.

As people watch content on Babelgum, they are served complementary content. Eventually users will be able to sign in and the site will customize based on their interests.

Babelgum also actively markets their content, even running Google and Facebook ads. They are using publicists to promote *Bomb It* and arranging interviews with the artists in the film. They also run regular contests to engage their audience and bring awareness to their site and programming. For *Bomb It* they flew a lucky winner to participate in a graffiti event in São Paulo, Brazil (an example of utilizing live events to promote online content).

They have a 50/50 revenue share deal with their content providers, but Babelgum is relatively unique in that they will pay minimum guarantees for some (usually exclusive) content.

They require exclusive Internet free on demand (IFOD) rights — in other words, streaming. They also obtain mobile rights. Two million users have downloaded Babelgum's iPhone app.

They are experimenting with different arrangements with filmmakers. For *End of the Line*, a documentary about the declining global fish resources, they did a day-and-date promotion for the theatrical release. However, the filmmaker broke the film up into enhanced segments, different than what was in the actual film.

They also have an iPhone app with over 2 million downloads. Babelgum reports that more people watch their channel over the iPhone than on the web!

SnagFilms

SnagFilms is committed to documentaries, which is commendable in and of itself. SnagFilms is a website where you can watch full-length documentary films for free (with interstitial advertising). Their main focus is a widget that allows you to "snag" a film and put it anywhere on the web. A customer can then set up a theater on their website to show one or more "SnagFilms." According to Snag, their widgets have been embedded a billion times on 25,000 websites.

Widgets can be for a single film, or you can obtain a multifilm widget, aka a "Snag multiplex." NGOs can use the widgets to get documentaries out into their target communities. Individuals can share movies by posting the widget to their Facebook profiles.

Snag offers two ways to monetize your film:

- Ad revenue share on a 50/50 net basis (after deducting costs)

- Click to Buy now, in which Snag takes 8.5 percent of the sale as an affiliate fee.

Snag works with festivals and other curators to feature channels on their site, such as National Geographic, PBS, CRM, E1, ITVS, and the Sundance Channel.

They have co-world premiered films with festivals and have run a film day-and-date during a festival run to heighten awareness for the film.

Anyone can submit to Snag; however, if your film has been in a certain select festivals, you can submit via SnagFast, which is a quicker way to get it programmed/curated.

Their term is three to five years and worldwide, and they want exclusive rights but are flexible and can be non-exclusive, I am told. They do generally require sublicensing to third parties, which is partly due to their third party only streaming partner relationships, and partly due to the Snag feature.

DOWNLOAD TO OWN/ RENT COMPANIES

Here are a few of the top download-to-own and download-to-rent options.

iTunes

www.apple.com/itunes/

iTunes is currently the largest source of revenue in the digital space where music, movies, and TV shows are sold as downloads. Movies may also be rented. iTunes provides trailers and comments, as well as consumer ratings for downloads.

You must submit your content through aggregators and they have notoriously strict guidelines for compression. Viewing can be done on any Apple device: a computer, iPod, iPhone, or on your television through Apple TV.

Amazon Video On Demand

amazon.com/Video-On-Demand

With thousands of titles available, Amazon Video On Demand allows users to download or rent movies in a manner similar to iTunes; however, the movies are only playable on Amazon's viewer or a compatible platform and are not transferrable to an iPod or DVD. Rights terms for filmmakers are 50 percent for electronic sell-through and DTO (download to own).

This service has the benefit of being part of Amazon's search engine for its customers, which I would argue is one of the most important proprietary media search engines. Hence it is important to be on Amazon somehow. If you do not manufacture DVDs for whatever reason, you should consider a combination of Create Space and Amazon Unbox.

Customers watch your content either on their computer or through some tested device that runs a version of the Unbox Video Player or the TiVo DVR. Customers can also stream content to their TV via a Roku box or a number of other devices (including their computer).

SUBSCRIPTION STREAMING

Subscription services may be the wave of the future. Instead of buying content piece by piece like music on iTunes, you would subscribe to a company and watch any film in their catalog whenever you want. This will inevitably lead to a scramble for control over content. But the subscriptions might result in enough revenue for sites to be able to pay advances for content, just as cable companies do (and once did handsomely for independent films).

Netflix Watch Now

Netflix Watch Now is a form of subscription streaming. If you belong to Netflix, you can stream any of their Watch Now films for free as part of your membership, either to your PC or to your television (through a Roku or Xbox). Eventually, you will be able to stream Netflix (and many other sites) on your television without this additional hardware.

If your film is on Watch Now, Netflix customarily pays a flat fee that can be sizable or paltry. They usually pay more for the license if they can have Watch Now day and date with the DVD release.

AN ASSORTMENT OF OTHER COMPANIES

There are a plethora of companies providing streaming and download methods for customers to watch films and other media for free or for a fee via the Internet. As I mentioned before, this is not meant to be a complete list.

The Auteurs theauteurs.com

The Auteurs appears to be a co-venture between the founder of Celluloid Dreams (a foreign sales company) and The Criterion Collection. Their website states their intention to be a "website with a uniquely curated library of films delivered through high-definition streaming and download on demand." They "wish to be an online cinematheque where film lovers around the world come together to watch, discuss, and read about the best of cinema. Focusing on editorial coverage of international cinema and a highly interactive, community-based design, it is our intention to create a global community of the most interested and interesting film fans in the world."

Film Annex filmannex.com

Film Annex's mission is to provide a new channel for promoting filmmakers and their works as well as distributing their films. Film Annex is also an expansive network of specialized Web TV's that target particular themes, interests, and viewership.

Filmmakers can show their films for free, in which case, they will create revenues through advertising revenues, or they can sell their films for a price they set up. The filmmaker decides on the sales prices for each film, the type of player (e.g. Quicktime, Flash, Microsoft Media, etc.) and the quality/size of each movie file. 100% of the sales revenues go directly to the filmmaker.

Film Annex also gives filmmakers the opportunity to generate advertising revenues through their web pages. 100% of those revenues go directly to them.

Film Annex offers a non-exclusive license, while the filmmakers retain ownership. Film Annex will cover all expenses of research, programming, legal fees, web design, and above all promotion and advertising. The agreement between Filmannex.com and the production company has no time limitations and the film can be pulled off the site at any time. The filmmaker is allowed to present his work on other platforms in addition to that of Film Annex.

Guba guba.com

Guba allows users to watch, share, download, and upload videos for free, in a manner very similar to YouTube.

Jaman jaman.com

Jaman is an online on-demand movie service. Users create an account and download movies to watch for a small fee. Jaman can also suggest titles based on the user's ratings and most-frequented genres.

CinemaNow cinemanow.com

CinemaNow allows users to download or rent films via an on-demand service. CinemaNow also provides TV shows and music downloads.

Joox joox.com

Yet another online platform for sharing, renting, and watching films online. Indie films welcomed.

Brightcove brightcove.com/en/

A video platform with a more commercial slant. Brightcove targets the distribution of the videos of businesses and organizations, providing a place in cyberspace for everything from news videos to movie trailers.

filmmak-
ers will
now be able
to charge
their audi-
ence on a
download,
rental or
subscrip-
tion basis
from their
own sites

CHAPTER 34

DIY DIGITAL RIGHTS

Only recently have resources emerged for monetizing one's own digital rights.

I believe this will provide significant competition to the free streaming and download-to-own sites. If a filmmaker has a large enough fan base, that filmmaker will now be able to charge their audience on a download, rental or subscription basis from their own sites.

Here are some new companies and methods that can help you DIY your digital rights:

Distribber

As discussed previously, iTunes requires that filmmakers go through an aggregator to become part of their service. With Distribber, filmmakers can avoid the traditional gatekeeper deals that "aggregators" require.

Distribber charges a one-time flat fee (currently $1,295) to encode, match, or create chapter breaks, and to chaperone a film through the iTunes QC process. The filmmaker keeps all rights and 100 percent of the money collected. There is a $79 per year charge that covers the processing of quarterly reports and checks.

Distribber is now finishing deals with many of the other major download and streaming companies, with the intention of offering clients a one-stop menu of outlets. Each filmmaker will be able to choose a combination of platforms that serve his or her film's goals and that work within his or her other rights commitments.

So if you think you will sell a decent amount on iTunes, this deal does make sense. Even though the $1,295 fee feels high initially, when you realize that you get to keep 100 percent of your revenue, it's pretty cool. Distribber acknowledges that if you are not going to sell a lot of content, the $1,295 and their services will not work for you.

Youreeeka

Youreeeka is a groundbreaking DIY solution for filmmakers. It is one of *the* first, if not the first company to offer filmmakers a way to sell their films off of their own websites in an relatively seamless fashion.

For a low startup fee of $99, you give Youreeeka your content in *any* format including many tape formats. Youreeeka will create a streaming and/or downloadable "product" for you to sell from your website. In addition, you will receive embeddable text that will essentially give you a widget that you can share around the Internet. This allows other people to post your store to their site, giving your store the ability to become viral.

For this service, besides the $99 setup fee, the split of revenue from sales is 60 percent to you (the producer) and 40 percent to Youreeeka for their services as a wholesaler. Besides the encoding and technology, the 40 percent also includes any credit card fees (including international) and streaming/bandwith costs that Youreeeka incurs when your film is sold.

There are a few options that you as the producer set in creating your product(s):

- Whether you want to provide streaming, download to own, or both. Most of their clients choose streaming, since it prevents the user from making copies and passing them along.

- For streaming, you can choose any viewing period for the consumer: one day, one week, or unlimited. You can also offer a menu of different times for different pricing. The consumer has a library (similar to Amazon's VOD) where he or she has access to purchases.

- For download to own, you can also offer different resolutions (the most common one being iPod). The rationale is that even if the iPod version is passed around, it is of too low quality for a large screen. Their download files are agnostic, meaning that they can play on iPods as well as MP3 devices.

You can also offer other files to be downloaded, such as PDFs of a teaching guide for an educational version (sold at a higher price). Since they also have a fulfillment company, you can package any type of merchandise with the streaming or download (e.g., a hat and a week of streaming for $14.99).

To get a sense of the player with the "buy" button in action, check out Taylor Steele's surf film site, poorspecimen.tv.

MeDeploy

MeDeploy is a fascinating hybrid blend because it allows you to handle your rights in a DIY manner as well as become part of a distribution catalog. MeDeploy's mission is to enable any blog or fan-oriented site to be able to offer films of their choice for sale on their site. For instance, a surf blog would be able to choose from a variety of surf films and offer their top 10 picks. Currently, if a blog has a top 10 list with a link to a sales site, such as Amazon, a customer is directed to that other site to buy or rent a film, with a relatively low revenue split in exchange for the recommendation. Moreover, when the customer is sent to the sales site, they have to leave the recommender's site. MeDeploy's solution keeps the customer on the recommender's site *and* allows the blog to take a higher percentage of the purchase.

The customer does not know that MeDeploy exists, nor is the customer directed to a separate site for the purchase. Fan sites can now be their own gatekeepers of content. In other words, any site can promote any film and profit from it. Obviously, this could be an incredible opportunity for blogs and filmmakers alike, because both will be able to profit from the films they promote, thereby increasing the incentive for a site to promote a film. The caveat is that it might further blur the line between journalism and commerce.

Let me use bombit-themovie.com as an example. We have about 20,000 unique users that come to bombit-themovie.com. Not mind-blowing, but a healthy amount. Through MeDeploy, I could offer my visitors a variety of graffiti films that they would access through me (in addition to my film *Bomb It*, of course). I can now promote a number of films, make a little money, and approach similar filmmakers about promoting mine in return. MeDeploy is currently negotiating deals with the major studios to have access to their content.

There is one simultaneously great and one potentially tricky side to this. As a filmmaker, you need to become part of MeDeploy's catalog. This allows anyone to sell and promote your film. It's great, because exposure is what you need. You can now enlist all of your established blogger fans on the Internet to set up a store to sell your film for a profit.

The tricky part is that the ability to allow many sites on the web to sell your content *may* violate other Internet agreements you have. You just have to be aware of the rights deals you have already made and be cognizant of how your participation may affect those deals. Hopefully MeDeploy will enable you to turn off certain territories so that you don't violate those deals.

CONTROLLING YOUR RIGHTS IN A DIY SCENARIO

Two issues that you will need to face when deciding whether to sell your digital rights on your own are:

1. Territory. Do you sell to the world, the U.S., or some variation in between? This decision will be governed mainly by whether or not you have deals in any territory that require exclusivity, in which case you will have to figure out a way to block sales to that territory.

2. Whether or not to institute some form of digital rights management, or DRM.

DIGITAL RIGHTS MANAGEMENT

DRM is a term that applies to coding digital media in such a way as to limit what platform it can be played on, as well as how many copies can be made and/or how many devices it can be installed on.

In the free Internet culture, and specifically among iTunes consumers, DRM is an anathema that prevents consumers from doing what they want with the digital products they buy. You might be among those DRM protesters.

However, as a content producer who needs to maximize revenue on a product, you might feel that you need some form of DRM for your digital content. Whether you choose to do this goes back to a core decision that you as a content provider must make: Do you feel that any copy of your film (whether paid for or not) benefits you and your mission as a filmmaker/content provider? Do you feel you need to produce DRM-free content for consumer goodwill?

If you made a film without any desire of monetary recoupment, but solely with the intent of getting a message out to as many people as possible, you probably want your film to be copied and passed around as much as possible.

However, if you mortgaged your house (not a good idea) to finance your film and there are only 1,000 potential buyers in the world for your film, you need to maximize revenue from each of those potential buyers — and if any of them receive a copy from someone else, that is a loss of income.

These are two polar extremes, and it is unlikely either will match your situation exactly. It is likely that your needs are somewhere in between. It is also likely that your feelings about whether free media begets more revenue will be somewhere between the extreme of yes and no.

However you feel, you do need to have an opinion about these issues in order to make an informed decision about whether you will apply some sort of DRM to your own digital content.

SECTION 6 CONCLUSION

The new opportunities outlined in this chapter indicate the coming explosion of revenue-generating opportunities for filmmakers. The services listed in this chapter just became available in mid-2009. I am sure more companies and services are on their way to link consumers with filmmakers.

Before entering into any sale of your digital rights, I highly recommend that you do the following:

- Evaluate your film and its potential market.

- Consider how you are going to best reach that market.

- Determine which service will help you sell to that market.

- Make sure that you don't give up exclusive digital rights without proper compensation.

- Receive counsel, legal and strategic advice, on the various agreements you enter into.

Section 7
Foreign Sales

The orientation of this book is primarily for film-makers in the United States. However, I believe the principles espoused in this book can be put to use in almost any liberal democracy in the world (and to varying degrees other forms of government as well).

In addition, any foreign filmmaker could apply these techniques to releasing a film in the United States.

More importantly, as many of the delivery techniques become global, I believe there will be a blurring of the distinction between domestic and foreign sales, with digital rights leading the way. Many sites exhibiting or selling either digital products or merchandise can also sell to a worldwide audience.

CHAPTER 35

CONVENTIONAL FOREIGN SALES

THE OLD MODEL

The old model for foreign sales was essentially an international version of the old model for domestic rights. A filmmaker would get a foreign sales agent or company who would handle all foreign sales. These sales agents worked on a sales-fee basis. Depending on the strength of the film, an advance or minimum guarantee would often be paid against the sales of the film.

The sales agent/company would then take the film and make territory-by-territory deals. A popular film would have a series of overall deals, one in each territory, with a particular all rights distributor in that territory. The distributor in a territory would pay an advance to exploit all rights within that territory. In addition, a sales agent would often be engaged in advance of the film's production so as to use these foreign sales to help finance the film.

Foreign sales agents still exist and can be quite helpful for independent films. However, it is much harder to get an advance because overall deals in foreign territories are diminishing, just like overall deals in the United States. The reasons for this decline in overall deals are the same as well. Conventional theatrical for independents is harder to come by throughout the world. DVD sales are declining. Television sales remain the strongest of the traditional rights sales in foreign territories.

There are two kinds of foreign sales agents to consider: the traditional ones who focus on overall deals, and the ones who focus on television sales. The latter type is becoming more prevalent because television sales are the most lucrative market available in foreign markets. As Broderick points out, ironically, you can make more money sometimes only selling your television rights. While in an overall deal filmmakers receive an advance (and the hope of receiving backend someday), in television deals filmmakers receive a fixed payment (which is often larger than the advance on an overall deal).

DEAL POINTS TO CONSIDER WITH A FOREIGN SALES AGENT

When working with a foreign sales agent, whether it is for all rights or strictly television, there are some deal points that you need to be careful about and consider:

1. Term

Previously, foreign sales deals tended to be long-term because of the amount of work involved in developing a foreign sales presence. I think that most foreign sales agents work a film hard for the first year or two and then place it in the catalog. Therefore, I would strongly push for a much shorter term of no more than three to five years. My current TV sales deal for *Bomb It* is eight months. You can also offer a shorter term with a renewal, and/or have the term tied to performance guarantees.

2. Territory

This depends on what other territorial obligations you have. If you change sales agents, eliminate any territories in which you already have deals, similar to the suggestion I made for digital rights. I recommend keeping a spreadsheet of your current territories, who the rights were sold to and controlled by, and when they expire.

3. Rights Granted

Even in all rights deals, you should try to exclude your digital rights. At least put in a clause to have your sales agent make best efforts (or some kind of effort) to retain the digital rights for territories. In your television-only deals, you should make a strong effort to exclude digital rights, or only allow their inclusion on specific deals on a case-by-case basis.

Make sure that festival screening fees are included in the revenue stream. For docs, you want to have educational rights removed from the agreement.

4. Advance

I feel that it is relatively hard to get an advance on foreign sales these days for most independent films, but it is still possible. However, filmmaker Darrin Hollander, *Rise Up*, feels that you should always make sure your sales reps "have skin in the game." This skin is an advance that motivates the sales agent to earn back that advance. A good sales agent will be investing in your film even without an advance, since they will be paying for the creation of promotional material as well as the costs of attending markets.

5. Sales Fee

Standard is 25 percent plus expenses.

6. A Cap on Expenses

Expenses for foreign sales agents can be add up. They go to markets to sell your film, they create promotional material, etc. What expenses are deducted from your revenue and how great an impact will they have on your revenue stream? Here are some guidelines on types of expenses and capping them:

- Only allow deductions for direct expenses that are paid for creating marketing materials directly related to your film, such as key art and sell sheets.

- Allow no market expenses to be deducted, or require that the market expense be prorated across all films represented by that agent at that market.

- Since even these direct expenses can add up, you can also require a total cap on expenses of, say, $50,000.

- Even better, have an overall cap and then a maximum percentage that can be deducted each quarter. For example, if you only have $20,000 of sales in a quarter, $5,000 would go to the sales agent as a fee and only an additional $1,000 would go to pay back expenses (if the expenses were capped at 5 percent) instead of all of the leftover $15,000 going to pay back the sales agent for expenses. This is a tough provision to fight for, however.

- The best: No non-approved expenses deducted whatsoever.

7. Escrow Account for Sales

A number of foreign sales companies are notorious for not paying. It is very difficult for independent filmmakers to track foreign sales.

One solution is to require that all money be put in an escrow account that allocates money earned to the sales agent and you, the producer, based on the terms of the contract. This costs a point or two (as well as a setup fee), but is well worth it if your agent will agree to it.

8. Arbitration and Venue

If you have to pursue your foreign sales agent to get your money, it is usually cheaper to do this in an arbitration hearing. More importantly, since you are the poorer one seeking money, the venue of any trial should be in your city as opposed to the foreign sales company's home city. (Good luck suing someone based in France or Taiwan.)

9. Limit on Assignment

Most contracts have an assignment clause. What you want to limit is the sales agent's ability to sell the foreign sales agreement itself to other foreign sales companies without your approval.

Miscellaneous Approvals

Try to get the following approvals in your contract so you can maintain some control in certain areas:

- Approval over art and marketing materials.

- Approval over any re-edits required for delivery length or ratings.

- Involvement with or approval over any dubbing.

BARRIERS TO SALES

When thinking about a global audience, we must first consider what barriers might exist to potential sales. There are a number of barriers that you need to overcome in order to have a successful international release:

1. Language

Hence the need for subtitled versions. The more languages, the better.

2. Marketing

The holy grail for international sales will be how to access audiences in foreign countries. It is hard enough in your country, in your language. One day soon, Facebook and Twitter might have internal translators. However, different countries and regions have different favored social networks. Some countries still use Friendster.

3. Video Standard

Each country/continent subscribes to a different video standard. North America, some of South America, and Japan are the primary markets for NTSC. Europe, China, and Latin America are PAL. France and the former Soviet Union are Secam (which can also play and screen PAL material). This barrier is starting to fall with the rise of multi-standard DVD players.

4. Region Coding

DVDs are customarily coded to play in only one region. For films that have a significant budget and can afford to produce DVDs at a profitable quantity in each region, this might make sense. However, for independent filmmakers it is cost-prohibitive to encode a DVD for each region. I recommend that you not region code your DVDs. I also suggest that your U.S. DVD company not region encode any DVDs they create for you. If they don't region code them, it is easier to use their DVDs to sell to foreign territories.

U.S. DVD companies region code because it is presumed that you will have other foreign deals that might require it, in order to prevent market bleed. But since DVD sales are dropping overseas, this requirement is less likely. And just because they are not permitted to sell the film in a foreign territory doesn't mean you can't — it is much easier to sell a U.S. DVD in a foreign territory if it is not region-encoded. There are many DVD players in foreign countries that will play NTSC videos despite being PAL, but those same DVD players often have trouble playing region 1 encoded DVDs. Having a region-free DVD will save you re-authoring and mass replication costs.

★ When You Might Want Barriers

You may find yourself wanting to create some barriers to the viewing of your material. This will derive from either:

- Having a deal in a particular territory that needs to be protected so that you will not be sued for breach.

- You don't want your media released in a territory until you have set up all avenues to monetize the content in that territory. (For example, you would not want the film on DVD in England until you have your screening on Channel 4 and can sell the film through a local distributor who is paying for the content.)

Sales via the Internet can be regulated per territory by shutting off sales those certain territories. This is normally done by disallowing the country of registration for the credit card. If you needed to shut off sales to Italy, you or your fulfillment company would not accept sales to credit cards with Italian registration or other payment methods originating in Italy.

CHAPTER 36

HYBRID FOREIGN SALES

I believe that the split rights model of distribution outlined in this book can be applied to foreign markets, just as it can be applied to one's domestic territory. Using *Bomb It* as an example:

- We have done a decent amount of theatrical via festivals and requests.

- We are in the process of authoring international multi-language DVDs.

- We have a company representing the film for foreign institutional sales and screenings.

- We have a TV sales agent and have made a number of foreign TV sales.

- We are parsing out the digital rights.

I will discuss the particulars for each of these foreign aspects below.

CONTACTING FOREIGN BUYERS

Hollander suggests that you can contact any foreign buyer directly, although it can be tough since foreign sales are based on relationships. If you are dedicated and a good salesperson, it might work. In addition to markets, you can also contact buyers when they are in their home office. You can get the location and contact information for most buyers from the major markets' official websites or from sites such as allbusiness.com.

Markets are the most common place for films to be sold internationally, and there is already an existing circuit: Cannes in the spring, Toronto and AFM in the fall, Berlin in the winter. MIP still is strong for television sales. IDFA is the preeminent international market for documentaries.

While it is possible to attend these markets as an individual selling an individual film, it is very expensive. One tip is to get a day pass from a friendly foreign sales agent and work the floor on that day.

FOREIGN THEATRICAL/LIVE EVENTS

<u>Festivals</u> The most readily available of theatrical screenings are the foreign film festivals. Aside from the most prestigious festivals, mid- and smaller-size ones are used to paying a fee for screenings. Sometimes they even allow filmmakers to take a cut of the admission — you just need to ask. These screenings can be a very lucrative source of revenue.

If they don't/can't pay a fee, here are some alternatives:

- Have them buy a bulk of DVDs to sell in the festival shop.

- Require them to give you the translation that they make of your film. This is why it is better to have a subtitle list ready as a delivery requirement rather than a dialogue list — then you have the chance of receiving a subtitle list back from the festival. A subtitle list can be quickly modified to bring into DVD Studio Pro for your multi-language DVDs or for your specific language download being offered to territories on the web.

- Require them to give you back any submaster that they make of your film (e.g., translated and/or transcoded into PAL). For some reason festivals often put up a fight about this. I always ask, "What are you going to do with the film, as you have no rights to it? I would rather not have duplication-ready masters lying around outside of my control." This is a source of additional high quality screeners.

- Of course, they should pay round-trip shipping.

- One exception: They will generally not pay a fee if they are flying you to the festival (unless you have a hot film!).

<u>Cinematheques/Museums</u> Many countries have a national cinematheque and these often pay better than festivals. You can ask them to pay an advance against a percentage of the door. Sometimes these cinematheques will both pay for your film and fly you out.

<u>New Screening Networks</u> As I mentioned in Chapter 18, indiescreening.com is enabling people to organize grassroots screen-

ings in England. They did tremendously well with the *Age of Stupid*, setting up over 300 screenings in the U.K.

DVD

I strongly recommend having your foreign DVDs ready to go when you release your domestic DVD. If you do not release them close to the same time, your domestic DVD might be pirated because of its higher import price and its relative unavailability. This will make it more difficult to sell your foreign DVD later.

<u>Authoring</u> At the very least, release an English language version of the film. If possible, you should consider subtitling the film in as many languages as you can handle. You might have subtitle lists from festivals. There are developing systems for crowdsourcing your subtitles DIY subtitling is one of the most arduous parts of the DIY foreign sales process. You can pay professional services to create subtitles, but it will cost around $2,000 a language.

Distribution

<u>Your Website — Direct Sales</u> You can, of course, sell your foreign DVDs through your website. If you have deals in place that preclude you from selling your DVDs in various territories, your fulfillment house or shopping cart will have to be able to selectively turn off those markets.

You might also consider replicating and fulfilling from Europe for a PAL title. This will reduce shipping costs tremendously and also provide peace of mind for European customers, as they are buying locally. Delivery times will also be reduced.

Of course, any form of marketing that you used for your domestic DVD sales can be applied internationally.

<u>Wholesale</u> While it might be tougher to deal with a foreign-based DVD company, it is still possible. If you have a hot title, why not try and get an advance? Just carve out the same restrictions as if it were your home territory DVD company.

You might have better luck through distributors and retailers that cater to your niche. Any fulfillment service should be able to handle these bulk orders as well.

TELEVISION

There is still a strong television market for independent films, especially documentaries. Keep in mind that if you do make a TV sale, you should try to have your DVDs available for sale in that territory, since television is a great way promote your film. You can even use that TV sale as an entrée into a local DVD deal.

Here is what one TV-sales-savvy filmmaker indicated as the best available territories and the potential rates one can expect from a doc with some moderate interest (all figures are in U.S. dollars and will likely change as soon as they are printed):

- U.K. $40,000

- Germany $20,000 to $30,000

- France $20,000 to $25,000

- Italy $15,000

- Benelux $10,000 to $15,000

- Spain $10,000

- Former Soviet Union $8,000 to $10,000

- Japan $10,000

Other potential markets are Latin America (often sold as a block), Korea, Taiwan, Australia, and South Africa.

DIGITAL RIGHTS

Much of what was covered in the digital rights section is applicable here. In addition to the companies that offer worldwide streaming and download-to-own rights, there are some (and will be more) foreign national companies that offer the same services as Vudu, iTunes, etc.

This is yet another reason to be very careful about the disposition of your digital rights. Even services that purport to be worldwide do not have a presence in large portions of the world, and it would be wise to be careful about making exclusive deals with them without a significant advance.

This is also the advantage of going through an aggregator and/or distributor (especially the latter) because they will have set up arrangements with these companies already.

SECTION 7 CONCLUSION

Global sales are one of the most challenging yet exciting markets that have the potential of breaking out for independent filmmakers, due primarily to the power of the Internet.

As we discussed in Chapter 34, you can already DIY your digital rights globally. Many streaming sites operate globally. iTunes and iTunes-type stores are popping up across the world.

Hopefully the grassroots screening models will continue to expand across the globe.

What remains to be developed are ways for filmmakers to connect with (and market to) their global audiences, across language and social network boundaries — although the prevalence of Twitter in the recent Iranian uprising indicates that this might happen faster than we think.

Section 8
Sanity and the Future

Some final thoughts and a look to the future.

CHAPTER 37

KEEPING SANE

I moved this chapter from the beginning of the book to the end because I didn't want it to be such a downer right away (not that the new 50/50 isn't a downer!).

As you may have surmised, the new mode of distribution is very time-intensive. This not only takes time away from making films, but the process for many filmmakers is antithetical to their creative process. ("Soul sucking" is a term I heard from one filmmaker.)

Except for producers, filmmakers (especially writer/directors) are generally not businessmen/women. In fact, many of us — myself included — went into filmmaking (or another creative art form) to get away from "business." If I wanted to be in business, making and selling widgets, I would go out and do that. I chose not to do that, so why am I faced with it now?

Furthermore, many filmmakers are introverts and are often not con-stitutionally made up for some of the tasks required in distribution and marketing (salesmanship, for instance). We are at a point in time where developing a business sense is necessary for filmmak-ers. Because selling yourself is such a big component of all aspects of film, I suggest that all filmmakers develop some self-promotional skills. How much you move toward a business mentality is a choice you personally have to make.

Ted Hope is more emphatic on this issue. He states that filmmak-ers have to get beyond the old art-versus-commerce divide. It's all part of the same process. The sooner we collectively realize that, the better.

This paradigm shift is one where filmmakers move from a project-to-project model to a career development model.

In the career development model, filmmakers are not "marketing," rather they are developing a relationship with their audience, which in turn builds a long-term support structure.

A great resource on this concept is Scott Kirsner's book *Fans, Friends and Followers*. Go out and buy it and read it.

If this still is not convincing, here are some other thoughts that might help:

★ Change your attitude toward business and marketing.

To paraphrase Rosenbush: Marketing gives you the opportunity to reach the audience that *wants to see your film!* Your fans exist. You just need to find them. The way you do that is through distribution and marketing.

★ Make your films inexpensively.

I said this before in chapter 3, but it bears repeating. Keeping your costs low means that the money you earn on your own or through distribution entities will allow you to recoup faster. With some exceptions, alternative distribution models are just taking shape and they haven't fully monetized yet, so it's best to set reasonable expectations.

Swanberg has purposely kept the costs of his films low so that it is easier to recoup his investment and move on to new projects. He does this because he does not like distribution — he prefers making films, and by making and selling films cheaply he can create more.

★ The film community needs to accept distribution as something that's just as important as production.

Distribution is as much a part of a producer's and director's role as production.

In chapters 2 & 5 I make a case that films need to hire distribution and marketing producers just as they hire line producers.

When considering jobs to earn a living while writing your masterpiece, instead of assistant editing, how about Internet marketing? Is learning how to market creatively on the Internet any more soul-sucking than logging tapes? Perhaps then you can become one of the new breed of distribution producers and make your name that way.

HOW TO NURTURE YOURSELF CRE-ATIVELY AND PSYCHICALLY DURING YOUR FILM'S RELEASE

I was only half joking when I subtitled my first *Filmmaker* magazine article about my experience distributing *Bomb It* "Or How I Spent Six Months Wanting to Kill Myself Every Day."

Here are some thoughts on how to survive:

1. Cut yourself some slack.

You are not alone in feeling that the soul-sucking aspects of distribution prevent your creative juices from flowing. This is a common feeling among filmmakers. Film distribution is time-consuming and draining. In addition, filmmakers have reported feeling that the part of the brain needed to function in a business environment will often push aside the creative part of their brain. Perhaps acknowledging the problem will help you carve out some creative space.

2. Network with other filmmakers.

Not only for ideas about how to do your distribution, but also to commiserate. It helps to know you are not alone.

3. Create time to be creative.

This is always difficult and easier said than done (especially when there are 70 emails in your inbox every day when you wake up). But try to discipline yourself to write or do something creative for an hour a day, perhaps when you first wake up or before you go to sleep. And if you can't do this, don't beat yourself up — I couldn't either.

4. Meditate.

Again, best done first thing in the morning, even for five minutes. If you can't do this, either, don't despair! It's hard when your mind is racing with everything you need to get done.

5. Do yoga.

Niles took up yoga during the release of *Note by Note*. He credits his continued sanity to it. Hatha yoga is actually a form of meditation, and you will have a decent chance at what you know as meditation immediately after practiciing Hatha yoga.

6. Do something other than filmmaking and screen-writing.

It might be hard to motivate yourself to write a script (and I have no idea how you would find time to shoot a film). Play an instrument, draw, paint, take photographs. Anything to keep the creative part of your brain oiled.

7. Remind yourself of why you are releasing the film.

You are releasing your film because of the goals you established. So embrace it.

8. Embrace the relationship with the audience.

Film is about connection. Connecting with an audience. Have that interaction feed your soul. This is why live theatrical events are so important. Don't take the audience for granted. Don't become blasé or jaded.

9. Set an end date.

Understand that during the release, you need to devote yourself to a business mentality, but set a day for that to end — at least mentally. Know that you will go back to being a creative person when the release is over. While the film will always be with you, it won't always be a full-time job.

CHAPTER 38

THE FUTURE

Where do we go from here? Are DVDs dying? Will we ever be able to fully monetize a film from digital rights?

Here are some thoughts on the future of film distribution and marketing from the people we have been hearing from throughout the book:

Dentler observes that if you look at the history of consumer media, you always have different models for different types of publications. Some things are free, some things you pay for. He uses print media as an example, pointing out the difference between the *Wall Street Journal* and the Free Press.

Hyams feels a pricing structure will develop based on when a consumer wants a product: The sooner they want it, the more they will pay, in whatever form. For example, if they want to be the first one to see a film, they will pay $14.95 (a person), if they want to watch it later that will cost $8.99, even later, $4.99.

Broderick sees a growth of semi- and non-theatrical screening events and live appearances that will continue to help drive DVD sales. He also feels that the country-by-country segmentation of the market will erode and films will begin to be available globally.

Sloss feels that distribution will change the shape of independent films. A new generation is viewing storytelling differently than those who came before (us of the indie film generation, as it were). We can't force our methods and models on new consumers. They will decide how they will consume and engage with media.

Weiler sees an increasing socialization of media, where people come together as a community through various platforms. Filmmakers will increasingly give their audiences tools to become engaged in their narratives. Content creators and audiences will become mutually supportive allies in the creative process.

I would agree with all of these sentiments. The one thing that is certain is that independent film is not dead — it's evolving into new and exciting forms that we can only begin to imagine.

PEOPLE NEED TO TELL STORIES

People have been gathering around fires to tell and listen to stories since the birth of humankind. The form and delivery of those stories will change, but that need will never change.

MY THOUGHTS ON THE FUTURE

Here is some of what I see happening in the coming years:

As the noise of overwhelming content increases, a premium will be paid for quality and curatorship. Consumers will not only pay for specific content that meets their interests, but they will pay service fees for institutions that pre-select this content for them. I don't see this as a way of reducing choice, but actually a way of increasing choice. It will be easier for a film to find its natural audience. Or conversely, it will be easier for an audience or consumer to find the visual media that appeals to them individually.

Consumers will pay for experiences that they cannot get any other way. It is up to filmmakers to invent these new experiences for them.

Filmmakers will discover new techniques and forms of storytelling that take advantage of not only new technology and new forms of communication between people.

Filmmakers will experiment with alternative structures of storytelling, relying more on different forms and lengths allowing viewers a multifaceted way to engage with story and characters.

There will be new forms of collaboration between artists in media creation that transcend territorial limitations and utilize the technology of the Internet for long-distance collaboration.

Filmmakers will embrace a long-term approach to their careers and will judge projects on how each one fits into that career.

Filmmakers will create long-term relationships with their audiences and engage them as active participants in their filmmaking process.

Filmmakers will experiment with new forms of live events, breathing new life into this ossified form.

SOME THINGS THAT NEED TO OCCUR TO FACILITATE THE DREAM:

Consumers (and filmmakers as consumers) need to realize that they need to pay for content. If content isn't paid for, content creators can't sustain themselves and continue to create content.

Filmmakers and content creators need to consider what kinds of products and content audiences will be interested in paying for. This not only means considering whether to meet niche or mass desires; it also means reinventing the notion of the types of products that filmmakers traditionally create. And by "product" I do not just mean merchandise. Think creatively in terms of what you can create for your audience that they will want to purchase to keep you in business. Think in terms of the ways that your audience consumes media, and how you can work with those new patterns. Break out of old habits and mindsets about what film is and what the work of making film involves.

Institutions need to be flexible with the restrictions that they place on filmmakers and their rights. They must understand that the landscape is changing rapidly and they must be open to new ways of doing business to help filmmakers survive. Those companies who are able to work with filmmakers in this way will be the ones that continue into the next generation of film distribution.

Filmmakers need to share information to help each other in this turbulent time. The only way that I was able to release my film was through the generous advice of filmmakers, distributors, and publicists. My goal in writing this book was to expand on that knowledge and share it with the rest of the filmmaking world. Please contribute to the website — give your tips and advice. The only way we can continue to thrive and enrich our lives is through our shared experience. The stories we tell as filmmakers are only one aspect of that shared experience. I look forward to your comments, thoughts, criticisms, and ideas.

Jon Reiss
ultimatefilmguides.com
jonreiss.com/blog
twitter.com/Jon_Reiss
facebook.com/ThinkOutsidetheBoxOffice

APPENDIX: ADVICE FROM FILMMAKERS

★ Curt Ellis (King Corn, The Greening of Southie)

Five Pieces of Advice for Independent Filmmakers

- Build your email list incessantly and from the beginning.

- Preserve your right to sell to your core fans. Don't hand that to a distributor.

- Make a film with general appeal *and* an organized target audience.

- Save as much time, energy, and money for distribution as you spend on production.

- Try to build a strategy that takes advantage of self-distribution streams first, and conventional distribution streams after that. They can build on each other and reinforce each other, and a distributor can get your film into places you can't ever reach on your own.

TOP DIY DVD SELLERS

The following filmmakers are some of the top DVD sellers in the DIY world. Here are their do's and don'ts:

★ Ben Niles (Note by Note)

- Connected with Steinway (his film is about the making of a Steinway piano). Niles went to a dealer convention and the dealers went nuts after seeing the pieces of the film he brought.

- Every time he would screen the film in a new town, he would contact Steinway, who would put him in touch with a local dealer.

- He knew he had a high-end audience, so he created a high-end product.

- He listened to his attorney and didn't sign anything he would regret.

- Finding and listening to his consultant (who happens to be Peter Broderick).

- Realizing that he had to make a choice about how to release the film and stick with it.

Things he feels he did wrong:

- Trying to sell his PBS underwriting on his own.

- Not having enough time to develop his next project.

★ Jim Tusty (The Singing Revolution)

Six Pieces of Advice for Independent Filmmakers

- Distribution is as important as production. You need to embrace the distribution process.

- No one will care about your film as much as you.

- No one will know your film as much as you.

- Luck helps.

- But in the end, it's the story that has to resonate with people. No amount of marketing will sell a bad product.

- Identify niche audiences and focus on them.

Your Top Don'ts for Self/DIY Distribution

- Don't think positive audience reaction to your film at festivals will generate an audience. It's not about "likeability." It's about "marketability."

- Don't take it personally. You need the world more than the world needs your film.

- Don't resent Hollywood. They're no more competition for your film than *People* magazine is competition for *Atlantic Monthly*. They have mostly different audiences. Focus on your audience.

- Don't spend every last dime on production. It does you no good to build a Mercedes and then not have any money leftover for gas. Distribution is the gas that powers your film.

- Don't start another production while distributing your first film. You need time, focus, and attention.

★ Marty Ostrow (Renewal)

<u>Five Pieces of Advice for Independent Filmmakers</u>

1. Think about self-distribution.

2. Be prepared for work that will rival and surpass the effort you put into making the film. Self-distribution is extremely labor-intensive!

3. Discover the organizations who will most care about your film and let them become the frontline disseminators of information about your work.

4. Get your film in festivals and send it out for reviews.

5. Take advantage of social networking sites to increase awareness about your film and the subject your film is about. We have been completely dependent on the web to broadcast information about the film, with no budget for advertising, print, or otherwise.

JON REISS

Jon Reiss began his career as member of the punk rock documentary collective Target Video, and went on to make five films with the radical performance art group Survival Research Laboratories as well as multiple groundbreaking (and banned) music videos including ones for Nine Inch Nails, Danzig, Slayer and The Black Crowes. Named one of "10 Digital Directors to Watch" by Daily Variety, his features include the award-winning documentary *Better Living Through Circuitry*, a striking exposé on underground electronic music culture, *Cleopatra's Second Husband* a dark thriller and *Bomb It* about the world wide explosion of graffiti and street art and the subsequent battle over visual public space. Jon also teaches at the Film Directing Program at Cal Arts and runs a distribution tools website to complement the book: ultimatefilmguides.com

Jon can be contacted at:
jonreiss.com/blog
twitter.com/Jon_Reiss
facebook.com/ThinkOutsidetheBoxOffice